DIVINE INTERVENTIONS

Heartwarming Stories of Answered Prayers

DIVINE INTERVENTIONS

Heartwarming Stories of Answered Prayers

Guideposts
Danbury, Connecticut

Inspiring the world to believe anything is possible with hope, faith, and prayer.

Published by Guideposts Books & Inspirational Media
100 Reserve Road, Suite E200
Danbury, CT 06810
Guideposts.org

Acknowledgments

Every attempt has been made to credit the sources of copyrighted material used in this book. If any such acknowledgment has been inadvertently omitted or miscredited, receipt of such information would be appreciated.

Cover design by W Design Studio
Cover photo by Dreamstime/Shuang Wang
Interior design and typesetting by Müllerhaus
Indexed by Maria A. Sullivan

ISBN 978-1-959633-96-9 (hardcover)
ISBN 978-1-959633-97-6 (softcover)
ISBN 978-1-959633-98-3 (epub)

Printed and bound in the United States of America

Our prayers have two stages. First, we pray for something. And then second, we pray for the courage to deal with the rather shocking reality that the prayer was actually answered.

—Craig D. Lounsbrough

Contents

Introduction

Divine interventions happen each and every day, but we may not always recognize them as such. One dictionary defines divine intervention as "a miracle or act of god (or gods) that causes something good to happen or stops something bad from happening." A divine intervention, simply put, is when God steps in and changes the outcome of a situation. There are times we know without any hesitation or doubt that God was watching, protecting, and providing for our needs at exactly the right moment. It is when we reflect on these times that it becomes clear to us that the mysterious work of God changed the outcome in a favorable way.

The Power of Divine Interventions

When we experience a divine intervention, it changes us. This was the case for my colleague's mother, Jo Ann, who experienced a divine intervention that saved her life. She was traveling with her husband, Jim, and older sister, Jorja, from New York to North Carolina for their youngest brother's funeral. Jo Ann was devastated by the news of her brother's passing, and she hadn't been able to eat or sleep for days. Because she was exhausted, she decided to lie down in the back seat for the ride.

While driving through Pennsylvania, Jim, Jo Ann, and Jorja stopped for something to eat. Waiting for a table at the restaurant, Jo Ann and her sister opted to use the restroom. As Jorja washed her hands, she talked to Jo Ann, who was still in a stall. Suddenly, Jo Ann went silent, and Jorja heard Jo Ann's eyeglasses fall to the floor. Jorja knew something was terribly wrong and tried without success to open the stall door. She yelled for Jim, who ran into the ladies' room, busted down the stall door, and found Jo Ann unable to speak. The paramedics came quickly after they received the 911 call and rushed Jo Ann to the hospital in Harrisburg, Pennsylvania.

When asked what happened, Jo Ann remembered fumbling with the button on her pants, breaking out in a cold sweat, and feeling disoriented, but she couldn't recall anything after that. Although Jo Ann didn't experience any chest pain, she had suffered a heart attack and needed bypass surgery to alleviate her blocked coronary arteries. After hearing the full story of how the three of them wound up at the restaurant in Pennsylvania, the doctor told Jim and Jorja that had they not stopped for dinner when they did, Jo Ann could have died. He went on to explain that she would have had the heart attack in the back seat and perhaps neither one of them would have noticed. The decision to stop for food on a whim saved Jo Ann's life. In addition, Jo Ann later learned that this hospital is one of the leading heart hospitals in the country.

It has been more than fifteen years since the divine intervention that saved Jo Ann's life took place. To this day, Jo Ann and her family thank God for His intervention. He made Jim, Jo Ann, and Jorja stop for dinner when and where they did. And He inspired Jo Ann's favorite saying: "God is good all the time. All the time God is good."

A Timely Book with a Timeless Message

In reading this book, *Divine Interventions*, you will be encouraged to continue to pray and trust God's intervention for your life. You will be strengthened spiritually to recognize, as you read about the mysterious and powerful divine presence that makes a way when there is no way, that God can turn tragedy into triumph and send help in the nick of time. Whether you are crying out for a financial miracle, longing for answers to an unanswered prayer, or struggling in a difficult situation, the timeless message of hope will empower you to keep believing that all things are possible.

This book will help you understand that God is always in control and He is able to do the impossible. Your spiritual lenses will widen to show you the divine presence that surrounds you. When God steps in and changes the outcome, gratitude and joy fill not only your miraculous life but the lives of each and every human being. As you read these stories of divine intervention, your faith will increase and your spirit will be lifted.

—Rev. Dr. Pablo R. Diaz
Former Vice President of Ministries, Guideposts

1

God's Promises Regarding Prayer

God never made a promise that was too good to be true.

D. L. Moody

Humans are special in God's eyes.

After all, He created us in His image . . . something even the angels don't claim. He breathed His very life into us. Think of that. We were just inanimate, two-dimensional drawings in the dirt until God blew His life into us and expanded us into amazingly complex beings.

We are reflections of His brain, reflections of His wisdom, reflections of His humor . . . and reflections of His heart.

When God created Adam and Eve, He came down to Earth and touched them personally. Scripture indicates that God walked, talked, and spent time with them. Imagine it. If you've ever had children, you know how talkative they can be at the end of the school day when they are bursting to talk about things that happened and/or new things they learned. Maybe Adam and Eve were somewhat like that. Maybe when God walked and talked with them, they almost burst with information about the funny thing the kangaroo did that day or the tasty new berry they found. Maybe they asked questions about the intricacies of their work or reflected on the expanse of the heavens or exclaimed about the sweet scent of the flowers.

We can only imagine what they discussed. But we would probably not be far off the mark to believe the fellowship was sweet and the joy bubbled. For our God is a God of relationship.

Even after Adam and Eve betrayed their friendship with God by sinning, God still was evident in human lives. He still found ways to communicate with the people He loved, and that holds true today.

Though all of us have the taint of Adam and Eve's betrayal on our souls, God still longs to be in relationship with us. He still longs to breathe life into our souls through His communion. And that's what prayer is all about. God has promised that He will never leave us nor forsake us, and He created prayer so His beloved humans are still able to turn to Him as their friend.

Let's think about some of God's promises regarding prayer.

He Promises to Be Accessible

Take a moment to let this sink in—the God of the universe is accessible to you. You don't have to be rich, famous, or important. You don't have to be a pastor, a Bible teacher, or even the strongest believer.

You don't have to schedule an appointment to meet with Him or wait in a long line. There's only one prerequisite for receiving God's attention. You simply have to call on Him.

Jeremiah 29:12–13 promises, "When you pray, I will listen. If you look for me wholeheartedly, you will find me" (NLT).

He Promises to Reveal Things to Us

Some of the most precious moments for parents are moments when we are teaching our children or telling them about things that interest us. The God of the universe is the ultimate source of information for His children. Do you have questions? He promises to answer them. Jeremiah 33:3 says, "Ask me and I will tell you remarkable secrets you do not know about things to come" (NLT).

He Promises to Say Yes

"Mom, can I go shopping with Faith?"

"Yes, just be careful and be home by nine."

Again, to use the parental analogy, what a joy it is as parents to be able to say yes when our kids make requests. Of course, there are times we have to say no because there are dangers our children don't understand or the timing isn't right or for other reasons. But as one spiritual mentor said, "I make it a habit to say yes to my kids anytime I can. That way they have confidence to ask me . . . and to learn to have confidence to turn to God with their needs."

Naturally, there will be times when what we ask does not line up with God's plans for our lives, but God will at least open the door and hear our request. Keep in mind Jesus's promise in Matthew 7:7–11: "Keep on asking, and you will receive what you ask for. Keep on seeking, and you will find. Keep on knocking, and the door will be opened to you. For everyone who asks, receives. Everyone who seeks, finds. And to everyone who knocks, the door will be opened.

"You parents—if your children ask for a loaf of bread, do you give them a stone instead? Or if they ask for a fish, do you give them a snake? Of course not! So if you sinful people know how to give good gifts to your children, how much more will your heavenly Father give good gifts to those who ask him" (NLT).

So when you turn to God in prayer, don't do it apologetically. He enjoys blessing you. Jesus promises in John 16:24, "Ask, and you will receive, that your joy may be full" (NKJV).

He Promises to Help Us Figure Things Out

Do you sometimes face situations you don't know how to handle? Maybe you've encountered difficulty in a relationship—you don't know how to communicate with someone, good or bad. Maybe it's a problem with your work; things don't seem to be clear or adding up right. Maybe you don't understand some scripture or have questions about God.

Whenever you need knowledge or wisdom, follow the advice of James 1:5: "If you need wisdom, ask our generous God, and he will give it to you. He will not rebuke you for asking" (NLT).

He Promises That Prayers of Trouble Are No Trouble!

Sometimes it seems like life is just a lot of difficult situations strung together—the path from one problem to another seems short.

But your heavenly Father is aware of this. He doesn't get tired of listening to the troubles we face and lending a hand. He doesn't scold as we expect him to. So if you're in trouble, no problem! Even if it's of your own making, don't try to prove you can handle it on your own. Heed the words of Psalm 50:15: "Call on me when you are in trouble, and I will rescue you, and you will give me glory" (NLT).

He Promises That Our Prayers Make a Difference

Does it really matter if we pray? Won't God do what He wants no matter what we ask or say?

Probably none of us understands how prayer "works," but we can rest assured that when we pray, it makes a difference in the world. James 5:16–18 says, "Confess your sins to each other and pray for each other so that you may be healed. The earnest prayer of a righteous person has great power and produces wonderful results. Elijah was as human as we are, and yet when he prayed earnestly that no rain would fall, none fell for three and a half years! Then, when he prayed again, the sky sent down rain and the earth began to yield its crops" (NLT).

If you know Christ, you are a righteous person and your prayers have great power and wonderful results! Does that mean the sick will always be healed or the weather will always cooperate? No, sometimes God has other plans.

But even when our prayers don't seem to change situations, they still affect lives and make a difference in the world—and in our lives.

He Promises to Forgive

Yes, being human, we may sin at times. Sometimes a little seed of rebellion or pride or disobedience kicks in. But God is prepared for imperfections in His beloved humans. That's why Christ came to Earth and died on the cross and rose again—so that we, too, can be forgiven and be victorious over sin.

Not only that, but when we've done wrong, instead of hanging our heads or hiding, we can remember Hebrews 4:15–16: "This High Priest of ours understands our weaknesses, for he faced all of the same testings we do, yet he did not sin. So let us come boldly to the throne of our gracious God. There we will receive his mercy, and we will find grace to help us when we need it most" (NLT).

He Promises That Our Prayers Can Be Preventive

We know our prayers can help us when we land in trouble or that they can bring forgiveness from God when we sin. But our prayers can also be preventive maintenance. Mark 14:38 says, "Keep watch and pray, so that you will not give in to temptation. For the spirit is willing, but the body is weak" (NLT).

It's kind of like driving. We watch while we drive and avoid situations that may lead to wrecks or other harm. Similarly, as we travel life's roads, we keep our eyes open. And we pray that the Lord will help us avoid temptation that crosses our paths.

Temptation is real. Nip it in the bud with prayer.

He Promises to Read Our Hearts

Our human minds are so finite. Sometimes we just can't sort through the jumble of thoughts to be cohesive and clear. Sometimes we can't even organize our thoughts enough to articulate them in prayer. We are needy, but we don't know what to say or where to begin.

Thankfully, God is still with us in those moments! Romans 8:26 says, "Likewise the Spirit helps us in our weakness; for we do not know how to pray as we ought, but the Spirit himself intercedes for us with sighs too deep for words" (RSV).

Even if we end up babbling to God like a toddler with nonsensical words, the Holy Spirit is able to not just read our lips but read our hearts and minds!

He Promises to Give Us Peace

We know that God wants to say yes to us in His plan and timing. But what if He seems to be saying no or seems to be delayed in His answers?

There's still amazing value in prayer, for the very act of praying puts us in the presence of God. And that brings us an amazing sense of peace. When we've taken our concerns to God and placed them at His feet, we're better able to let go of our concerns and let Him worry about them.

So is anything making you anxious today? Have you prayed about it? Remember Philippians 4:6–7: "Don't worry about anything; instead, pray about everything. Tell God what you need, and thank him for all he has done. Then you will experience God's peace, which exceeds anything we can understand. His peace will guard your hearts and minds as you live in Christ Jesus" (NLT).

Want to know what else God promises about prayer and how He works through prayer? That's the design of this book . . . to *show* you some of the mighty deeds, miracles, and incredible power God displays when His humans pray . . . to help you glimpse Him through His divine interventions!

2

Miracles Happen

Prayer is the instrument of miracles.

Marion G. Romney

Have you ever been pressed against a wall of impossibility? Maybe the diagnosis says there's no cure and life is ebbing away. Perhaps the estrangement with someone you love seems unbreachable. Maybe you've done all you can do to pay your mortgage but are about to lose your home.

These are the times that try our souls. But in the dark moments of life, God's light shines brightest. All of Scripture reflects God's words in Jeremiah 32:27: "I am the LORD, the God of all the peoples of the world. Is anything too hard for me?" (NLT).

One of the most amazing miracles in the Bible happened because the people of Gibeon made a treaty of peace and became allies with Israel. So when the king of Jerusalem, one of the Amorite kings, decided to attack Gibeon, the Gibeonites cried out for help, and the leader of the Israelites, Joshua, and his army came running.

Joshua's army didn't face only the king of Jerusalem's army. The king had called on others to help. It was five against one when the five kings from the hill country and their armies joined forces against Joshua and his army.

Based on this, the surrounding nations certainly must have concluded that the odds favored the five kings. But the Lord told Joshua, "Do not be afraid of them; I have given them into your hand" (Joshua 10:8, NIV). And despite the long odds, Joshua and his army were winning the battle! However, as the day passed, the Israelites needed more time. When darkness came, the other armies could easily retreat and later regroup.

Joshua needed a miracle. He needed the sun to keep the darkness away. So Joshua called on the Lord. And amazingly . . . the sun appeared to stand still for a whole day until the enemies were defeated!

Just as Joshua called on the Lord and then stood confident, so can we. We can stand confidently before God when we need our miracle to happen. When we come to God in prayer, even in impossible situations, He hears our cries. It doesn't matter what kind of impossibility we face; He can give us wisdom and change hearts for those relational impossibilities. He can heal the intricacies inside our bodies. And He can even deal with the physical elements of the universe. His power is unlimited.

Call upon the Lord for a miracle—just as the people who tell their stories in this chapter did. And you, too, can experience miraculous answers to prayer!

Our Prayer and His Gift

– ALICE KLIES –

I couldn't believe I was about to deliver my baby girl almost three months early. At twenty-six weeks' gestation, I had ended up at the local hospital, and hours later, an ambulance transported me to a larger hospital that specialized in premature births.

My baby presented herself in a breech position, with the umbilical cord wrapped around a foot. The outcome didn't look good. And the extra wow factor? I was forty-four years old!

When Ray and I married, each of us had grown children who were well on their own journeys. This pregnancy shocked us and rocked our many plans to enjoy our new lives together. Our new house, recently purchased, was almost complete. The sunroom would now be a nursery. Travel plans and a carefree life of "just the two of us" no longer existed.

"Are you ready, Alice?" a neonatal doctor asked. He then nodded at two nurses who tended to wires and dials on an incubator nestled against a wall. Now they stood at attention with their hands poised in the air. I thought they looked almost comical, like statues with funny white masks across their noses and mouths.

"Yes," I spoke so softly that the doctor had to lean in to hear me.

"Okay, then."

I wondered if he smiled beneath his mask.

My husband's fingers tightened on my shoulder. His head fell forward inches from mine. He brushed my bangs from my eyes and whispered, "It will be all right, Alice. We'll get through this."

"Pray with me, Ray." I pushed my face closer to his. Tears trickled down my cheeks and mingled with his.

"Heavenly Father, please watch over our baby and Alice. Please, God, bring us all through this."

I sobbed, "Please, God, please be with the doctors and bring our baby safely into this world."

I hoped that at this very moment, a steady hand was making an incision across my belly and about to bring baby K out of her warm sanctuary into a world she wasn't supposed to be in for almost three months. The comical-looking nurses, the tension in the room—it all felt surreal.

"We have a girl. One pound nine ounces."

The doctor's announcement brought me back to reality.

Ray's arm tightened around my shoulder. My cries were muffled as I buried my face against his chest.

"Is she alive?" I asked.

Ray turned his face toward the two nurses who were nearly running. One of them held something very tiny in one hand. Suddenly, the incubator and nurses were gone. Ray gazed back to the doctor.

The doctor stepped close to me, leaned over, pulled down his mask and said. "The nurses are taking your baby to the Neonatal Intensive

Care Unit. She will be evaluated and attended to there, and when you have recovered, you and your husband will see her."

I looked deep into Ray's eyes. "Do you think she will live?"

"She'll be just fine."

But my husband told me later that his heart had thumped in his chest as he heard those words. *One pound nine ounces? How can she possibly live?*

My husband told me later that his heart had thumped in his chest as he heard those words.

The doctor calmly stitched me closed. When he finished, he put his hand on Ray's shoulder. "Congratulations, Dad."

Then the doctor moved closer to me and said, "Your baby is very tiny, but we have an amazing staff in the NICU, and they will do everything possible to help her grow. All the best to both of you."

After a short time in recovery, I was moved to a room. When an aide lowered me into a bed, I looked at the bed next to mine. A young woman sat on the edge of her bed holding her baby close to her chest. The baby's noisy suckle pierced my ears. I started to cry.

How could they put me in a room beside a mother with a full-term baby when I don't even know if mine will live through the night?

Hours seemed to pass before a nurse asked us if we were ready to see our baby. By this time, I started to feel the effects the C-section. The nurse handed me a pillow to hold over my tummy in case I coughed and explained the procedure of visiting our baby in the NICU.

We chose the name Lindsey, after the actress who played the Bionic Woman on a television series. We figured she needed a bionic name since she was so tiny. But we still didn't expect the blaring alarms, blinking lights, wires, and tubes that accosted us as we entered the NICU.

When my wheelchair stopped in front of an incubator, my mouth dropped open. Before us was a birdlike figure. Lindsey's minute frame was only eleven inches long. Her skin looked transparent. Blue veins ran through her body, resembling a road map to nowhere. Her miniature fingers weren't much longer than the sulfur on the end of a wooden match. A white cloth covered her eyes. A nurse quickly explained our baby was jaundiced and needed the mask for the bilirubin light providing phototherapy.

I felt like someone stood on me, pushing the air out of me. I grabbed Ray's hand. Gasping to talk, I started to ask questions.

"Wh-what are all the wires? Is she breathing? Why is that alarm going off? Can I hold her?"

The neonatal nurse stepped close to me. She gathered my hands into hers and began to explain.

"The tube is designed so we can feed her directly to her tummy. She will be fed this way until she is old enough to know how to suckle. We will have you pump your breast, and we will store your milk for her feedings. This wire"—she pointed to the one taped to Lindsey's chest—"will set off an alarm if she stops breathing. We can then massage her chest to encourage her to breathe."

The nurse patted my hands. My blank stare must have revealed my shock.

The nurse continued. "Other wires tell us what her body temperature is. Preemie babies are born without the thermal layer of fat directly under the skin that controls temperature. Since your preemie's nervous system wasn't developed, she can't shiver or sweat. If we don't monitor this, she could burn up extra calories she can't afford to lose."

I drew in a deep breath and laid my head against Ray.

"Why don't I feel any better about this? I feel like I'm going to get sick. What are we supposed to do?"

Ray bent down to embrace me. "It will work out, Alice. The doctors and nurses will see that she will be given every opportunity to live. We will be by her side every step of the way. God will be with us on this journey; just wait and see."

He lightly kissed my forehead.

"You can't hold her, but would you like to touch her?" the nurse asked. "Come over here, closer to the incubator, and put your hands through these two holes. That way, you can stroke her cheek or fingers."

Ray pushed the wheelchair to the incubator. My hands shook when I brought them forward toward the holes. Once again, tears started to drown my cheeks. Ever so gently, I reached to hold Lindsey's hand, touch her cheek, and stroke her frail torso.

From this moment, I knew God gifted Lindsey to us. He certainly had a plan for this baby, and I intended to give everything I had in me to see His plan through.

For the three months in NICU, we prayed daily for everyday miracles for our tiny child. Friends, strangers in our church, and even the nurses prayed for her. Not only did our prayers for her to live get answered, but she overcame all kinds of odds and trials from then to now, thirty-one years later.

Our gift, through answered prayer, can be a testimony to many.

When the Lord Sets the Table

– RUTH P. VERRATTI –

Knitting is a requirement for marriage. At least, that's what I thought as a little girl. My mother knit beautiful sweaters with pictures and designs for each of us. They were works of art. And she was happily married. Therefore, I needed to learn to knit for my husband.

I tried. Oh, I tried! I clearly remember the look on my mother's face when she saw the length of the arms on the sweater that I had knitted for my love. They landed somewhere close to his knees! The sweater would have fit perfectly on a horse.

There goes that theory of how to have a successful marriage!

If I were to unravel the fabric of my life and study the yarn, year by year, day by day, moment by moment, what a vast array of situations would meet my eyes.

From contrasts to constants, there were "green" times of growth, "gray" times of despair, "rose" times of joy, the tangles and knots . . . and oh, those dropped stitches!

But the Master continues to knit.

I was raised in a Christ-centered, loving, and very active home. My father's job required extensive travel, which in turn demanded a lot of my mother—six children, moving every three years, and a husband with one foot in business and the other in ministry.

Then it happened. Dad called a family meeting and dropped the bomb. He and Mom had felt God's call to leave his high-salary job and to enter full-time ministry as a traveling speaker.

This was not a salaried position. No. This was a "Children, I know God will provide" position.

To a fourteen-year-old girl, this meant many things. It meant challenges and changes, loss of status, loss of security, and loss of friends. However, as I struggled to regain my footing, I realized that I was embarking on a journey that would change my life forever. On this journey I would see, over and over, a God who was much bigger and far more powerful than the stick figure that I had drawn Him to be.

The first year was a maze of questions and answers, tears, and celebrations, as I watched my parents learn to relax in the arms of the One who was carrying them. I witnessed a battle being fought between Satan and God over my family. We experienced—and recovered from—extreme illnesses, and we faced empty kitchen cupboards—yet never went hungry.

> Mom prayed. And yes, God rolled up His sleeves and went to work.

One day, Mom answered the phone. After a brief conversation, she turned to us children and explained that company was coming for the weekend, arriving the following night for dinner. Confidently, she said, "Children, even though we have no food to serve them now, we will watch God provide."

Mom prayed. And yes, God rolled up His sleeves and went to work.

We lived in one of the suburbs of Toronto, Ontario. Our friends who lived on a farm north of the city called to tell us they had a frozen half of beef that a customer had failed to pick up and they didn't have room in their freezer for it.

"Could you take it off our hands?"

My older brother was sent to pick up the meat. *Thanks, Lord.*

That evening, we left our weekly prayer meeting at church to find a fifty-pound bag of potatoes leaning against our car.

The following morning, a neighbor called to see if we could use half a bushel of apples.

A friend stopped by with a loaf of bread.

By late afternoon, my mother had set the table with all her best china and silverware. The doorbell rang. There stood a woman with a beautiful arrangement of flowers in her hands that she thought we might like on our table.

As my mother closed the door, she turned to us and said, "Children, when the Lord sets the table, He does it right!"

God continues to knit my journey—one lesson after another, teaching me of a God with power and wisdom beyond the farthest galaxies of my mind.

As time picks up its pace and life begins to fly past the windows of the present, I am inclined to pause and ask myself, *Does my life reflect a total trust in the one almighty God? Does the structure of my daily existence allow God space and opportunity to display His power and glory, or do I default to my own strength and that of the world I live in?*

How many times has my heavenly Father longed for me to just let go, to place the situation in His loving hands, and to watch Him go to work in His own perfect time and way?

“Now to him who is able to do immeasurably more than all we ask or imagine, according to his power that is at work within us,” says Ephesians 3:20 (NIV).

Ask Him in prayer . . . and then let Him have the knitting needles. He’s got this. He continues to knit.

A Mac and Cheese Miracle

– KAREN WINGATE –

Scraggly sagebrush blurred into a gray mesh as our car dipped from La Veta Pass and sped toward the alpine San Luis Valley in southern Colorado. After receiving a call to his first ministry, my husband had moved our possessions to our new home two weeks earlier. Our two children and I stayed behind in Ohio to finish medical follow-up after our newborn daughter's surgery.

As we rode from the Pueblo airport, I shook my head, wondering where God had led us. The landscape and seclusion from larger cities lining the front range of the Rocky Mountains made me feel like we had landed on the other side of the moon.

My despair deepened as we entered the ramshackle rental house the church had found for us. Billows of dust rose out of a decades-old carpet. The fireplace, which sounded like a wonderful idea in the sub-zero temperatures of a Colorado winter, was clogged and sent plumes of smoke into the room the first time we tried to use it. Black particles floated in the water, so we had to frequently change the filter on our well pump. We had to burn our trash in a barrel in the backyard. I switched from disposable to cloth diapers because wet plastic diapers merely smoldered for hours. The floorboards in front of the toilet were so thin that I feared our feet would fall through every time we walked into the bathroom.

Worse yet, the landlord lived five hours away in New Mexico. We had to wait until he came to town to address recurring issues, fix it ourselves, or learn to live with it.

Eager to follow God's calling, we decided every ministry career must have a lean beginning. We would dig in and do the work, trusting God to meet our needs.

Each week, our paycheck stretched thin. Determined to be a stay-at-home mom so I could care for our baby's special needs, I decided the best way I could contribute to the family finances was to save as much as I could. That wasn't easy. Many times, it came down to only shopping sales, buying generic brands, and learning to do without our preferred foods.

Innocent about our financial woes, Katherine, my four-year-old, waltzed into the kitchen one morning.

Her next question shocked me. "Why don't you pray for a sale?"

"Mommy, I want Kraft mac and cheese. Can we have Kraft mac and cheese for supper?" She emphasized the brand name.

The time had come, I determined, to pass on my frugal habits to my children. "Kraft costs too much," I told her. "We need to buy the store brand or wait till Kraft goes on sale, and I haven't seen a good sale price in a long time."

Her next question shocked me. "Why don't you pray for a sale?"

Where did Katherine get that idea? Had my prayer habits been as obvious as my spending behaviors? What else was she observing?

I believed in prayer. I believed in praying for specific things. I had taught my girls that God cares about the smallest needs. But this crossed the line. I could not bring myself to pray for something that sounded so trite and, to my penny-pinching state of mind, lavish and selfish.

I blurted my annoyance. "You pray about it."

Undaunted, she folded her hands over her stomach. "Dear God. Please make Kraft mac and cheese go on sale."

There was that emphasis on the word *Kraft* again.

Disoriented by her simple faith, I turned toward my kitchen sink. The inflection in her voice expressed unyielding confidence in a God who would do what she asked.

O God, my spirit pleaded. *I would never dream of asking You for something so insignificant. Surely, you want Your children to ask for things that have more spiritual value than a box of macaroni and cheese. But I beg You. For the sake of this child's faith, would You do something?*

I couldn't even articulate what that something might be.

The grocery store flyer came the next morning, tucked in the folds of the daily newspaper. I knew I needed to look, but I hesitated. I was afraid of disappointing my child, afraid I would unwittingly tarnish her faith. I didn't think I could explain to a four-year-old that God just doesn't work that way, that He wants us to wait, or that He wants us to be content with what we have.

Coward! my conscience accused me. I unfolded the flyer. *If I'm lucky, Katherine will have forgotten.*

But Katherine stood in front of me, shifting her feet from one side to the other.

I gulped. Front and center was a box of Kraft macaroni and cheese labeled with the cheapest sale price I had seen in months.

"Katherine!" I said, my voice as small as my faith of yesterday. "Kraft mac and cheese is on sale, and it's a good price. In fact, it's the best price ever."

She jiggled on her toes, clapping in glee. "Let's go to the store."

That was it. She acted as if she wasn't surprised at all. She seemed to believe that God works this way all the time. *After all, didn't we pray about it?*

After my assurance we would go later when Daddy got home, she ran off to her toys, leaving me to ponder. Newspapers print ads well ahead of their delivery date. That newspaper was already printed before Katherine made her request. That didn't stop the Lord God. He knew of a little girl's desire long before grocery store executives decided which items would go on sale in a particular week.

I once heard a conference speaker say that God is more apt to answer the prayers of three groups of people: prayer warriors, new Christians, and children. Prayer warriors have the experience of righteousness, giving them a backdrop of confidence in knowing how to pray according to God's will and interest. But God often says yes to the prayers of new Christians and children in order to build and validate their faith.

Katherine wasn't the only one whose faith in God's provision was cultivated that day. Our family has clung to that story and repeated it to each other many times in harder moments. The trademark of God's faithfulness has reminded us that God cares deeply about the tiniest details of our lives. He really does love us lavishly, and He knows about our needs and desires even before we ask.

And God's miraculous answer to her prayer was a picture of how God was caring daily for our family despite a paltry salary so we could do the work He called us to do. He had even provided sales on simple low-cost items like boxed macaroni and cheese dinners. *Kraft* macaroni and cheese.

No Medical Explanation

– TRISH PROPSON –

Be ready to leave for Children's Hospital. A Life Flight will be waiting."

The nurse's harsh command numbed me as she whisked my four-year old daughter into the lab.

My daughter's screams faded down the hallway as she fought to break free from the nurse's grasp. I was forced to wait outside, and the words cut through my soul.

Our journey had started with a routine trip to the pediatrician. Alyssa had strep throat for the tenth time in three years. The doctor recommended a tonsillectomy. We had kept hoping she would outgrow the problem, but we finally agreed to surgery.

As a routine preoperative procedure, the doctor ordered a series of blood tests. When the doctor's office called us back in to repeat the tests, I assumed the lab had messed up. But I was a little concerned when the doctor's office called to repeat the blood tests a third time. The nurse said the test results were not conclusive, asked questions about bruising and nosebleeds, and told me to bring Alyssa in immediately. Her odd behavior raised suspicions.

A week later, the office set an appointment for us to see the doctor. I anxiously awaited, knowing the news was probably not good. I spent hours in prayer that week pleading with God to spare my daughter.

It wasn't the first time I'd prayed about Alyssa's health.

When I was pregnant with Alyssa, I woke up often in the night feeling unexplainable dread. I sensed that something might be wrong with the tiny life growing inside me. For nine months, I asked for a miraculous healing and prayed for God to spare her life.

My fears were relieved when I had an easy delivery. The unease returned when nurses recorded a high fever and whisked her away to the ICU. I was scared but not surprised. They carefully monitored her and gave her IV antibiotics.

We waited and prayed. When they finally released her, explaining that it may have just been faulty equipment, the roller coaster of emotions I was on steadied. I thanked God for His faithfulness, and we took her home.

She seemed healthy as she grew. She was prone to colds and always seemed to have a stuffy nose. She contracted her first case of strep throat at eleven months.

We never gave the infection a second thought. I reasoned it was all normal for a toddler as we dealt with ear infections, sore throats, and other minor health issues.

Our pediatrician was a kind man who had cared well for all of our children. On the day of our appointment, he entered the room with less pep than normal and chose his words carefully, "Your daughter's case may be very serious. We repeated the tests to make sure we were right before proceeding. Your daughter has a bleeding disorder. We are not sure what type or how serious it is. We will have to run a long series of tests to determine her prognosis. She cannot have the tonsillectomy until we rule out hemophilia."

His last words hit me like a javelin and spun the scrambled thoughts in my mind even faster. *Hemophilia? People die from that.*

"What next?"

He explained that a complicated series of blood tests would assess various clotting factors. Each three-week round of testing would move us into more serious levels of the disease.

"Don't worry. The disease is very rare, and the problem is usually found in the first rounds," he said, trying to assure me.

But the concern on his face did not comfort me at all. I began to pray even before I left his office.

The testing began immediately, to Alyssa's dismay.

"No more pokes," she whimpered pitifully.

Her whimpers turned to wails when we arrived at the lab. Her strong will unleashed like a tornado. I held her tightly as the nurse drew blood from her tiny arm. I feebly promised my red-faced little girl ice cream. She grudgingly accepted before fiercely proclaiming, "Not going back there—ever!"

The nurse warned us that it might be two to three weeks before we got results, so we tried to put the horrific experience at the back of our thoughts, never forgetting to pray for healing. I hoped that this test would be the last and we could move on.

The nurse finally called with results. My hope turned to fear when she told us to come in for the next level of testing. This meant the disease was more complicated than we had hoped.

I didn't tell Alyssa but as soon as we parked the car, the screaming began.

"No pokes, no pokes," she wailed.

I carried her kicking and screaming to the lab where two nurses solemnly greeted us. Two of us held her down as the nurse did the draw, informing me that the results would be available in three weeks.

Alyssa was furious. I was shaken. Ice cream didn't help.

Alyssa was furious. I was shaken. Ice cream didn't help.

We needed an avalanche of prayer. I contacted my friends, who put the call out to the church and other prayer circles. Hundreds began praying for healing.

Our lives for the next three horrible months consisted of blood draws, waiting for results, and praying.

I frantically researched each new level of the disease, knowing hope was dwindling. We found comfort knowing God loved our child more than we did.

We had at least nine rounds of blood testing. Each time, the battle with Alyssa got harder and our desperation loomed larger. Each time, the results were negative, the doctor grew more concerned. Specialists were assigned to her case and explained the seriousness of the what-ifs.

This last test would determine if Alyssa had hemophilia. The nurses knew us well after months of testing and were more than familiar with Alyssa's antics during blood draws. They seemed indifferent. But it was probably their way of hiding their emotions—feeling helpless or hopeless—when dealing with terminally ill children.

I, on the other hand, was trying desperately not to fall apart. I trusted God with my child, but also knew a whole team of medical professionals thought this was serious enough to warrant immediate transfer by helicopter to the children's hospital for emergency tests.

I prayed fervently in the waiting room boldly asking God for a miracle.

Three weeks later, we met with the doctor.

"I don't know what to say," he began.

I broke down and cried.

"The tests confirm it," he said calmly with a tone I did not recognize.

"What?" was the only word I could squeak out through my tears.

"Well, the team has reviewed the test findings, and we repeated the test to make sure." He continued. "There is absolutely no medical explanation for this: Your daughter has no evidence of any bleeding disorder. Suddenly, she is fine."

His voice lowered as he conceded, "There is just no medical explanation."

"Praise God! He healed her!" I burst out.

Our normally jolly doctor was cautiously skeptical. "I wouldn't go that far."

"I would, and I do," I exultantly smiled as I scooped Alyssa into my arms and practically danced out of the office. I knelt to pray right there in the waiting room.

There was no medical explanation. There was no reasonable explanation. Many have tried to explain it since. I have tried to rationalize it and the result is always the same: There just is no medical explanation.

I know in my heart that the prayers that hundreds of God's faithful people prayed on Alyssa's behalf made her well. God answered my prayer for divine intervention, but He also showed me that He is capable of great and mighty things beyond my comprehension.

Divine Protection

– FRAN CAFFEY SANDIN –

"Mark, don't run in the house!"

My command faded as a strong nine-year-old farm boy continued to race toward our patio, where some children had arrived early to celebrate our daughter's eighth birthday.

"Don't run!"

Deaf to my warning, he propelled himself like a rocket through three ninety-degree turns into the back playroom of our home and, without stopping, ran headlong through a thick, full-size sliding glass patio door.

Three girls on the patio began screaming and sobbing. Mark stood motionless, gazing downward with his arms extended about six inches from either side of his body. As he shook his hands, glass slivers showered and clinked onto the patio. Large jagged edges of glass like the giant teeth of a scary shark leaned out from both sides of the doorframe.

I expected to see a pool of blood, deep gashes, or broken limbs.

Surely, I will need to get him to the emergency room, I thought.

Surely, I will need to get him to the emergency room, I thought.

Instead, Mark remained motionless with a dazed expression. I placed my hand on his arm and asked with a quivering voice, "Mark, are you okay?"

"I'm fine," Mark responded with a strong, steady voice.

I promptly took Mark by the hand, walked him into the adjoining playroom, and checked him from head to toe. Except for a small red spot on his nose that didn't even require a bandage, he seemed perfectly well.

"I'm okay. I'm okay, Mrs. Sandin," he kept saying. "Please let me up so I can play."

The girls stopped crying when they saw Mark was not injured.

I explained, "Don't worry. Stay away from the glass, and we'll move our party inside."

I continued to monitor Mark for any signs of bleeding, broken bones, or head injury. Satisfied that he was all right, I focused on his big, beautiful brown eyes, placed my hands on his shoulders, and warned, "Mark, you must never, ever run in the house again."

"I'm sorry, Mrs. Sandin."

Then Mark began playing with the other children as if nothing had happened. The children's chuckles and laughter were a healing balm to my soul while I gingerly brought party supplies back into the house. Thankfully, nothing but the door was ruined. The small group of Angie's friends played games in the playroom and then enjoyed birthday cake and punch in the kitchen.

Mark's mother and I were dear friends. When she came to pick up Mark and his sister, I explained that early that morning before the party I had prayed aloud, "Lord, thank You for Angie and for this special day.

Please keep all the children safe, put Your guardian angels around them, and let us all have a happy time."

When I told her about Mark's incident, we both rejoiced in answered prayer! I asked her to let me know if Mark had any symptoms later. Fortunately, Mark never suffered any adverse effects.

That evening, when my physician husband, Jim, came home and viewed the damage, he was astounded. Standing by the saw-toothed glass, I felt the tears flow as I contemplated what the devastating consequences could have been. But God caused a miracle to happen that day, and Mark was not hurt. I felt so thankful.

Jim and I embraced as we gave thanks to our heavenly Father for answering the simple prayer I had prayed that morning.

I have learned that power in prayer depends not on the length of the prayer or flowery words but on the condition of the heart. Miracles happen because God can do anything according to His will when we call upon Him with devotion and sincerity.

Mark's miraculous, dramatic incident occurred several years ago, but the impact of God's answer is forever impressed on my heart.

Maybe we should each ask, What should I pray about today? A miracle may be waiting.

The Cowboy Angel

— DELORES TOPLIFF —

Lord, send help. My friends are so cold and scared. He knew I was getting quite concerned, too, if not as frightened as my friends. With the sun already low in the sky, I stomped my feet against the bitter cold. If I stood still too long, I'd risk frostbite.

Two friends from Minneapolis had helped me drive cross-country to pack up my former residence in British Columbia, Canada. My husband and I had raised our family in the far north, but after he passed away, I decided moving to Minnesota would mean more time with my grandkids.

This was a working vacation for my friends. After days of packing, we needed a break, so we decided to explore one of the nearest peaks in the Rocky Mountains. The weather was sunny but normal, with a November daytime temperature of thirty below zero. My friends and I bundled up, and a neighbor insisted we borrow his larger car, saying it would be more reliable.

All went well until his vehicle stalled and died in the middle of nowhere. Was it the alternator? Something worse? I managed to get his car started a few times. Each time, it drove a short distance before it shuddered and died again. After years of living in the cold north, I was confident things would turn out well, but my friends looked terrified.

"Are there wolves out here?" the younger one asked. I assured her that the wolves wouldn't bother us.

If only we had blankets, I thought.

The other friend's eyebrows hiked. "Just how cold does it get?"

"I've experienced sixty below zero twice for short periods and been fine, but it's much warmer than that now." Okay, that might have been a slight exaggeration. "Don't worry. We'll get help, but even if no one stops, we can build a snow shelter." Their expressions told me my attempt at lighthearted humor was failing.

The car drove in fits and starts back to the Alaska Highway, and something beneath the hood sounded worse every time it started up. Finally, I maneuvered to the safety of the highway's shoulder between miles 120 and 137, where we had no cell phone service and no houses or vehicles in sight. Our warm down coats and boots wouldn't be enough if I couldn't start the car again to make the heater work.

At last, two hunters stopped. They looked and listened. "It's probably your fuel pump. We'll go to our hunting camp, gather our gear, and come back."

Except they didn't. We waited, hopeful, as the late afternoon light faded, but we never saw them again. *If only we had blankets,* I thought.

I had brought a shovel and small bucket of sand in case we got stuck. I routinely also carried a small coffee can of clothes-dryer lint with a few feathered wooden sticks for a fire starter if needed.

I glanced at my friends to see the worry etched on their faces. I needed to get help, but the distances were too great to walk.

I don't recommend hitchhiking, but I reasoned that if I could reach my good friends who operated a restaurant and garage at mile 147, we'd have the help we needed. I had to try. "I'll be back in no time," I promised with more confidence than I felt. "Let's all pray right now that I catch the right ride and person."

"Oh, let's do it." We bowed our heads and asked God to help us.

We'd been driving south toward my home. Now I crossed the highway to catch someone heading north. Soon I heard a vehicle coming and pulled off one leather mitt to stick out my thumb. The car whizzed past without slowing. People in a second vehicle slowed and gawked, but the car was full, and it kept going. Still, if they had stopped, I could at least have sent a message asking for help.

Finally, in the dim, cold glow of the setting sun, I saw a heavy-duty black pickup with Montana plates heading north toward Alaska. The driver saw me, glanced at our parked car with its flashing hazard lights, and came to a stop. A tall, handsome dark-haired cowboy stretched his way up and out of his truck. He wore a fringed brown-leather jacket with a matching Stetson clamped on his head.

He grinned. "Stranded? It's pretty cold to be out hitchhiking."

He might just have been the most wonderful sight I've ever seen. It was all I could do not to hug him. "Yes," I said. "Some hunters stopped by earlier and thought it must be the fuel pump. They said they'd come back, but it's been hours, and there's no sign of them."

He nodded. "I'm glad to help. What's your plan?"

"There's no cell phone signal here, or I would have called. But if you can get me to mile 147, my friends at Mae's Kitchen and Ed's Garage will help. My passengers are from Minneapolis. They have cold winters there but nothing like this, and they're panicking. They need blankets right away, even before the car gets fixed."

"If I had some, I'd give them. Hop in. I'll take you where you're going." I hesitated, but something made me trust him. After assuring my friends that I would be back as soon as I could, I settled in the cab with my seat belt fastened.

He turned my way. "We'll be there in no time."

I didn't ask his name or destination. It was enough that he'd stopped before dark and was willing to help. We raced past highway mile markers, and I sagged with relief as I saw the welcoming lights of the restaurant and garage. "This is it," I said.

The cowboy parked and followed me inside. He tipped his hat and accepted the pile of blankets my friends stacked in his arms. "I'll run these back to the ladies while you follow in the tow truck," he said. And that's what he did.

An hour and a half later, we had reached home, enjoyed hot food, and were toasty warm again. Our conversation turned to our mysterious rescuer. "Who was he?" my friends asked me.

I shrugged. "I don't have a clue. A rugged, handsome Montana cowboy willing to help."

My older passenger shook her head. "He was more than a rugged cowboy."

My other friend nodded. "We were both praying. We believe he was an angel sent by God."

Could that be? I'd certainly been praying too. I didn't picture angels—or answers to prayer—looking like the tall, handsome cowboys in cigarette ads, but who knows? Maybe they did sometimes.

A Tale of Two Tails

– HEATHER TRENT BEERS –

Some opportunities to pray come like a summer breeze through an open window: the wind rustles the curtains, you acknowledge the air flowing through, and they're gone.

Other opportunities get your attention like a threatening storm. They crash through and wake you at night, whip your hair around as you lean against the gale-force winds, and demand your attention until the squall passes.

Most of my prayers are the summer-breeze sort. *Lord, help me meet this deadline.* Or *God, help that cashier have a better day.*

This summer, I had two back-to-back threatening-storm prayer opportunities.

Our cat, Cedar, is the sweetest kitty. She entertains us with a whole passel of antics. During her evening tromp from one end of the house to the other, she sounds like a herd of bison drumming the Kansas plains. At bedtime, she jumps into our bed for ear scratches and cuddles. Sometimes, she starts a midnight soccer game down the hallway with any mouse unfortunate enough to sneak in. She's an excellent mouser.

One Sunday morning in mid-June, Cedar joined us for our morning coffee, as usual. But instead of jumping into my lap, she lollygagged on the floor. And she hadn't jumped into bed with us the night before.

"Something's wrong with her," I told Dennis, my husband.

"Maybe she's worn out from having the family here yesterday," he offered.

I could see that. Our kids and three grandsons had been over Saturday for dinner. Cedar was a fan of mice but not so much of little boys.

When I called her name, she ignored me. Unusual for her. Her eyelids looked heavy. When I picked her up, she cried. That night, she slept in a different room. Monday morning, she hunkered under a chair.

I called the vet's office. They were busy, but they could work her in if we dropped her off.

Cedar was a rescue, so I worried she'd think we were abandoning her.

"It's okay, sweetie," Dennis reassured me. "She's in good hands."

I kissed her goodbye and went home to wait for the doctor's call.

The preliminary tests and X-rays were inconclusive, so the doctor wanted to keep Cedar overnight for observation and to give her fluids.

When we brought her home the next day, she ate and drank, but she still wasn't herself. Instead of hanging out with us, she found out-of-the-way places in other rooms to rest—behind the couch in the den if I worked in my office or under my office chair if I knitted in the den.

By the end of that first day home, she was favoring her front right paw and limping. But when I checked her paw for pain, she didn't wince or seem uncomfortable.

The next morning, she held her paw at a right angle, as if it was broken, but she still didn't cry out when we pressed on her paw or the "wrist" joint. Was it paralyzed? What was happening to our kitty?

After a very long week and more X-rays, we finally got the verdict: brachial plexus avulsion, which is a neurologic diagnosis with a poor prognosis.

The doctor cautioned this could be Cedar's new normal. No jumping up on our bed to sleep and cuddle with us at night. No more tromping like a wild woman through the house. No more getting underfoot and meowing for treats. There were no medicines to help.

> The doctor cautioned this could be Cedar's new normal.

So we prayed. We laid our hands on her several times a day and said, "Cedar, we bless you in the name of Jesus. We release the healing power of Jesus into your body." Then we kissed her, rubbed her ears, and reminded her she was the best kitty ever. Sometimes, worry nibbled at the edges of my peace. I prayed for God to heal Cedar, but would He?

One day during a moment of worry, Luke 18:1 floated into my thoughts: "Jesus told his disciples a parable to show them that they should always pray and not give up" (NIV).

So Dennis and I continued to pray, separately or together, many times a day.

When I didn't see immediate improvement, I reminded myself to never stop or lose hope. So we kept praying and thanking God.

By the beginning of July, Cedar had improved in little bits and was completely well! Not a single trace of lameness, and her daily tromps had resumed.

A few days later, while Cedar sat on my lap, a notification from the Nextdoor app popped up on my phone's home screen. Oh no. Someone's dog had been spooked by fireworks and had run away. I offered a summer-breeze prayer: *Lord, help them find their pup. And thank You, Lord, for healing our kitty.*

Our driveway alarm sounded, so Dennis and I headed outside to greet our visitors. I didn't recognize the car.

A young couple emerged from their SUV. Before they could speak, I asked the young woman, "Are you Heather?"

"Yes!" she said. "How did you know?"

"I saw your post on the Nextdoor app."

Heather told us their dog, Pretty Girl, had been gone four days now. The kids were inconsolable, and the whole family had spent hours and gallons of gas driving up and down country roads, keeping a lookout.

I was sorry to tell them we hadn't seen Pretty Girl either. But I promised to keep my eyes peeled.

The next day, as I watched Cedar bat a golf ball around, I thought about Pretty Girl. God had answered our prayers for Cedar the month before. Our life was so much fuller with her in it. Heather and her family surely felt the same way about their fur baby.

God had healed our Cedar, so I committed to pray for Pretty Girl's safe return.

Others on the Nextdoor app were on the lookout too. Someone had seen Pretty Girl over by the state line. Others recommended that Heather check the local shelters and call the police.

I kept watch on the updates. Every few days, I messaged Heather through the app and kept praying.

Three weeks later, I was still praying. *Lord, I know You can get Pretty Girl to her family. Please send Your angels to protect her and guide her home.*

Every day, I thought about Heather and her family. I didn't know if they were praying, but I knew they were hoping. And I worried they might lose hope as to how this whole thing would turn out. A total stranger knew I was praying for her dog's return. But what if Pretty Girl didn't come back? Or what if she wasn't okay? What then?

As I got ready for church on Sunday, August 4, I propped my phone on the shelf in front of the mirror and put on my makeup as I listened to Gungor's song, "Beautiful Things." The lyrics said, "Could all that is lost ever be found? . . . You make beautiful things out of us."

I hoped so.

Red letters popped up on my phone from the Nextdoor app: "Urgent Alert." Then a picture of a dog and this message in caps: "SHE IS HOME!" When I clicked into the app, I saw Heather's post. Pretty Girl had come down their driveway that morning and was waiting at their truck—four weeks after Heather had posted that the dog had run away!

Tears poured down my face, and I thanked God for healing Cedar, for leading Pretty Girl home, for teaching me to pray and not give up, and for being faithful despite my misgivings.

Later, I learned that the day Pretty Girl returned—August 4—was Heather's birthday. What a perfectly timed gift!

Sometimes, prayer opportunities float in and out like a summer breeze. And sometimes they arrive like a brewing storm. If we accept His invitation and stick with Him, we learn about His faithfulness and the reward of His good timing and not giving up hope.

A Doctor-Approved Miracle

– JANIS VAN KEUREN –

Tubes hung from my mother's limp body while monitors beeped and clicked revealing the unseen conditions of her heart, lungs, blood pressure, and other vital organs. I stared blankly out the window of the intensive care unit.

My mind was reeling. It was not supposed to go this way. Although the surgery was complex, especially for an eighty-four-year-old woman, the surgeon had assured us the typical recovery would take no more than four weeks in the hospital and a skilled nursing facility. He also assured us that he had performed this surgery on other patients her age.

I had left my home in Arizona to be with Mom in California for the procedure. Much prayer had gone into this decision, so why had Mom experienced numerous complications?

I looked at the world outside the window where life proceeded normally. The contradiction churned inside me because nothing in my life was normal at this moment. So I turned my attention to the Lord, crying out to Him for my believing Mom, citing Psalm 91:14–16:

"'Because he loves me,' says the Lord, 'I will rescue him; I will protect him, for he acknowledges my name. . . . I will be with him in trouble . . . With long life will I satisfy him and show him my salvation'" (NIV).

Emotionally drained and separated from my family, I had difficulty feeling the Lord's comfort. As I stood immobile at Mom's bedside, scenes from that morning flashed through my mind.

When I had arrived in the intensive care unit (ICU), the nurse on duty spoke in an urgent tone. "Your mother's blood pressure is dropping, and you can visit for only fifteen minutes."

Mom could hardly talk. I squeezed her fingertips and told her she would be okay, trying to encourage both of us. I whispered a silent prayer and hoped my love for her and my wobbly faith could pull her through.

I returned to the ICU waiting room. My best friend, Cecelia, greeted me with compassion and concern. Within moments, we heard a chilling voice over the loudspeaker, "Code Blue! Code Blue! Intensive Care."

I feared it could be for my mother. My friend and I grabbed hands and began praying through our tears.

Soon a doctor appeared in the hallway and shouted at me, "Your mother has had a heart attack."

Was he saying she would die?

My friend sobbed and said, "This is not what the Lord showed me was supposed to happen."

Every fiber of my being wanted to believe that she had heard the Lord's distinctive voice saying Mom would pull through. But the heaviness in the room and among the hospital staff demanded I face reality.

In desperation, I called the pastor we had known when we lived in California. He dashed to the hospital to pray with me. He said, "Pour out your heart's requests to the Lord. Then entrust your mom into His hands."

How was I to pray for healing, to believe God would do this miracle, yet let go of her to God?

That night, I wrote in my journal, "How can I trust You, because what You want and what I want look vastly different? I want Mom restored to health, but You aren't healing her." Then I realized what I was doing.

"Lord, I want to direct You. I want to make You heal her. If I give up now and surrender Mom to Your will, I will feel as if I have let her down. I'm burdened carrying her on my every prayer," I wrote from my broken, stubborn heart.

That weekend, as Mom's life hung in the balance, my husband, Tom, and our two sons flew in from Arizona. Friends rescued our sons, providing time for them to relax and play.

In the quiet moments, Tom and I prayed and agonized over the what-ifs of Mom's condition and how to handle different scenarios. Nerves frayed like worn fabric, we called a minister from Mom's church to come and anoint her. Relief washed over me as I sensed God's hand.

When the minister arrived, Mom's condition had not changed. Machines pumped rhythmically to keep her alive. As we gathered around her bed, the minister removed a bottle of oil from its pouch, anointed my mother, and began praying. Heads bowed, we all focused on the Lord, hearts united, entreating God for a miracle.

The minister prayed, "Through this holy anointing, may the Lord in His love and mercy help you with the grace of the Holy Spirit. May the Lord who frees you from sin save you and raise you up."

Then we all prayed, my heart hoping God would heal Mom.

As we ended our prayer, Mom suddenly started coughing and rapidly breathing above the respirator's pulses of oxygen. For the first time in three days, Mom's eyes opened.

A new flame of faith flickered in my heart. During the next six weeks, she had multiple setbacks. One day, the medical reports looked good, and I cheered. The next day, the doctors discovered problems that made my stomach flip with nauseating despair.

A new flame of faith flickered in my heart.

Daily, I stood by Mom's bedside holding her hand, talking to her, reading scriptures, and softly singing Christian songs, even when she was not completely alert. Each morning, I met with the doctors and fired my arsenal of questions at each specialist. Their answers were harsh and realistic. One doctor even said it would be a miracle if she pulled through.

During this time, the Lord reminded me to thank Him every day for something. At first, I was only grateful to God for not having to pay for hospital parking multiple times a day. Gradually, my vision expanded, and I saw the Lord's hand and comfort in many people and situations, even though Mom's condition remained tenuous. I had the love of family and friends who came to the hospital on a moment's notice, more than one warm home to collapse in at the end of an exhausting day, people in many states praying for Mom, counsel and expertise on medical reports from friends who were nurses, and friends caring for my family back home in Arizona, to mention only a few.

Mom overcame major hurdles but was unable to breathe on her own, despite many attempts.

One hopeful morning, the chief surgeon suggested we meet in the hospital before sunrise. Waiting breathlessly, we saw Mom's lungs kick in and draw their own breath for the first time in months. The miracle was on its way.

There was still an extensive recovery ahead for Mom, but after two and a half months in the hospital, she came home. And the doctor who said it would take a miracle, stopped me in the hall on Mom's last day there to agree a miracle had occurred.

The Lord graced us with Mom's life for four more years.

Through this experience, I learned to find a nugget of God's blessing in all circumstances, to trust His Word, and to not rely on myself.

I also realized God still does miracles. Sometimes we only have to ask.

Feasting with Angels

BARBARA PARENTINI

The university hospital towered against the blue-black predawn as I eased the car past the front entrance. My husband, Brian, tapped his fingers in a nervous rhythm on the armrest. He had admitted that morning he was anxious about this surgery and didn't want it to turn out like the first one, many months before. When the valet took the keys, we hurried through the doors to the elevators.

Once inside the pre-op area, we were ushered into a beehive of activity. Doctors and nurses bustled in and out to Brian's bedside to introduce themselves, discuss medical information, and get him ready for this surgery. His surgeon pushed the curtain aside to say hello and gave a reassuring smile before leaving the room.

Once we were alone, I held my husband's hand and prayed. I whispered, "I love you," and leaned down to kiss him.

"I love you, too, honey. I could never have made it this far without you and the Lord." I smiled as his tired eyes searched my face.

As the nurse slowly pushed his bed past me toward the hall, Brian's eyes followed mine. His parting smile concealed the hint of worry, and within moments his handsome profile disappeared behind the operating room doors.

I scanned the spacious waiting room, anticipating a wait of several hours for my husband's surgery. Families and friends huddled in small groups, speaking in low voices. I was exhausted, and my legs felt like lead as I sank into a cushioned chair in a quiet corner. I closed my eyes and whispered prayers for Brian's good report, and once again, trusted God with my husband's life. After six surgeries in six months, I had come to better understand what "pray without ceasing" meant.

Over the previous eighteen months, we had walked through the Valley of the Shadow more than once. Prayer was no longer a monologue, but rather quiet time and personal conversations from my heart with the Lord.

Every two hours, I received the same message from surgery: "Still in the OR. Doing well."

I called my family with an update and prayed with my aunt and her husband. They had stayed close to us on our journey, fasting and praying each time Brian underwent surgery.

In the afternoon, to pass the time, I strolled along banks of windows overlooking the front of the hospital. Life below seemed untroubled and carefree. Couples drove away to evening destinations, and parents hurried home to their families. I daydreamed about the beach retreat we had planned last summer. How we loved to relax and restore by the ocean! Maybe next year.

By evening, I was getting concerned. Brian was still in the OR, and no one had offered a reason. After taking a seat closer to the reception desk, I felt an overwhelming desire to pray that God would send angels to minister to my husband.

"Oh, Lord, Brian hasn't eaten for two days, and he is still in surgery. Please send Your angels to minister to him and feed him Your heavenly food that nourishes him, strengthens him, heals him, and comforts him with Your love and hope . . . on all levels. Thank You, Lord."

I continued to thank and praise God for what He was doing for my husband. I prayed for God to minister to the surgeon's needs, as well, to give him wisdom, skill, and supernatural strength. I prayed that the healing hands of Jesus move through the doctor's arms and hands to guide him as he worked.

I looked around the empty waiting room and approached the receptionist. Her eyes softened as I asked for news.

She repeated the message I'd heard all day. She then told me that the recovery area would close soon, and Brian would be sent to another building of the hospital complex to recover in the surgical intensive care unit. She encouraged me to go downstairs for something to eat before the cafés closed. I agreed to take a break.

"It's *paid* for? What do you mean? Who paid for it?" I asked.

The cafeteria buffets were empty, so I walked next door into a quiet café. One customer paid for his order at the cash register, and a couple waited behind me while I ordered.

When my sandwich was delivered to the cashier, I reached into my purse. She said, "You don't need to pay anything. Your sandwich is paid for."

"It's *paid* for? What do you mean? Who paid for it?" I asked if she was sure I didn't owe anything, certain there must be some mistake. I looked around me in disbelief. "Where is this person? I'd like to say thank you."

The clerk scanned the small dining room. "It was some lady. She had on a brown coat." She shook her head. "I don't see her now. She must have left."

I was pleased but perplexed by the anonymous gift. I wandered back to the empty waiting room upstairs and sat down as the receptionist prepared to leave. After I had eaten most of the sandwich, a clear, quiet voice spoke to my heart: *I heard your prayers. I answered your prayers. I sent angels to feed Brian. And I sent an angel to feed you.*

My mouth fell open. I tingled with goose bumps, and tears filled my eyes. I took a deep breath. An angel!

Delighted by the affirmation of God's presence, I felt angels swirling about in my thoughts as I navigated the labyrinth of walkways to the distant wing of the hospital.

As my husband's time in the OR approached seventeen hours, I longed to know how Brian was doing. I began to speak with an older woman. I told her about Brian's miraculous recoveries and how Jesus had healed him. She shared her own faith and spoke of God's goodness. When a nurse called her name, she got up to leave.

"I enjoyed talking with you. I hope your husband does well," she said.

I thanked her for her kind words. "By the way, what is your name?"

She turned and smiled, her face aglow in the soft light. "Angela."

I paused and repeated her name in utter amazement. "Oh . . . Angela. Have a good night."

My heart soared with joy and gratitude, and I knew Brian was going to be just fine.

And he is.

Ten Things about Miracles

– DIANA AYDIN –

1. **Miracles can be super small.** It's easy to dismiss a miracle if it's not on the scale of parting a major body of water! But maybe miracles are God's way of communicating with us. As someone once said, "A coincidence is a small miracle where God chose to remain anonymous."
2. **God is a creative genius!** Seriously, I'm constantly amazed by His miraculous designs–from cliffs that look like wedding cake to a fiery rainbow. Even something as ordinary as cabbage is wondrous when you examine it closely.
3. **Love uncovers the miraculous.** It's no surprise that many miracles involve sweethearts or family members (and especially, it seems, mothers!). There's something about the bond of love that brings wonder to light.
4. **Miracles don't always look like miracles.** Sometimes you don't realize wonder has occurred until after the fact. That's

something I learned from my parents, who met in the first grade but didn't end up connecting until much later. Isn't it amazing to think of all the "miracles in progress" unfolding at this very moment?

5. **It's all about perspective.** What's a miracle for you might not be for someone else. God speaks to you in your own language. And He'll use whatever is meaningful to you not someone else.
6. **God uses people as miracles.** I've been blown away by the number of times another person has participated in the wonder in my life. Like my friend Gladys, whose words of comfort reached me at the very moment I needed them most.
7. **Miracles are completely surprising.** You can beg for them, plead for them. But they always seem to happen when you least expect them.
8. **Sometimes you gotta think like a kid.** Stop asking questions and put on your inner-child wonder vision. You never know what you might see.
9. **Miracles often happen at low points.** As C. S. Lewis said, "God whispers to us in our pleasures, speaks in our consciences, but shouts in our pain." In moments of darkness, God swoops in with a nudge or sign to remind you He's got your back.
10. **Prayer is powerful.** I've noticed that prayer often comes before a miracle. That's not to say you pray and instantly wonder unfolds. But keeping an open dialogue with God is key.

3

Tragedy to Triumph

There is terrible suffering in our world today. Tragic things happen to good people. God does not cause them, nor does He always prevent them. He does, however, strengthen us and bless us with His peace, through earnest prayer.

REX D. PINEGAR

The winds howl and go on a rampage, leaving destruction behind. The gun goes off, striking innocent victims and breaking hearts. The earth shakes, toppling structures and terrifying hearts. The heavens open up, and the deluge sweeps away everything in sight. Fire roars, and angry flames devour everything in their path. And dozens, hundreds, thousands, or even millions of lives come to a standstill. Whether nature-created or man-made, disasters bring us to our knees begging for help and mercy.

And that's where we should be.

Sometimes tragedies are on a large scale and public, and sometimes they happen on a personal level. The land was facing a severe drought when God sent Elijah to go to an area called Zarephath and stay with a widow, whom He had instructed to serve Elijah food. She did, ready to obey God by using the last of her flour and oil to prepare bread for Elijah.

But an odd thing happened. The flour and oil didn't run out. Elijah told the widow that both would last all through the famine so she and her son would not die of starvation! (See 1 Kings 17.)

However, sometime later another tragedy struck. The widow's son became ill. He got worse and worse and finally died. But again, God cared. Elijah prayed over the young man, and he came back to life. The widow's response? She probably said quite a bit! But 1 Kings 17:24 records, "Then the woman told Elijah, 'Now I know for sure that you are a man of God, and that the LORD truly speaks through you'" (NLT).

Every tragedy—small scale or large scale—involves individuals. For instance, we may see a video of a tsunami wiping out houses in Japan . . . each one of those houses is someone's home, and God cares about each individual.

In this chapter, you will read stories about individuals like the widow who suffered from no fault of her own. And you will see how

God overcomes the tragedies in our lives to bring triumph. Sometimes it's direct triumph in our lives; sometimes the triumph is that we see a new reflection of God.

Take heart from these stories and know that God can unleash the same power in your own life. Tragedy doesn't surprise an all-knowing God. And He cares about us incredibly more than we can even think or imagine.

F. B. Meyer said, "The greatest tragedy of life is not unanswered prayer, but unoffered prayer." So, in your tragedies, turn to God. Follow the wisdom of Lamentations 3:55–57, "I called on your name, LORD, from the depths of the pit. You heard my plea: 'Do not close your ears to my cry for relief.' You came near when I called you, and you said, 'Do not fear'" (NIV).

God Spared My Life

– DAVID HATCHER, AS TOLD TO LORI HATCHER –

God, help me! Please don't let me die. I'm not ready!"

Lying on my bed, shaking with fear, I knew I was dying. And if I died, I knew I'd go to hell. Earlier that night, I'd swallowed drugs I'd never taken before, added alcohol, and plunged myself into a living nightmare.

For weeks, I'd been discontented with my life. Only seventeen years old, I'd tried much of what the world said would fulfill me. But it never did. Every high had a low, and every low just got lower.

I had enough of a religious background to know I needed God. I tried to change. But when I visited my childhood church, I came away feeling emptier than ever.

As the drugs and alcohol took effect, I became sleepier and sleepier. Somehow I knew if I fell asleep, I would never wake up. I'd lost several friends to drug overdoses, so I knew it could happen.

"It's not fair, God," I said. "I want to quit. I want to change, but I can't do it by myself. Please change me."

God, in His mercy, spared my life that night. I awakened the next morning with only a dim memory of my terrifying experience. When friends came by looking for drugs, I still went with them.

We were sitting on a brick wall on a street corner when Jolene, a lady selling World Book Encyclopedias, walked up to us. She was looking for families with children, so we sent her down the road. She walked away, then turned and came back.

"I feel led by the Lord to speak to you guys," she said. "Six months ago, my husband and I were using drugs and alcohol. Our marriage was falling apart. He was packing his bags to leave when someone knocked on the door. This man from the church told us how Christ had changed his life. He said Jesus could do the same for us."

She continued, "When we prayed to receive Christ as our Savior, God began to change us. He took away our desire for drugs and alcohol. Now I can drink as much as I want to—but I don't want to."

As I listened to her words, my body began to tingle. Memories from the night before flashed across my mind. Overwhelmed with emotion, I realized the God of the universe was answering my prayer.

Jolene stopped. Until that moment, she'd been talking to us as a group, but then she singled me out.

"God wants to save you today," she said.

"God wants to save you today," she said.

She explained how humans sinned and fell short of God's standard. Because we couldn't pay the punishment for our sin, God sent Jesus, the sinless God-man, to suffer and die in our place.

"If you'll confess, repent of your sin, and accept God's offer of forgiveness," she said, "God will save you. He'll come to live in your heart and change you into the person you were created to be."

My heart leaped with joy. *Yes! This is what I need. This is what I want. . . . But how can I do this in front of my friends?*

This Holy Spirit–filled woman spoke again. "You know, the Bible says if you're ashamed of Him before men, He'll be ashamed of you before the Father."

Her words removed the final obstacle. Right there, on the side of the road, with cars passing and my friends watching, I bowed my head and asked Christ to be my Savior.

On July 2, 1980, on a street corner in Woodfield Park, Columbia, South Carolina, the old David Hatcher died, and a new man took his place. Over time, God took away my desire for drugs and alcohol and replaced it with a desire to find joy through my relationship with Him. No longer a slave to addiction and fear, I've spent the past thirty-seven years changing to become more like my Savior.

Now I'm free from the pointless struggle to earn God's love. Instead, I rest in the security "that he who began a good work in [me] will carry it on to completion until the day of Christ Jesus" (Philippians 1:6, NIV).

Hanging On Tight to Jesus

– TERESA SHIELDS PARKER –

I saw her coming down the hall toward me, and I knew what she was going to say. If I could have found an excuse to turn around, I would have. But she was right there. This time, though, I'd be honest.

"Hi, sweetie," Betty said embracing me in a big bear hug. "Is this your last day at work before you go off to college?"

"Yes, ma'am," I said, bracing myself.

"I just want you to know that I'm praying for your mama. I know God is going to answer us if we keep praying. He will deliver her. I know it," she said with tears in her eyes.

I stared at her with all the wisdom of a seventeen-year-old high school graduate and let loose. "Well, you can stop praying. I've been praying for her as long as I can remember, and she hasn't gotten any better. As a matter of fact, she's worse. I really think God is fed up with listening to our prayers for her."

I tried to walk away, but she had hold of my arm. "Look at me. God is a God of the breakthrough. He will set her free. Prayer works because God works."

Her eyes bored into my soul, and her tears fed a part of me I didn't know existed.

She was just a woman from my church who happened to work where I worked for the summer. She was simply a woman who cried wet prayers for my mother.

Mom had been emotionally ill for most of my life. I was looking forward to going off to college to get away from her madness.

She had what was described as a nervous breakdown. She hadn't gotten out of the house in months. She was afraid of crowds, afraid of people looking at her or singling her out. She was paranoid with schizophrenic tendencies.

At her worst, she would sit and stare into oblivion, ignoring everything and everyone around her. I never knew what kind of mood she'd be in when I got home from school. One day, she'd be dancing in the kitchen to jitterbug music and baking cookies. The next day, she'd be stark raving mad, waiting for me with a belt.

Although I wasn't a model child, the spankings weren't for something I'd done wrong. They were simply because she was angry about something. Sometimes she would say that I had done something, but I had no idea what she was talking about.

I came to understand later that she was taking her anger at herself out on me. As a child, it always messed up my mind. I was always trying to figure out what I did wrong and what I could do right to avoid another beating.

She spent many summers in a nearby mental hospital or the psychiatric ward of the local hospital. Maybe the stress of raising three kids, along with taking care of the house, laundry, meals, and grocery shopping was more than she could handle.

One thing was consistent throughout my childhood: every day I prayed for my mother. My father prayed for my mother. People in my dad's church prayed for my mother. Friends of mine at the church across the street from our house, like Betty, prayed for my mother. Grandma and Papaw prayed for my mother. My uncles, aunts, cousins, and everyone I knew prayed for my mother. Most of them seemed to cry when they were praying or when they told me they were praying.

When I'd ask my dad what was wrong with her, he'd simply say, "Your mother is sick."

Even as a little kid, I knew she wasn't physically sick, like with a stomachache, mumps, or even chicken pox, which I deemed the worst of my childhood illnesses. Her sickness was of the mind and emotions, a kind of soul sickness that defied any definitions.

I heard one of my younger cousins say my mother was "crazy." I defended her and said she wasn't crazy; she was just sick.

"Yeah, she's sick," he said. "Sick in the head." He laughed and ran off to play.

What did he know? Those words, though, stuck with me. As I got older, I understood more of what was going on with Mom, but the cure always came back to prayer. Nothing else worked; not medicine, doctors, or hospitals. Our hope was in God. Only He could fix her.

When I walked into the house after seeing Betty, I saw a letter on the bureau. I got lots of mail from Oral Roberts because I was always writing to him to pray for my mom. When I saw the letter with his logo, I opened it, only to find it was actually a prayer request for healing that Mom had written to him.

Her words were devastating: "Many times, the emotional pain of living here on earth gets so unbearable that I just want to take a knife and kill myself and my three children. I want to take us all out of this horrible world."

I read the words over and over and over again. She was asking for prayer so she wouldn't do this. Maybe that was a good sign?

Still, I was leaving for college in a week. I couldn't leave my little sister and brother here with her if she really wanted to stab them. I stuffed the letter in my jeans pocket and hurried to my room.

"Okay, God, this is getting really serious," I wrote in my journal. "I don't know what to do here. I know You opened doors for me to go to school. I know it's the next step, but I don't think I can leave with her like this."

That evening, Dad asked me to do the grocery shopping, and I told him I needed his help. What I really needed was to talk to him. After he read the letter, he said, "Your job is to go to college. My job and God's is to make sure your brother and sister are safe. I'll talk to the neighbors to make sure they know to watch out for them. But your job is to go to college."

Then my dad prayed as only he could pray, through tears, for his wife and my mom. I will always remember his wet prayers that seemed to well up from the deepest ache in his soul. "Father God, heal my wife. Heal the woman I love. Restore her. Renew her. Resurrect her by Your Power."

I left for college knowing if anyone could get through to God, it was Dad, and Betty wasn't far behind because I knew she would never stop praying.

The phone call alone should have let me know that something different was up.

"It's your mother," my college suitemate said in hushed tones.

"You mean, my dad, right?" She shook her head, "No," and mouthed the letters *M-O-M.*

My mother had not once called me at college. It was always Dad. Sometimes he'd put Mom on the phone, but she never talked.

"What's up, Mom?" I said in the phone.

"God healed me," she said matter of factly.

"Really?" It was hard to tell from her voice if this was real or another one of her fantasies. "Tell me about it."

She told me about a woman who had invited her to go to a Full Gospel Business Men's Fellowship meeting near our home. The first miracle was that Mom didn't say no. Yvonne came and picked her up. The second miracle is that Mom went.

Mom said the speaker that night was talking about emotional illness and strongholds. At the end of his message, he said, "God is going to touch three people tonight. If you are one of those, I want you to stand."

> "God is going to touch three people tonight. If you are one of those, I want you to stand."

The third miracle was that my agoraphobic, anxiety-ridden, manic-depressed, clinically ill mother stood. The speaker talked to each of them and told them each something different. My mother remembered only what he said to her: "God is going to touch you tonight, but you are not going to be instantly healed. You have been trying to fit the Word of God into your life. You need to fit your life into the Word of God. You have been trying to find words in the Bible that will prove you can do whatever you want. You have to fit your life into what God's Word says. You have to do what God's Word tells you to do."

"Mom, how are you going to do that?" I asked.

"I'm going to hang on as tight to Jesus as I can," she answered.

Over the next several years while I was in college and living in different locations, I watched as my mother became a real mom to my brother and sister.

I saw in her a drive to become a godly woman. She still took medication, although not as much. She still saw her therapist, but she was daily walking out her life's issues with God as her guide.

When she passed away in 1992, the words many spoke to me were that my mother was a true friend and had a heart of mercy and compassion. Beyond that, she had a love that wouldn't stop for her grandchildren.

In my mom's life, I saw firsthand how God can start a person on a healing journey that will be demonstrated in how she lives her life here on this earth.

Oh, and remember Betty? The next time I saw her was at the newspaper office when I was working during Christmas break. I ran up to her, hugged her tightly, and said, "Betty, forgive me for what I said to you the last time I saw you. God healed Mom! Thank you for praying. God did listen."

"Yes," she said. "I never once doubted He would. He always works in His own time and in His own way."

And this time, we both had tears in our eyes.

An Attitude of Gratitude

– KELLY WILSON MIZE –

The Christmas lights were extinguished, the holiday decorations were put away, and the satisfaction of a season well celebrated gave way to the promise of a fresh new year—a bright future filled with limitless possibility.

That is, for everyone but me. In my world, the new calendar year meant a new reality that was too excruciating to imagine, much less accept. The doctor was sympathetic but confident in her diagnosis.

My baby was going to die.

Two days before Christmas, in the middle of a rare Alabama ice storm, my husband and I received the devastating news. We plodded through the holidays, knowing it could be our son's first and last Christmas season. Every joyful carol was a reminder of our family's fate, and twinkling lights illuminated only the awareness of our sickening new normal.

Ordinary, everyday tasks became almost unbearable: taking a shower, cooking, cleaning, unsuccessfully nurturing a heartbroken marriage, and taking care of a baby who we were told would soon leave us.

Our beautiful, firstborn, six-month-old baby boy was diagnosed with a rare neurological disease and would likely not live past his second birthday.

Through tears, the doctor had explained that any future children we had might be stricken with the same fate. There was no treatment and no cure. Life support would soon be a major concern, and we would need to make other important decisions. I desperately asked the neurologist, "Have you ever been wrong?"

Her answer hit hard. "In fifteen years, unfortunately not."

We could do or say nothing else—except to pray.

Then, on a dreary winter morning soon after the diagnosis, I stood in front of my bathroom mirror, attempting to prepare for yet another hopeless day, tears washing away what little makeup I had applied.

"God, please help me!" I cried, physically dropping to my knees, a position that had become second nature.

At that moment, I heard God whisper, *Philippians 4:5*.

Though I was familiar with the passage, I rushed to find my Bible, to see the words, read them, hear them, *feel* them. I was starving for any small morsel of God's presence in my dire situation. "The Lord is near. Do not be anxious about anything . . ." (Philippians 4:5–6, NIV).

As I carefully read the words I had read a hundred times, I noticed something I'd never focused on before in the next verse: ". . . by prayer and petition, with thanksgiving, present your requests to God. And the peace of God, which transcends all understanding, will guard your hearts and your minds in Christ Jesus" (verses 6–7).

With thanksgiving? I focused on the words cynically.

I definitely wasn't *feeling* one bit thankful for anything. But as I thought and prayed more, the concept began to make perfect sense.

When we ask God for something, the request should always be prefaced with thanksgiving. Because only then are we in a position to receive the precious, invaluable peace He promises.

I began to thank God for everything I could think of—extended family, a warm home, my husband's job.

When I was thankful, even in that seemingly hopeless situation, I was able to experience God's peace. The very idea of peace had been unfathomable in the month leading up to that day—a distant, fading dream I couldn't imagine ever experiencing again.

Then, one day in early spring, after countless tests, doctor visits, and turmoil, we had an incredible breakthrough. Three months (almost to the day) after the original diagnosis, not one but *two* neurologists in a neighboring state found my son's condition to be that of a normal, healthy, nine-month-old baby. All previous test results and diagnoses were suddenly and gloriously dismissed.

All previous test results and diagnoses were suddenly and gloriously dismissed.

Dumbfounded, I remember asking the doctor, "What should we do now?"

"Go home to Alabama," he replied.

So we did—praising God all the way. The trip home was a joyous passage. Spring's bright beauty, in such stark contrast to the darkness of the winter, reflected the condition of our hearts.

That precious baby boy recently finished his sophomore year of college and has a beautiful eighteen-year-old sister. During that time of darkness, I promised God that if He would just let me keep my baby, I would tell the world what He had done. I've kept that promise and shared this story many times in many different ways.

God does not always choose to heal. But we can be assured that He will never leave us alone during those terrible times of waiting and suffering. I have learned that when I take the time to express thanksgiving as a part of my prayers, like I did on that cold, desperate winter morning, it makes a monumental difference in my state of mind. Gratitude leads to a peace that is beyond human comprehension: miraculous and perfect.

And that perfect peace is not just for hopeless, desperate, wretched days . . . it's for *every* day. We can access it any time we choose to be grateful.

Finding the Right Combination

– ZETA COMBS DAVIDSON –

What happens to a bright, conscientious young woman when she tries to be a perfect wife, a perfect mother, and a perfect teacher?

That described me after a ten-year hiatus of being a stay-at-home mom while my two children were small. Such an enthusiastic set of goals might work for some people, but it didn't work for me.

After not sleeping any during the night for an entire week, I got up one morning, showered, dressed, and could go no further. Who would have thought an articulate, achieving teacher could be not only slowed to a crawl—but completely stopped? I knew I was losing weight—nothing tasted good—but thirty-two pounds without trying?

Focus? My concentration skills had left me. Normally gregarious, smiling, and talkative, I had slowly become withdrawn and reclusive. Every circumstance I encountered seemed negative—I simply could not think positively about any situation.

And I had no idea what was wrong.

We finally got an appointment with our primary care physician. Terry Calhoun took one look at me, ordered a blood test, had the nurse take my vitals, and sat down facing me. "Zeta, you are suffering from clinical depression created by a chemical imbalance—you have coped with your feelings of 'no matter what you do, it's not good enough' until you can cope no more. You've used all the serotonin in your brain."

You may have heard of this mental-health condition—I had not. My family's philosophy had always been, "Get up and get going—get over whatever is holding you back."

"This condition is known as the common cold of mental illness," Dr. Calhoun continued. "You must rest; you are totally worn out."

Never before had I suffered an illness that couldn't be treated with one prescription, let alone taken longer than a week or two to get well.

My chest burned. My anxiety level topped out at what felt like well above 100 percent. My hands shook; I was fearful of riding in a car; the future looked bleak at best.

I knew if I had a physical illness, or an injury such as a broken arm, it would have to be treated to heal; the same was true of clinical depression—I couldn't worry about what others thought. The emotional pain that had reversed my personality hurt more and far longer than any broken arm might.

The doctor sent me to the hospital for a weeklong stay, and the psychiatrist who saw me asked two very straightforward questions: "Do you know that untreated depression can lead to suicide? Has anyone in your family ever died by suicide?"

"My dad did," I answered.

"Would you ever do that?"

Pulling at the back of my hair on first one side and then the other, I responded, "I hope not; I hope not."

After resting at the hospital, I waited three more long weeks for an appointment to see another recommended psychiatrist. Medication started at the hospital did not make any difference. My bedroom became my domicile; I didn't leave it.

Depression medications take about three weeks to make a person feel better. Each week, my husband would take me for an appointment. Three weeks went by; nothing happened. The new medication only kept me from sleeping. Three more weeks passed. My only encouragement was a remark our friend Bill heard from the director of a local mental-health agency. I said it over and over and over in my mind, *Depression can almost always be treated successfully if the right combination of medicines can be found.*

Bill's wife, Sandy, stayed with me when my husband, Don, had to be away on business one day. I knew I was little or no better when I saw the look of questioning hurt on her face. I knew those new medicines had not worked.

> "Mom, we say we believe in prayer. Why don't you have a prayer meeting for Zeta?"

That very week, two things happened—the psychiatrist started me on still another combination of two antidepressants, and Sandy's son quipped to his mother, "Mom, we say we believe in prayer. Why don't you have a prayer meeting for Zeta?"

Within the next couple of weeks, Sandy did just that—planned a prayer meeting at her home. Don had told her, "Don't expect Zeta to attend; she won't leave our bedroom."

I don't know why I went; I just did. Sandy seated us in a circle with me at her right. She had her Bible open; she must have read a scripture. Then she asked the person on her left to begin the prayer time.

One by one, our closest church friends—John, Marilyn, Charles, Sharon, and Bill—prayed for me, followed by our pastor, Brad Dixon. When it was Don's turn, he wept as he pleaded with God for my return to health.

Prayers of praising God, requests for my healing, and thanking God in advance filled an entire hour. When it became my turn, I could not say a word.

To this day, I am convinced that this new combination of medicines and the prayer meeting changed me. When I awoke the next morning, I felt more like myself than I had in several months. A still, small voice whispered to me, *You must share all of this story with your psychiatrist.*

Dr. Olomon could tell at my next weekly appointment that I was better. I kept putting off saying anything—even though the still, small voice said, *You must share . . .* She kept writing notes on my chart; then she was ready to close the chart.

Finally, I spoke, "Dr. Olomon, I believe my being so much better is possibly because of two things—I believe you found the right combination of medicines. And I don't know what you will think, but—" Then I blurted out the details of the previous week's prayer meeting. She immediately hugged me.

What has happened since? During my eighteen years of teaching, I had the privilege of being nominated for Teacher of the Year, and my children have grown and have children of their own. I still take that same combination of two medicines. Plus, I will always have these words marked in my Bible in James 5:16: "The prayer of a righteous person is powerful and effective" (NIV).

Seeing with New Eyes

– MICHAEL CREANGE, AS TOLD TO SUSAN PANZICA –

I've been a drug addict for many, many years. My mom came to live with me after she lost everything in Hurricane Sandy. I was one of seven children, yet she picked me. Later, I realized it was because she was so worried about me.

I started drinking at an early age. My friend and I would steal beers from his stepdad's basement. Eventually, we began cutting school. Once, at ten years old, I forged an absence note from my mother that went something like this: "Dear Mrs. Kroswell, Please excuse Michael for missing school yesterday. He had tuberculosis and almost lost both legs."

If Mrs. Kroswell hadn't figured out I was the one writing the note, she certainly did when she saw that I signed the note, "Love, Mom."

In my twenties, I worked as an elevator mechanic. I got married and had a child, a beautiful baby girl. I was living the American Dream. Then the unthinkable happened.

I fell down an elevator shaft, which required a number of back surgeries and put me on the dark road of addiction. For years, pain management facilities became my pushers. They gave me whatever I wanted—oxycodone, hydrocodone, morphine. I felt like a kid in a candy store. I used pain as an excuse to keep increasing my dosage, and the pain management centers gladly obliged. My life became a blur of drug-filled days as I moved on to more illegal drugs.

I would drive down to Newark, New Jersey, to the inner city, with a thousand dollars in my pocket to spend on heroin. There wasn't a time driving back home that I wouldn't think of my daughter. I had no money to give her since I spent it on drugs for myself. An addict will always find an excuse for the things he or she does. But in the end, addicts will always wind up putting themselves first. Always.

Through the years, I convinced myself I was able to function. I gave my daughter as much love as I could possibly give. I tried to be there for her in times of joy and times of sorrow. She was the world to me. And a little girl always sees things through innocent eyes.

But my wife knew. She looked at my lies, my manipulations, and she saw what was most important to me—drugs. And she grew tired of it. If she caught me taking painkillers or found where I had hidden them, I immediately got defensive, "My back hurts! I need them!"

When my daughter was about four years old, I was working in Paterson, New Jersey. Addicts, dealers, and homeless people were the only ones on its inner-city streets. Gunfire was common. A security guard in a dilapidated building told me if I needed anything, he would be able to get it dirt cheap. One night after work, I took my daughter and returned to Paterson, driving down a dark, dead-end street to the back of a broken-down building. I locked my car, told my daughter I would be right back, walked into the building, and met the security guard.

But the dealer was late. Twenty-five minutes later, I left the building with four bricks of heroin. It was pitch-black outside when I got to the car. My daughter was sitting there, terrified. She was shaking, and her face was wet with tears.

When I got into the car, she hugged me like I was her hero. Through gasps, she told me that a man came up to the car and banged on the window screaming at her to let him in.

Events like this caused me to hate myself. Each morning, I would wake up and look in the mirror at a failure. The guilt and shame were just too much.

My wife divorced me. "I don't want to come home and see you dead," she said. "You love something more than your family and hate yourself for it."

She was right. I didn't blame her. After that, I plunged deeper into my cave of sorrow, not believing I would ever find my way out. I pushed everyone away from me, even my daughter, so no one would hear the sadness in my voice.

When my beautiful daughter got married to a wonderful young man, I saw their love for each other. And knowing she would be taken care of, I no longer cared whether I lived or died.

It got so bad that whenever family members came to visit my mom, I went into my bedroom until they left. I just wanted to be alone. After they left, I could see the hurt on my mother's face, but that wasn't enough to change me. That bedroom became my tomb.

Then about eighteen months ago, something happened that I still cannot explain. I was sitting in my bedroom looking out the window when a Presence filled the room. It kept getting bigger and bigger. It was God's love. This love was so overwhelming that all the shame I had disappeared. My tremendous hatred for myself, my past, my guilt, my feeling of being a failure—one by one they faded. All that was left in that room was God's love and me. Experiencing that one little word—*love*—changed everything.

Since that moment, I haven't used anything. I've been clean for a year and a half. That doesn't mean I didn't go through withdrawal and all that comes with it. But instead of feeling empty and lonely, now I wake up and His love is there to greet me. I go to bed at night, and that love is there to tuck me in.

> Experiencing that one little word—*love*—changed everything.

During the day, I look around and God's love is there with me. It's as if He's holding my hand. He loves me just as I am, and there is nothing I can do to make Him stop loving me. "God is love" (1 John 4:16, NIV). And it is a perfect, endless love. Since that day, I've been aware of that love everywhere I go. I still have days of loneliness when the road I'm on feels very difficult, but I know I am not alone anymore.

Three months after this experience, my daughter gave birth to a baby girl. When I went to the hospital, I wanted to hold her. My daughter gently said, "Dad, she's pretty tired. Why don't I hold her, and you hold her hand?"

Despite the positive change she saw in me, my daughter still didn't trust me. And I couldn't blame her. I knew only time and God's love would show her. Six months later, I visited her at her home. As soon as I arrived, my daughter said, "Dad, can you watch the baby, please? We have to go to the store."

I played with that little munchkin, holding her in my arms, delighting in her laughter. God's love works miracles every day. All I have to do is keep my eyes and heart open to experience them. My daughter and I have never been closer.

Two months ago, my mom died. One late afternoon while she was still in the hospital, we were alone—very unusual with seven kids and over twenty grandkids! Her eyes were dark and sunken as she told me she remembered that when I was a child, strangers would come up to her and tell her how beautiful my eyes were, so blue and twinkling with laughter. For years they were empty, and she felt so helpless. But now, she said, they were alive again. This time, the tears in her eyes were from happiness.

She knew she was dying, but she was not afraid to die. Just when I could really appreciate all she had done for me, she would soon be gone. I started crying and said haltingly through my tears, "Mom, I'm so sorry for all the pain and worry I caused you."

She took my hand, looked me in the eyes, and said, "Michael, you are the answer to all my prayers. I can go now because I know you're going to be okay. I know you will never go back."

In time, I learned that many people had been praying for me—family and friends, individuals and groups, churches, people I never met. Maybe, in a way, the pain I owned—the condemnation, the sense of desolation—was itself some kind of prayer.

My story doesn't end here. This is only the beginning. Every day, I'm learning more about God's love and experiencing it in such a powerful way. Finally, I'm seeing with new eyes and feeling with a new heart, a heart made new by being washed in the eternal fountain of His love.

Seven Ways to Pray after a Tragedy

– BOB HOSTETLER –

Those of us who pray in times of tragedy may often do so because we feel helpless, because there seems to be little else we can do, but that doesn't mean that prayer is a last resort. Prayer is not inaction. Prayer, rightly understood, is action. It is hard work. It is resolve. It is revolution. It does not exhaust our concern or fulfill our obligations to those who suffer, but it can and should be the source and foundation of our efforts. After all, God says, "Call on me in the day of trouble" (Psalm 50:15, NIV). And the Bible exhorts us: "in every situation, by prayer and petition, with thanksgiving, present your requests to God" (Philippians 4:6, NIV).

So go ahead. When tragedy strikes, strike back first with your prayers. Follow these biblical examples of prayer in times of tragedy:

1. **Pray your confusion and frustration**—Various kinds of healing oil and ointment were used as medicines in the ancient Mideast. One of the most highly prized was a "balm" that was

produced in the region of Gilead, east of the Jordan River. When the prophet Jeremiah mourned the tragedies that he and his people faced, he cried, "Is there no balm in Gilead? Is there no physician there? Why then is there no healing for the wound of my people?" (Jeremiah 8:22, NIV). When tragedy strikes, it is okay to cry out to God, as David did in Psalm 22 (and Jesus echoed while suffering on the cross): "My God, my God, why...?" (verse 1, NIV).

2. **Pray for mercy**—When I hear a siren or read of a tragedy, a prayer leaps to my lips almost unbidden: *Lord, have mercy.* It is a heartfelt and helpful way to pray, for those who suffer are in desperate need of mercy and relief from pain and sorrow.
3. **Pray for freedom from fear**—The twenty-third psalm is rightly beloved by many people, partly because it gives strength to those who are facing or have faced tragedy. Pray that those most affected by tragedy will be able to say, "Even though I walk through the darkest valley, I will fear no evil, for you are with me" (verse 4, NIV).
4. **Pray for comfort**—The rest of that verse in Psalm 23 supplies yet another prayer focus for times of tragedy: "Your rod and your staff, they comfort me." Pray for the victims and those who suffer loss in a tragedy to experience comfort, both from those around them and from the knowledge of the presence of God.
5. **Pray for healing**—Send prayers for healing to all who suffer—physically, mentally, and emotionally—from the effects of a tragic event. Pray for the healing of all who need healing, as Jesus healed all who came to Him in His earthly ministry (see Luke 9:11).

6. **Pray for hope**—One of the worst effects when tragedy strikes is the triumph of fear over hope, which can in turn bring about despair and depression. So pray that those who are touched by tragedy "may overflow with hope by the power of the Holy Spirit" (Romans 15:13, NIV).
7. **Pray for change**—When Jesus gave His disciples a model prayer, He told them to pray, "Deliver us from evil" (Matthew 6:13, KJV). That is a prayer that can be turned against any tragedy, past or future. Pray it often. Pray it in faith. Pray it and be ready for God to tell you how other efforts you might make can be added to your wrestling in prayer for the victims of tragedy.

4

Spiritual Guidance

Prayer is aligning ourselves with the purposes of God.

E. Stanley Jones

How amazing it is that when God was creating the world and the humans in it, He never left us to our own devices. Instead, He made a commitment to us. He developed us to be in relationship with Him. God reveals Himself to us in so many ways—through Scripture, through other people as directed by him, through nature itself, and sometimes even through supernatural means such as angels or miracles.

But communication is a two-way street. To thrive, relationships need participation. So how do we grow our relationship with God? The primary way is through prayer. Throughout Scripture, God frequently invites us to call on Him—not only in times of trouble, but in times when we simply want to communicate with Him. And He is always a ready source of wisdom and guidance.

Gideon is one of the people in the Bible who felt he needed some guidance. He was willing to do bold things but seemed a little hesitant.

When God called Gideon to rescue Israel, Gideon asked God for proof that He would save them. Gideon put a fleece on the ground at night and asked God to keep the ground dry in the morning and the fleece wet. Of course, the ground was dry but the fleece was soaking. Still Gideon's faith was not quite strong enough. The next night, he asked God to keep the fleece dry in the morning and the ground wet (see Judges 6:36–40).

God responded to Gideon's prayerful foray into faith, giving Gideon the courage to move on into God's call to rescue his nation.

As with Gideon, God always has patience with us as we grow spiritually. He can handle our doubts, our uncertainties, and our questions. Each answered prayer is like a transaction that builds the balance in our faith account.

In this chapter, you will read about people who sought God for direction—whether in ministry, in important decisions, or with the basic uncertainties in life. As we see in the pages ahead, God, the all-knowing, all-wise Creator, who is committed to His people, is always willing to guide us—in the most important battles of life and the most mundane steps of growth.

Today, are you needing special guidance? Whether you need overall direction in your big picture or want to discuss the minutia of life with someone, turn to the all-wise Lord. Psalm 37:23 tells us, "The LORD directs the steps of the godly. He delights in every detail of their lives" (NLT).

And if you need companionship or encouragement, God wants to accompany you on your life journey. Keep in mind the words of James 4:8: "Come close to God, and God will come close to you" (NLT).

Not beyond God's Reach

– BOB MCCAUGHAN –

There he goes, I thought. *Marty the unreachable.* Like a man stuck in slow motion, Marty bent over his walker as he pushed a large trash container down his driveway, inching it toward the curb for the Wednesday morning garbage pickup. Frail . . . about seventy, thin, haggard looking.

He wanted to do something useful, I suspected.

Strokes can really mess a person up, I thought. Marty had suffered a stroke just before he and his wife, Ruth Ann, moved in next door. He couldn't walk, and his speech was not intelligible. Even Ruth Ann said, "Half the time, I can't understand him."

It seemed to me that to try to share the gospel with Marty would be impossible. Since Marty was a homebound invalid, with no outside contact and unable to communicate, I thought it unlikely anyone would be able to befriend him.

Just the same, I had a profound burden for him. I prayed for him every morning and often during the day—for his recovery, his comfort, and of course, his salvation. I suspected that he and Ruth Ann were not Christians.

After several months of praying for Marty, I felt I had to do something. So one afternoon, I took a Bible off my bookshelf, and after making sure the print size was adequate for an elderly reader, I headed for Marty's house.

Kind of crazy when you think about it, I told myself. *People I don't have a relationship with, or for that matter people I hardly know. Here I am, hoping to share the gospel with Marty, a man unable to walk or communicate. Then there's his somewhat overbearing and even hostile-appearing wife, Ruth Ann. And I am going to go knock on their door and say, "Hello, I would like to meet and get to know Marty."*

But that is exactly what I did.

Ruth Ann seemed a little flustered when she greeted me at the door. There I was, Bible in hand, wanting to visit with her husband.

"Wait," she said. "I'll ask Marty and see what he says."

As I was ushered in, Marty was struggling with his walker, dragging one foot and moving slowly toward his favorite chair in their sunroom. Ruth Ann placed a dining-room chair close to Marty so I could sit near him. I introduced myself and mentioned that I had been praying for him.

"I was wondering, Marty, if I could perhaps read some Scripture and pray for you," I said, hoping for a favorable response. Marty nodded and said something.

I listened hard, but I could not understand what he was trying to communicate. I continued to share with him anyway, telling him more about myself.

Then a very startling thing happened!

In a labored but clear voice, Marty spoke. "I . . . want . . . to . . . know . . . the . . . Lord!"

Stunned, I realized, *God is here*!

For the next half hour, as I shared Scripture and explained the gospel message to Marty, he nodded frequently. I led him in a prayer, explaining that I would be asking him to not only trust Jesus as his Savior, but surrender to Jesus as the Lord of his life.

Stunned, I realized, *God is here*!

After we prayed together, I gave him the Bible I had brought for him.

During our time together, except for the time when Marty said he wanted to know the Lord, I never understood a word that he said. Nevertheless, he seemed to listen very carefully, bowing his head when we prayed. And he also seemed very grateful and interested in the Bible that I gave him.

Ruth Ann, however, appeared not happy at all; she clearly was not a believer. I left exhilarated but concerned. I would need to follow up with him; I just wasn't sure he understood what I had shared.

Sometime later, I asked Ruth Ann, "Would it be okay if I took Marty out for breakfast or lunch sometime?"

"Oh no! No!" she replied, "He is too fragile; he might fall."

I was in a quandary. Ruth Ann had made it clear she didn't like religion being talked about or advocated in her home, and Marty could not leave his home.

I continued to pray. I wanted to have some assurance that Marty understood the gospel. I frequently thought, *Did he pray sincerely with me? Would he be saved? Is he different? Is he manifesting fruit in his life as a new believer?*

I didn't know. And then . . . Marty died!

My wife, Lillian, and I went to the funeral. While we were waiting in the parlor for the service to begin, we didn't realize that we were standing next to some of Marty's family. The young woman closest to me clutched a Bible to her breast. She began to speak to Lillian and me.

"This is my daddy's Bible," she said. "He loved his Bible; he read it every day."

Then she opened the Bible to the front page and asked, "But I wonder, whose name this is . . . written inside?"

Marty's daughter was pointing to my name.

I realized talking with Marty's daughter was not chance. Once again this was God answering my prayers. Marty was in heaven!

Better Than Ice Cream

– BETH GOOCH –

Bedtime is my favorite time because that's when I have a big bowl of ice cream.

The dogs, walked and fed, settle into their beds. I shower, pull on comfy pajamas, and savor my treat. I keep various flavors on hand: cookie-dough ice cream, cookies-and-cream ice cream, mint-chip ice cream, and a chocolate-peanut butter concoction called Moose Tracks fill the freezer.

One night, however, something was amiss. The refrigerator made a *chug-chug* sound, and I slurped slightly melted ice cream.

The situation was serious.

A repair technician came the next day and delivered sad news. "It will cost more to repair this refrigerator than to buy a new one," he said, handing me an estimate.

The fridge still operated, but the *chug-chugging* continued, and the ice cream was too soft for my liking.

"You might as well find a new refrigerator now," my husband, Lester, suggested. "Don't wait until this one goes out and all the food spoils."

The only problem? Our refrigerator was an odd size. We had purchased it years earlier when our house was built. The cabinetmaker had fashioned a special structure that fit around the appliance, with perhaps a half inch of wiggle room. Tearing out the wood wasn't an option since it was attached to other cabinets.

I spent hours searching the internet, and every time I found a refrigerator that would fit, I hit a drawback. Some lacked the ice dispenser on the door, which we had grown to appreciate. Others were the wrong color. It had to match the other appliances, didn't it?

Weeks passed. But I couldn't find a suitable replacement at any local stores or online. I slurped soft ice cream as the *chug-chugging* grew louder.

One Sunday morning Lester woke me with a grim message.

"The refrigerator has breathed its last," he said. "We might not lose all the food inside if you can find a new one today and have it delivered tomorrow."

How could I get a new refrigerator delivered tomorrow? I had searched for weeks.

I pondered my dilemma as I sat at the kitchen table near the now-silent fridge.

Lester placed the Sunday newspaper in front of me, and I flipped to an appliance store advertisement featuring a counter-depth, side-by-side refrigerator similar to ours. I put on my glasses to read the fine print. Its dimensions were the same as our old one. But it didn't have an ice dispenser on the door, the color didn't match, and the price certainly wasn't what I had in mind.

Lester and I drove separate cars to church that morning because his job required him to go on duty shortly after our worship service ended.

The service ran long because several people were being baptized. Lester slipped out so he could arrive at work on time, but I had no excuse to leave early. I squirmed in my seat, imagining puddles of melted ice cream in the bottom of the old refrigerator. I wanted to bolt out the door and hurry to the appliance store. The sooner I got there, the sooner the new fridge would be delivered.

I silently prayed, *Lord, if I sit through this service, You've got to help me find a killer deal on a refrigerator!*

At that moment, my perspective changed. What was wrong with me? The people being baptized were making public declarations of their faith in God. Before me were new believers, each proclaiming his or her decision to follow Jesus. How could a new refrigerator measure up to that?

My desire to rush to the appliance store died, and I focused on the life-changing ceremony at the front of the church. When the service ended, I stood and joined the rest of the congregation in singing a joyful praise song. I even stayed behind and congratulated the people who had been baptized.

When I finally slid into my car, I gazed at the appliance store flyer that I'd brought from home. I'd intended to rush there and buy the refrigerator in the ad even though it wasn't exactly what we wanted and the price was too high.

Before wheeling out of the church parking lot, I called my brother-in-law Payton, who is the best bargain hunter I know.

No way would that dinky little shop have the odd-size fridge we needed.

"Payton, I have to get a new refrigerator, and I've had trouble finding one that fits the space in our kitchen. Any suggestions?"

"Try the little appliance store near my house," he said.

I thanked him, disappointed. He obviously hadn't understood about the refrigerator's unusual dimension. No way would that dinky little shop have the odd-size fridge we needed. I would have to stick with the store featured in the newspaper flyer.

My car seemed to have a mind of its own, though. As I exited the church parking lot, I turned right toward the shop Payton had recommended, instead of left toward the large appliance store.

As I entered the shop, a salesperson greeted me, and I handed him a scrap of paper with my refrigerator's dimensions. "You don't have anything this size, do you?"

He studied the paper and led me to a model that was the correct size, priced nine hundred dollars below the one in the newspaper ad.

"Wow," I said. "That might do."

But I couldn't help asking, "You don't have any with ice dispensers on the door, do you?"

The salesperson went to a computer and pulled up an image of a refrigerator that exactly matched my old one, even the same color, complete with ice dispenser on the door.

"We have one in our warehouse," he said.

It was too good to be true. "How much is it?"

"Eleven hundred dollars."

I handed him my credit card and arranged to have it delivered the next day, grateful that the price still matched our budget.

On the way home, I mentally listed which flavors of ice cream to buy after the new fridge arrived and called Lester to crow about our bargain. "I asked God for a killer deal," I said, "and He gave it to me."

There's no doubt the Lord answered my prayer by guiding me to the perfect refrigerator at the exact time we needed it. But He also provided a greater gift—stronger faith. When I remained in church that Sunday morning instead of rushing to the appliance store, the baptisms reminded me of God's work in our lives. I learned to put Him first in every situation and trust Him to handle the details. And that is even better than a big bowl of ice cream.

More than Enough

– SHARILYNN HUNT –

I slipped into a back pew in the small chapel with many residents from the nursing home. Each week, a visiting minister presented a short sermon for those who could function enough to listen and understand it and any staff member who could break away a few minutes for the service. It seemed a welcome relief from the busyness of my day as a social worker when I could join them.

On this November day, the pastor's lesson came from the Gospel of Matthew. He reminded us that Jesus told the people not to worry about earthly things such as food, drink, and clothes, for God even took care of the birds. Saying our lives were more valuable than His creatures in the air, He reminded us not to be anxious for tomorrow, for He would take care of us too.

As I sat in the congregation, no one had any idea how deeply this message spoke to my situation. Did I have enough faith to trust God for our family's provisions if I quit my job? After all, we were a two-income family like many with college-age children. But without my income, could we make it? Birds did not have mortgages or tuition payments. Surely, God knew the money we needed over the next year.

Plus, for two years I had balanced a full-time work schedule and attended graduate school part time at night. My day job no longer allowed for the hours my school program demanded. To complete my master's degree in rehabilitation counseling, I needed to volunteer several hours a week in social service agencies during the spring and summer semesters for college credits, while also attending my classes. Then in the fall, I had to complete a thousand-hour internship in a state agency.

With my present job, I performed the duties of the social worker, processed all admissions, and supervised a part-time activity coordinator. I wanted to give the director plenty of time to find my replacement over the holidays before the winter semester began.

The time had come to turn in my resignation.

Even though my husband and I had prayed about this situation, the chapel message spoke clearly to me. The time had come to turn in my resignation.

A few nights later, I awoke with my mind spinning in circles and my insides churning in a knot, anxious about the unknown. The thought of leaving my job, the pressure of another research paper due, Christmas expenses, and bills presented roadblocks to my inner peace.

I slipped out of bed and into another room. When I opened my Bible, the page fell to John 10:4: "And when he brings out his own sheep, he goes before them; and the sheep follow him, for they know his voice" (NKJV).

Within a few minutes of prayer, I wrote these words in my journal, impressed in my heart from the Holy Spirit: "You are about to embark on a new journey through which I will lead you every step of the way. I have a reason for you to finish school. It is a ticket to open a door where I need to place you. Because you are being trained to work with people who have disabilities, you will see the hurts and cries of My people. This will not be hard for you, for My timing is now! I have prepared the way, just walk in My steps and continue to seek Me first. Your efforts, your prayers, and your stand have not been in vain."

With God's peace in my heart, I returned to bed and knew He could provide for the birds and for us as well. And the way He answered those prayers for provision were totally unexpected!

Nineteen years earlier, my husband and I had bought land in the resort mountain town of Gatlinburg, Tennessee. We dreamed of building our beautiful chalet with a view nestled among the treetops. Then our financial situation changed, we moved a few states farther away, and for seven years the monthly payment felt like a noose around our necks. Eventually, due to the distance and the increase in building costs, we gave up our dream. We listed the property four or five times over the years with a local Realtor, but we never received a response from any interested party.

On the night of January 2, one week before my final day in the nursing home, we received a call from a Gatlinburg Realtor. She explained the owners of the property next door wanted to buy our lot. Would we be interested in selling our land?

Within twenty-four hours, we accepted a cash offer. The monies arrived the same week I changed from a full-time worker to a full-time student. For the next year, income from the sale covered all tuition costs for my classes, our daughter's last semester, and our son's first year of college. We even had enough money to buy a new refrigerator.

Upon my graduation a new journey began, and I held several positions over the years in the medical field of rehabilitation. Both of our children graduated from college debt-free and pursued successful careers.

I will always remember the winter night when a Realtor called and God said, "My time is now, and I have more than enough for you *and* the birds."

According to God's Script

– ELIZABETH GARRETT –

Beep, beep, beep. I tried calling Mom five times only to get a busy signal each time. After more than an hour of calling and hearing a busy signal, something in my gut shouted, "Call one more time."

Finally! She answered.

"Well, hey," she said. "You wouldn't believe who just called me!"

"No, probably not," I said and laughed.

"I've won four million dollars from Publishers Clearing House. They're going to come tomorrow and give it to me. I want you and Phillip to be here. Think you can make it?"

"Okay, hold on a minute. Really? Are you sure?" I raised my eyebrows.

"Why, yes! They are going to call me back in just a few minutes and tell me what time to expect them. I need to let you go, so I'll be available when they call." *Click.*

Hmm, I thought as I shook my head. *Something's not right. She didn't even sound like herself. Mom really needs to move closer to us.*

Driving more than a hundred miles one-way twice a week to ensure she received proper medical therapy took most of my time. I continued running my business, volunteering at church, and counseling other women, but I felt each area suffered from my busy schedule.

I asked God for wisdom, discernment, and protection over my mom. This included a request to transition her to a safe place where she could be loved and cared for on a regular basis. Specifically, I wanted her to move into our renovated guesthouse, and I just knew she would love it. Plus, I could serve as her advocate in situations like the current challenge.

Immediately after praying, I sat in front of the computer to conduct a search. I typed the contact person's name she gave me, and it matched up with the one on the Publishers Clearing House website. I checked several different places and noticed a spelling discrepancy. Hmm . . . red flag number one.

I called her back to touch base. "Hey, what's the latest?"

"Well, Publishers Clearinghouse called back and got some information from me for their records."

"What kind of information?"

"The address to see where they need to come in the morning. They're going to bring me a brand-new Cadillac too!"

"Really," I stated. "You haven't given them any money or access to money, have you?"

"Oh no. I have to let you go. I think that's them calling back."

As the afternoon unfolded and my work mounted, the truth reared its ugly head after several more phone conversations. She had written and mailed them a check for fourteen thousand dollars, supposedly for

She had written and mailed them a check for fourteen thousand dollars, supposedly for taxes.

taxes. They asked her to make the payee another elderly person who lived about an hour away.

I proceeded to make numerous phone calls to the postal inspector, law enforcement, the bank, and so on—a routine that lasted several days. The scammers even harassed her via the telephone throughout the weekend insisting they represented the company. To my amazement, they took the time to express mail her two fake checks in a handwritten envelope with scribbling.

Thankfully, we got her check stopped and intercepted by postal authorities, and we changed the bank account.

Eighty-five years old and living on five acres in what I referred to as the middle of the middle of absolutely nowhere, she existed in a vacuum without any close support.

God answered my prayer for the immediate situation and protected her funds, but what about her long-term needs?

Shortly following her financial landslide gone sour, her therapy at the hospital ended.

"Now there's no need for you to come down here every few days. I can make do going to the grocery store every other week," Mom said. "You've got your life. I'll be fine."

I still felt uneasy, especially after our recent clearinghouse issue.

During my first week off from caregiving trips, my husband, Phillip, and I sat at the breakfast table early on a weekday morning. He said, "You know, we should . . ."

"Move to my mom's," I said.

His jaw dropped. "How did you know what I was thinking?"

"I didn't. I just had the same thought."

We were stunned how both of us said it within seconds of each other. Before then, we never discussed moving, especially to her place.

Mom lived in rural northeast Mississippi, surrounded by red clay and kudzu, a vine bearing large leaves the size of your hand. Once rooted, it takes over everything in its path.

Philip's dad had lived in our guesthouse for six years and recently passed away, so we expected her to move into the guesthouse too. She kept saying she would move closer to us but had not done anything about it.

That very same day, Phillip's long-time friend and work associate suggested we move. During my prayer time that morning, God led me to the website where we eventually purchased house plans. I knew in my heart these things were more than coincidences.

That weekend we met with a real estate agent who gave us a fair value of the home, while my mother sought input from my brother who lived eight hundred miles away. The following Sunday, Phillip posted on a Facebook swap page that we were moving out of the state and needed to sell our toys—an antique Corvette and a Honda trike. A close friend and member of our group saw the post and messaged me within a minute. "What do you mean moving out of the state?"

I informed him of our plans.

He replied, "We're interested in your house. Can we come look at it tonight?"

That Sunday evening, he and his wife came over and toured our home, guesthouse, workshop, and other amenities. After the tour, we sat down at the kitchen table, held hands, and prayed for God's will. We even settled on a price.

I spent the next few weeks cleaning out twenty years' worth of storage. A friend who lived with us looked for an apartment, and the couple who bought our home prepared to sell their house—all within a month.

God moved mountains.

Only two weeks before we moved, my former house guest was accepted into a gated apartment complex in a nice section of town.

Since we planned on moving onto Mom's land, we decided to buy a decent used camper and live in it until our new house was built. With only a few days to go, we finally found an affordable travel trailer with plenty of storage. Now we would at least have a place to lay our heads. We just had to wait until our home closed so we could pay for it. No problem, right?

The couple who bought our home had an older house where they had lived for around ten years. Their house was on the market for only one day before it sold, but the inspector asked them to address a long, detailed list of concerns. Many factors still hung in the air until only hours before we met with the closing attorney, but we managed to close the deal.

During our first weekend as new residents in the middle of absolutely nowhere, we took a break from our busy lives and took Mom for a ride.

The crisp, autumn air signified leaves would be falling soon and moderate temperatures would cease.

Mom gazed out over trees covered in vines, which were starting to turn brown.

"There's frost on the kudzu!" she declared, grinning ear to ear. I hadn't seen her that happy in years.

Yes, frost covered the kudzu, and she was there to witness it. Like kudzu, Mom could not be easily uprooted as her roots dug deep.

God answered my prayer according to not my script but His—and far more creatively than I could have done on my own. It may have looked like mayhem to us, but we knew this was exactly how He wanted it, red clay, kudzu, and all. Mom was cared for, loved, and protected.

God had done the seemingly impossible.

Miracle on a Hilltop

– SANDI BANKS –

The jumbo jet screeched to a halt at Warsaw Chopin Airport, bringing me safely through the all-night flight from Colorado to Poland. Little did I know as I stepped off the plane that I was about to experience a divinely orchestrated crisis.

Gathering my luggage, I felt almost giddy—confident and excited about the seminar I would deliver the next day at the ministry conference. For months, I had poured my heart and soul into this hour-long message, carefully writing, editing, praying, preparing, internalizing, and memorizing it. I was thankful it had been heartily approved by the Polish conference board.

With my seminar pages safely tucked away in my bag, I snaked through the customs line, wearing a grateful smile as I mentally rehearsed the next day's whirlwind schedule.

I had been given the privilege of speaking to a large group of Polish women I had never met but for whom I had prayed for so long they almost seemed like family. I couldn't wait to see how God would use this message to reach them.

The conference director, Tomek, met me outside customs and drove me to his lively home, where I was warmly greeted by his family and the heavenly aroma of spicy pierogis, mushroom-barley soup, and hot poppy cakes. Steaming platefuls landed in front of me.

"Mmm, delicious." I complimented Tomek's wife, Zofia, as the flavors lingered on my tongue and delighted my American palate. We chatted and laughed our way through the meal.

Then it happened.

Tomek cleared his throat. "Uh, by the way, Sandi," he began nonchalantly in his rich Polish accent, as Zofia served dessert. "You know the seminar you prepared to give tomorrow?"

"Oh yes, it's all ready!"

"Well . . . you're giving a different one."

"A different seminar? What do you mean?"

Hesitating, he explained that somehow my seminar had been completely changed in the printed program. But he was not sure why or to what.

"Not to worry. It's okay. You will do fine," he assured me.

"What does the program say? What are they expecting?"

"Umm, well, I am not certain. Something about . . . *picture . . . yourself . . .*"

"Picture yourself. Okay, let's see . . . The inner versus the outer as in Peter? Seeing themselves as wise as in Proverbs? Work with me here, Tomek!"

"Wel-l-l-l . . . I don't think so. Something much different. I don't know. It will be okay," he repeated. "You will do fine."

I felt my face flush and my heart thump so hard I thought it was going to leap through my pocket any second. Tomek shrugged and returned to his plate of poppy cakes.

Politely excusing myself from the table, I snatched my jacket and Bible and headed up the hill behind their home. Reaching the top, I looked up into the heavens, raised my empty hands, and cried out to God in desperation.

Lord, help me! I need Your wisdom, Your direction. Tomorrow's seminar—it's not my message. It's Yours. I'm just the messenger. These are not my people, they're Yours. You created them. You know what they need to hear. Please give me the words.

God met me there. He began orchestrating something wonderful, flooding my mind with specific scripture verses, comforting promises, engaging stories, and solid truths. Then He ordered them clearly, concisely, beautifully into a brand-new message, one that would point them upward, while reaching outward, offering them liberating lifelines from His Word.

> I descended, feeling like Moses must have felt bearing freshly engraved tablets of truth to present to his people.

After nearly three extraordinary hours, I descended, feeling a wee bit like Moses must have felt bearing freshly engraved tablets of truth to present to his people.

That night, I crawled under the toasty-warm, wooly blankets, ready for a good night's sleep. It had been quite a day—international flight, shocking news, hilltop experience—but it appeared God was not through yet.

Scripture flooded my mind once again, and I felt compelled to climb out of bed and tiptoe into the next room, where a typewriter and I wrestled into the night. Promises from the Bible, the richest of treasures flowing from its pages onto mine, began to form what would soon be known as the Forty Day Adventure in Scripture—a journaling project to go along with the spoken message God had just given. For the next forty days, the women would mine the gold from forty chapters of the Bible—Genesis to Revelation—one day, one nugget, at a time.

Hours later, as thousands of Polish people, young and old, flooded the conference hall, I headed to the seminar building, carrying the handouts and journals for each person (another answered prayer). On the way, I grabbed a program from the table by the door. Hurriedly flipping through the pages, I found a paragraph on page 68, followed by the only word I recognized in the program: "Sandi."

"Excuse me!" I called to a Polish pastor I knew. "Could you please translate this for me?"

"Of course!" He began translating and I listened intently. When he finished, I was stunned: word for word, the paragraph perfectly described the seminar God had given me on the hilltop, long after the program had been printed.

"A miracle," I whispered.

Moments later, I stood at the podium beaming—God-confident as I looked out at those precious women, realizing how much God must love them. Joy flooded my soul, as my interpreter and I spent the next hour delivering the message, straight from God's heart to theirs.

Later that night, I lay in bed picturing God working miraculously behind the scenes weeks earlier, as the programs were being prepared—guiding the final draft for the print shop, making sure they heard the divine edits as their fingers raced across the keyboard.

No, not those words. These words.

Then I thought of God watching me slave away at my own keyboard and spend countless hours committing to memory a message He knew I would never give. Why?

Could it be that He was teaching me that He wants all His children to be diligent to accomplish, then willing to relinquish, whatever He gives us to do—to open the palms of our hands and let Him exchange our good for His best?

I'm choked up even now as I look back on that experience with God. There I stood, stripped bare of anything I could dare claim as "mine"—totally at His mercy. Humbled. Needy. He took my empty hands and lovingly began filling them with His gifts, one by one, then sent me to deliver those gifts to His beloved ones—but not without the blessings spilling over onto me a hundredfold along the way.

What happened in the hearts and minds of His people that day? Did the words He spoke through me touch a soul or change a life? Did the works of His Spirit during their Forty-Day Adventure through Scripture satisfy their hunger and draw them to Christ? Did any of them fall on their faces in worship, repentance, praise, or gratitude as He met and ministered to them?

Only God knows. One day He may allow me a glimpse of the miraculous work He accomplished in that extraordinary twenty-four-hour period in Poland.

In the meantime, I will always be grateful for what He accomplished in my *own* heart and mind that day. He opened my eyes to the majesty, the beauty, the mystery, the power, the gift of prayer—and the awesome God who answers, above and beyond anything we could ask or imagine, across a street, or across an ocean.

Four Ways to Find God's Guidance

– ELIZABETH PEALE ALLEN –

The entire Bible is a record of God's guidance of His people, both as a whole and as individuals. He directed Abraham into the Promised Land and led Isaac, Jacob, Joseph, Moses, Isaiah, Paul, and countless others. He wants to lead you too.

But how, exactly, are you supposed to find God's guidance? Be alert for these ways.

- **God guides through the principles and examples of the Bible.** "All Scripture is given by inspiration of God, and is profitable for doctrine, for reproof, for correction, for instruction in righteousness" (2 Timothy 3:16, NKJV). Read your Bible faithfully!
- **God often guides through the wise counsel of friends, peers, or your pastor.** "The way of a fool is right in his own eyes, but he who heeds counsel is wise" (Proverbs 12:15, NKJV). Talking with a Christian friend may lead to a new perspective on a situation.

- **God guides through providential circumstances.** When Joseph was sold into slavery by his brothers and soon afterward put into prison in Egypt, he may have felt abandoned by God, but later, when his position saved his family from starvation, he realized the important truth that God is in control. He told his brothers, "It was not you who sent me here, but God" (Genesis 45:8, NKJV). Look for God's hand in the circumstances that come your way.
- **God guides in answer to prayer.** "If any of you lacks wisdom, let him ask of God, who gives to all liberally and without reproach, and it will be given to him" (James 1:5, NKJV).

God wants to point you in the right direction—every day!

5

Love, Friendship, Family, and Community

The quality of your relationships will determine the quality of your life. And this is something worth praying about.

STORMIE OMARTIAN

God set us in families and eventually, as families grew, within communities. Even God's Son had an earthly family and community and chose a circle of friends. We were designed to live in relationship with God and with others. None of us was made to go it alone on earth. Friends and family help us grow, help us strive to achieve goals, help us overcome obstacles, and even help us grow spiritually.

That desire for companionship and love is built into our DNA. So it's only normal that the Creator of relationships would care about the connections between husband and wife, parents and children, families, friends, and community.

And it's no wonder that part of our longing for fulfillment in life includes other people. That's the way Hannah felt. More than anything, Hannah wanted a son. Her husband, Elkanah, loved her deeply, but Hannah wanted more. Year after year, she cried for a child and never conceived.

Each year, Elkanah took Hannah, along with his other wife and her children, to the temple to worship God and present sacrifices. And each time, Hannah prayed to the Lord from the bottom of her heart. Her emotion was so deep that the priest, Eli, assumed that she was drunk. When he scolded her, she told him, "I am very discouraged, and I was pouring out my heart to the LORD. . . . I have been praying out of great anguish and sorrow" (1 Samuel 1:15–16, NLT).

The Lord heard Hannah's prayers, and her child was soon born. She named him Samuel. Samuel grew up to be one of the most instrumental leaders in the Bible.

It's never wrong to pray for others. Whether we're asking God to give us children, asking Him to strengthen relationships, requesting that He guide us to groups of people who can be our friends or church family, or asking Him to work on misunderstandings or any other relational needs, He cares.

There's nothing like the encouragement and support of others! And there's nothing like communing spiritually with others. As we pray for others and they pray for us, we join together on a spiritual journey. We form a bond that includes the Lord in our care and concern. And when we pray together, even more power is unleashed.

In the following pages, you will read about people who took their relationship concerns to God. You will meet some who sought God's wisdom in relating to others. And you will meet some who championed a friend or family before God's throne and saw God work as a result.

Never hesitate to pray for and about the people in your life. Bringing someone's name before God is a wonderful way to say "I love you."

The Wedding Weather Miracle

– NAN JONES –

Only God's favor and the power of His hand could take care of our problem. But He is, after all, a miracle-working God.

For days, weather forecasters warned of impending torrential rain crossing our Blue Ridge Mountains the weekend of May 11, which was our son's wedding day. Our son's *outdoor* wedding day with no alternative bad-weather plan.

Three different weather systems were converging over the mountains of North Carolina bringing 100 percent chance of floods.

Matthew and Nina had purchased twenty-six acres and a fixer-upper along the North Carolina and Virginia border. Lush forest and mountain laurel abounded on their property. A soothing stream flowed near their house and carried its babbling melody down and across their land.

The wedding would occur across the stream on a level, open field beneath the chestnut trees. Matthew built a footbridge for wedding guests to cross the stream and a simple altar. The outdoor sanctuary was perfect in every way—except for the impending storm.

Friday night, the wedding party and family gathered to rehearse the ceremony. A slight drizzle fell off and on throughout the evening.

"Nina, what's the plan for tomorrow when it's pouring rain? There's no shelter in this field, and there's a one hundred percent chance of torrential rain."

Overhearing the conversation, I said, "It's not going to rain. I've asked the Lord to part the heavens on Bear Wallow Road between one and four o'clock tomorrow."

"Oh, really?"

"Yes, I believe He hears us when we pray and is concerned about the things that concern us."

Of course, after my brazen declaration of faith, I secretly begged the Lord to hear my cry.

I noticed the grin and the raised eyebrows of the gentleman standing beside me. "You do realize it's one hundred percent chance of pouring rain, right?"

"You do realize it's one hundred percent chance of pouring rain, right?"

"Yes, sir. But I believe the Lord will honor my request because I want those who don't know Him to see that He is a very personal God. Besides, I know that He likes to show off for His children."

"Interesting," he said. "Can't wait to see what happens."

Rehearsal ended, and we enjoyed our evening meal beneath a tent shielding us from the soft rain now showering down.

Saturday morning, the plan was for me to meet some of the ladies at Matthew and Nina's house about eight thirty to set the tables for the wedding dinner and finish flower arrangements. The closer I got to their home, the harder the rain fell.

By the time I arrived, there were pools around the tent edges where the reception dinner would be held. A gazebo, set up to house the desserts, sprang several leaks. We were all getting drenched running back and forth between the reception area and the house. Things were not looking good.

"I don't know what we're going to do about this rain," someone said.

"It's going to stop," I said.

"Sorry, but it doesn't look like it's stopping."

"It's not one o'clock yet. I asked the Lord to part the heavens over Bear Wallow between one and four."

"Oh," came a voice, and I saw more raised eyebrows.

I surely didn't want to sound cocky, so I explained, "I know the One in whom I have believed, and I know He sincerely cares about our heart's cry. He is a personal God."

As I continued to work, I continued to knock on heaven's door with my request. I prayed earnestly and with thanksgiving in my heart. Expectation, along with some trepidation, rose.

About eleven thirty, I hurried home to change clothes and join the rest of my family. Rain was hard and steady now. The radio sounded weather alerts, warning our mountain neighbors to prepare for flooding. The windshield wipers slung raindrops to and fro as I drove, dodging puddles pooling on the road.

Even so, I continued to pray, thanking the Lord for responding to my request.

When I arrived home, everyone was ready, complete with concerned looks on their faces regarding the weather.

"I know, I know. But it's going to stop."

More raised eyebrows.

We climbed in the car, carefully shaking off dripping umbrellas before placing them on the floorboards. As we traveled the thirty minutes back to Matthew and Nina's, the rain intensified, as did my prayers. I fought doubt in the name of Jesus because I fully believed I was praying according to God's will—to reveal Himself as a personal God who cares about our needs.

I rounded the last curve before their driveway and noticed a brightening in the sky overhead.

Thank You, Lord, I whispered in my heart.

Their driveway is about a quarter of a mile long. With each small increment of distance, the rain lessened. By the time we got to the top, the rain had stopped. It was 1:01 p.m. on May 11 on Bear Wallow Road. I turned off the wipers and parked the car.

I'll admit I sighed with relief, but mostly I was bursting with thanksgiving and wonder. Nina said, "Look, Mama Nan, my wedding miracle!"

"I know, sweetheart, I know. God is good."

In the days following their wedding, Matthew and Nina told me numerous friends offered their condolences for the nasty weather on their wedding day, saying they thought of the couple often as the creeks and river overflowed.

"Actually," Nina would reply, "it stopped raining over our house and land at one o'clock. It was perfect. I call it my wedding weather miracle."

A Gift from the Past

– PAM ZOLLMAN –

Mom," said Keith, my older son, "I have bad news." His voice sounded so sad, so crushed. Defeated.

I clutched the phone to my ear. No, not more bad news. I wasn't sure how much more I could handle.

It was March 2002, and my divorce had just been finalized. My family was scattered across the country. I was living alone in Honesdale, Pennsylvania, working for a magazine. My older son, Keith, was living alone in Houston, Texas, working for an architectural firm. My younger son, Bryan, was in Greenville, South Carolina, attending Furman University. My sons and I were grieving the loss of our family because Bill—my husband and their father—had walked out of our lives.

Keith had been forced to drop out of college after three years because his father would no longer pay for it, even though Bill made plenty of money.

As a new magazine editor, I didn't make much money and was struggling to pay for Bryan's college. In Texas, where our divorce took place, I didn't qualify for alimony, and our sons were too old for child support. I was struggling to make ends meet, and I was lonely too.

"What's wrong, sweetie?" I asked, trying to stay calm.

"I just found out that my job is over at the end of this month," he said.

I sighed. That wasn't so bad. When Keith had taken the job, he knew it would be temporary. He'd been holding out hope that the position would become permanent, but now it was ending two months early. "You'll get another one. You're good at finding work."

"Yeah." He hesitated. "But that's not the only thing."

"What else?"

"My apartment was robbed while I was at work today." Keith's voice quavered. "They took everything, Mom."

"Everything?" I repeated.

"My computer, my camera, my baseball cards, my jacket, my spare cash. They took everything of value."

"Oh no!" I said. "Will your renter's insurance cover it?"

There was a moment's hesitation. "I don't have any," he admitted. "I couldn't afford it."

"Oh Keith." I stopped myself from chiding him. He was suffering enough.

"I know, Mom. I know," my son said. "Is there any way you can send me some money?"

Now I hesitated. I got paid every two weeks, and I'd just gotten my paycheck. But I had no money. Every bit of this paycheck went to bills. "I can send you some in two weeks, when I get paid again."

"Nothing sooner?" His voice held out hope.

"I'm so sorry, Keith," I said. "I'll see if I can scrounge up something to put in your checking account."

"Oh . . . okay," he said, sounding deflated.

"Thanks." Then he admitted, "I'm not sure what I'm going to do about food until I get my last paycheck."

"You don't have *any* money or food in your pantry?" That surprised me.

"No," he said. "My checking account has only a few dollars in it. I was planning to go to the store tonight. That's what my spare cash was for."

"Let's pray about it," I suggested, and he agreed. So over the phone, over that long distance between Texas and Pennsylvania, we joined in prayer.

"Heavenly Father, Keith needs Your help. He needs money for food, and he needs a new job. He needs a safe place to live. We know that if we ask in Jesus's name You'll hear our prayers and answer them. We thank you in advance. In Jesus's name, we pray. Amen."

"Amen," Keith said. "Thanks, Mom. I needed that."

A few days later, I deposited ten dollars into his account. It wouldn't go far—maybe some ramen noodles, mac and cheese, hot dogs—but it was all I had.

I called Keith to let him know. After he thanked me, I suggested, "Why don't you move up here and live with me? You wouldn't have to pay any rent."

"But where would I work?" he asked. "Honesdale is a tiny town, and there aren't many jobs in your area."

"I don't know, but I'm sure you'll be able to find something."

I could almost hear him smile over the phone. "How about if I think about it?"

"Pray about it," I said.

"I will. And thanks, Mom, for everything," he said before hanging up.

Two days later, Keith called me, excitement overflowing in his voice. "You'll never guess what happened!"

"Something good, obviously," I said.

"Something absolutely amazing!"

When he didn't continue, I said, "What? What? Did you find another job?'

Instead of answering me, he said, "Well, I've been praying a lot about my situation. You know, asking God to help me with food and what I should do." He once again paused.

"And did He answer your prayer?"

Keith laughed. "Oh yes, He did! But it was really strange. Today, when I turned the page in Exodus, I found a thin, yellowed envelope that I had never seen before. And I've read the Bible all the way through, from Genesis to Revelation. I'm telling you, that envelope wasn't in there before." His voice was full of wonder.

"What was in the envelope?"

"That's the craziest thing!" he exclaimed. "When I opened it, there was a one-hundred-dollar bill inside!"

"What? That's amazing! How did it get there?" I asked in surprise

"I have no idea," he said. "I asked some people at church if they'd slipped money in an envelope into my Bible, but they all said they didn't."

"Maybe the person wanted to remain anonymous," I suggested.

"I don't think that's it," Keith said. "The envelope was really old. It had been sealed at one time, but the glue was coming unstuck, so it was easy to open. The bill inside was from 1950."

The year I was born, I immediately thought. How strange. That Bible had been my grandfather's, and I used it for a while. Then Keith expressed interest in it, so I gave it to him. He liked reading the notes my grandfather and I had written in the margins.

"Do you think your grandfather put it in there when you were born?" he asked.

That puzzled me. "Perhaps, but why didn't I find it when I was using it?"

"I don't know," he admitted. "And I don't understand why I didn't find it last year when I read the Bible all the way through."

"Maybe you weren't supposed to find it until you really needed it," I suggested.

"Maybe you weren't supposed to find it until you really needed it," I suggested.

"Maybe so." He laughed. "Ask and you shall find."

Then I explained to my son how he had mixed up the first two lines. Matthew 7:7 says: "Ask, and it will be given to you; seek, and you will find, knock, and it will be opened to you" (NKJV).

"I know, Mom," he said, "but in this case, I *asked* and then I *found* the mystery envelope in Exodus where God tells the children of Israel to go forward. I had asked God what to do, and I think He's telling me to move to Pennsylvania."

"You're coming to live with me?"

"Yes," Keith said.

My heart was overflowing with excitement, love, and gratitude. God answered our prayers in a unique—and mysterious—way. Who put that envelope in Keith's Bible? It had to be the work of our loving God.

When You're Drowning, Let Go!

– LISA K. ELLIOT –

Jesus, I feel like a blindfolded prisoner, prodded down the plank by three little pirates. They've taken over our ship and turned it upside down, and I think we're going to drown!

We'd hoped to start with one young child. But our first foster-care call came from a caseworker looking to place three brothers—ages three, four, and six—now living one hundred miles away from us.

"They just need someone to pay a little extra attention to them," she said.

Weeks later, our household of three—me, my husband, and our eight-year-old son—watched the boys bound out of her car with matching blue-and-white duffel bags. The oldest boy was too big to be six, the youngest too small to be nearly four, and the middle boy was a redhead speckled with freckles. They were all missing their front teeth, top and bottom.

The caseworker said they'd had multiple dental procedures in their first six months of foster care to address mouths full of rot and decay.

When I called their first foster mom, she said they'd come to her with little knowledge of toothbrushes, eating utensils, or indoor plumbing. Her home had been a "boot camp," transitioning them into unfamiliar ways of life.

Reluctantly, she admitted how badly she and her husband needed a break. But they would always keep the boys in their prayers.

My intuition told me there was more to this story, but I didn't ask, and she didn't tell.

At first, the boys were timid, quietly waiting for someone to tell them where to go and what to do. Then a frantic energy emerged.

Along with their meager belongings, the boys unpacked behaviors we had never seen and didn't know how to handle. If we told them not to do something, we could be sure they would do it. If we rewarded them for helpful behavior, they would be more destructive. Even compliments could be a catalyst to chaos.

By the end of the third week, all my emotional buttons had been pushed so many times I rapidly started losing sleep, weight, and sanity.

My saving grace was that I had a job with hours away from home while they were in school or day care. But the five or so hours we were at home with them seemed like a lifetime.

The boys' behavior got worse when my husband wasn't home, so he started leaving our farm early to help me handle the chaos.

Overnight, my son went from an only child to a lonely child because my husband and I spent all our time managing our new mess. Almost daily, he begged to bike to our neighbor's house after school.

Could we actually help these boys without hurting our son? If I could think of one single way we were helping them, I'd have tried to swoop in and "save the day." But after one month, I felt totally undone.

Lord, I've got nothing. No strength. No wisdom. No clue what to do.

With a leaden heart and a guilty gut, I gave the caseworker our two-week notice. However, instead of leading to relief, I got a bigger serving of grief.

"You know I'm going to have to split them up," she warned.

I knew that breakup would tear up the last of their former family life, but I saw no other way to go. *Lord, what do we do?*

That Sunday, I glanced down the church pew at three boys sitting neatly and sweetly between my husband and me, wide eyed and wonderfully behaved before the watching world.

Hating myself, I prayed again for grace, for guidance, for relief.

I don't remember one detail about the guest speaker that day, but I will always remember one thing he said that were words straight from heaven to my heavy heart.

"You've got to remember the Lifeguard Principle. Do all you can to save lives, but when you're drowning, let go!"

I had hoped to make their broken lives better. Instead, they had exposed all the ways I was broken and desperate for God's help. Every one of us needed to be saved from ourselves; Jesus was our only hope.

My grateful tears drew puzzled stares from the boys. As I assured them my tears were the "good kind," they were more confused.

I couldn't tell them that, without God's help, they'd move from home-to-home-to-home, feeling more disconnected and rejected with every hand off.

But with God's help, anything was possible.

After school the next day, I called my son's third-grade teacher, a former foster mom, to tell her what was happening at our house.

She said we were dealing with RAD (Reactive Attachment Disorder) and gave me the number of a career foster mom who helped kids with severe emotional needs.

I called immediately.

Before I shared any details, Jodi summarized the state of our household as if she lived with us. Finally, we had found someone who understood our circumstances and confirmed we needed help.

Anything we had done to parent our own son wouldn't help these boys; they craved "safety" at any cost. The more they manipulated our emotions, the more control they commanded. Lying. Defying. Assaulting. Anything it took to rule the roost.

We could minimize emotion and maximize their sense of security with age-appropriate chores. Because praise was poisonous, we could reward good work with more chores. We could teach consequences. Instead of time out, we could create and enforce a safe space called "restricted status" over which we had to be absolutely and unemotionally in charge.

I felt as if we'd just boarded the last lifeboat off a sinking ship.

When Jodi offered to meet our boys and help us correct our responses to their chaos, I felt as if we'd just boarded the last lifeboat off a sinking ship—with help, we might make their last weeks at our home their best.

The boys needed skilled emotional and behavioral support far beyond our ability. Every day I asked God to supply parents who could understand and love them "as is" and help them find their best lives, not just keep a lid on their behaviors.

When our time with them was to end two weeks later, the caseworker had nowhere else for them to go.

We gave her another week. And then another.

Still, nothing changed.

Lord, You said, "Let go," so, now what?

When I called Jodi to vent my frustration and ask her advice, I got God's answer.

"I think God brought us together because He wants me to take the boys," she said.

My heart leaped into my throat. Was I dreaming?

If Jodi took them, they would get everything they needed. If Jodi took them, she would keep them. The next stop would be the last. This foster family would be their forever family.

Thank You! Thank You! Thank You, Jesus!

When Jodi called next, she had good news . . . and not-so-good news. Her foster home was licensed for six placements, and she had a full house until her oldest son turned eighteen in six weeks. She couldn't take the boys before then.

If we chose to hang on, she would continue to coach us and help them transition from our home to hers.

I couldn't imagine surviving six more hours with them, let alone six weeks. Nor could I imagine giving them to anyone else.

Lord, we're desperate for Your help!

Daily, I prayed through the Psalms, offering both praise and lament as the weight of their care got heavier and harder to bear.

In response, God prepared me to be a fierce advocate for the boys in the courtroom, the classroom, and a psychiatric hospital room.

After the boys spent two fun nights at Jodi's house, meeting her kids and tending their animals—everything from dogs and cats to goats, pigs, and alpacas—they came home eager to tell us about all their adventures.

Eagerly stuffing those blue-and-white duffel bags with pajamas, toothbrushes, play clothes, and church clothes, they packed off to Jodi's again a few weeks later.

By then, Jodi's family had voted to welcome the boys, who eagerly accepted the invitation to become a permanent part of Jodi's family.

The last time we drove them to Jodi's, the youngest, who'd recently turned four, kept asking if we were getting close. Finally, he smacked the car seat and demanded that we "Stop saying no!"

After a second of silence, everyone laughed.

Wiping joyful tears from my eyes, I thought how we could have said no to foster care. Or no when the first placement offered wasn't what we wanted. Or when we thought we couldn't handle one more minute, let alone another month and more.

God let my head go under so my heart would surrender, fully accepting my weakness and trusting Him to be wondrous. He coached me to let go and know He alone would carry us carefully through every crazed, chaotic, frustrating, frightening moment.

Two years and five months after the boys left our home, we met them at a park to celebrate their adoption day. The first day all three *and* their one-year-old half brother officially began sharing the same last name with the family that chose them, not in spite of their considerable challenges, but because of them.

For more than three years, these foster households of faith had flooded heaven with petitions for help and hope and healing—lifeboats God launched to carry four boys safely away from violence and ambivalence to their new life within a forever family that follows Jesus.

The Golden Ticket

– KELLY WILSON MIZE –

The atmosphere in our home was bristling with nervous anticipation. I hadn't been so eager for my husband to get home from work since we were newlyweds. The answer to an important question could be revealed only upon his return—and the opening of a magical treasure box that only he could open.

Thirty plus years earlier, my husband, Wade, had been accepted to the US Military Academy at West Point in New York, a prestigious accomplishment that only one in ten high school applicants achieve.

In the late 1980s, Wade spent his college years as a cadet. He thrived as a student-athlete, formed deep friendships, and served his country as he completed the four years needed to graduate in 1990.

However, in his senior year, an unexpected turn of events led him in a direction he had not anticipated. At the age of twenty-one, he was diagnosed with Type 1 diabetes. Army officers, and soldiers in general, are expected be in perfect health, so this news meant his military career would be cut short. In spite of his diagnosis, Wade was allowed to graduate from West Point. However, instead of receiving a military appointment, he received an honorable discharge.

Wade was incredibly disappointed but accepted the setback as God's will and quickly found a job in his home state as a mechanical engineer. Soon after, he met me, and we were married two years later.

Fast-forward over a quarter century, three houses, two cats, and two kids. Our oldest child, Grant, was a sophomore at a nearby university and our daughter, Claire, a senior in high school, was visiting colleges. Her eventual university of choice was out of state—which meant, even with the multiple scholarships she had earned, it would be more costly than what we had budgeted. At this particular university, in-state tuition would make our daughter's dream college substantially more affordable. There was only one way to waive the out-of-state tuition: in-state tuition prices were available to veterans and their dependents.

But my husband had never considered himself a veteran. Throughout our marriage, I had learned to accept this self-assessment. In church services when veterans were invited to stand to be honored, he declined. When stores and businesses offered discounts for veterans, he did not participate. At Veterans Day celebrations, he never opted to be recognized. It was a unique situation: Wade had officially served in the US Army for the four years he worked toward his education at West Point but had not been allowed to serve past his college years.

Still, the classification of "veteran" could mean the difference in our daughter attending her first college choice or a runner-up. So with the encouragement of a friend whose husband was in the military, I did some research.

I found out that we needed one form—proof that my husband had been honorably discharged, a proof that he was not even positive existed and would require poring through the records system.

It had been more than thirty years, and Wade couldn't remember exactly. But he knew any documentation could be found, among other important items, in an army-issued trunk that was in our attic. I felt like our family was living the plot of *Charlie and the Chocolate Factory*—searching and hoping to find the golden ticket.

On that day of multiple phone conversations with the office of veterans at our daughter's chosen university, Wade finally arrived home. Claire and I tried not to pressure him, but we anxiously awaited his inspection of the trunk in the attic. It had not been opened in years!

That night after dinner, Wade made his way upstairs to the attic door, dusted off the lid of the trunk, and pried it open, while my daughter and I not-so-patiently waited downstairs.

He quickly found the form that we needed and eventually established his official classification as a veteran. I think that status was a gratifying realization for him, a redemption of sorts. It reminded him that the four years he worked so hard—academically, mentally, and physically at West Point—were not in vain. But even more than that, it was financially valuable—covering thousands of dollars' worth of our daughter's tuition over four years.

My daughter is now a freshman at her chosen school—Mississippi State University. She loves her roommate and her classes, and she is a member of the coed cheer squad! SEC (Southeastern Conference) football is highly celebrated in our part of the country, and our friends and family are excited to follow her journey. She is living her best college experience.

We are often asked why Claire chose that particular school. There are many reasons she wanted to go, but mostly, it just felt like home. And as we all prayed she'd choose the right school, the "golden ticket" in the attic trunk seemed to seal the deal, confirming God's will for her college choice.

If he had not been diagnosed with diabetes as a college senior and *had* received a military appointment upon his West Point graduation thirty years ago, Wade's assignment could have taken him anywhere in the world, and he probably would never have met me! The effects of that "setback" continue to unfold.

The effects of that "setback" continue to unfold.

My husband's college career ended in bitter disappointment. But even though the hard work he invested in the US Military Academy may not have resulted in an army commission, it earned him a second-to-none education. The turn of events after graduation allowed him to meet his wife of almost twenty-seven years, and his four years of service at West Point allowed his daughter to go to the college of her choice without breaking the bank.

Even when we don't understand God's plan for our lives, we can trust Him. He has the power to bring good and satisfying outcomes from what we perceive to be rejection. Sometimes, we are blessed enough to see circumstances, as the Bible promises, work for the good (even decades later) of those who love God and who have been called according to His purpose.

In my family's case, God used a young soldier's faithful service and perseverance in ways that young man could never have imagined.

This Is the Place for Me

– GAIL M. JUSTESEN –

Share your mom with others; I'm still using her, you know.

These words came through to me one spring day in 2010 as I was emptying the dishwasher.

Taken aback, I wondered if someone was in the kitchen with me, as the urging seemed almost audible. I knew the time was coming soon to place Mom in a facility after caring for her for several years.

My husband, Gary, and I had agreed early in our marriage that we would care for my parents someday. It had been a wonderful privilege. Both suffered from Alzheimer's disease, and Dad had passed six years earlier.

Mom's physical health had allowed me to care for her easily, but the mental deterioration had spilled into all her abilities for self-care and reason. I found myself at that difficult decision time. My three siblings understood and supported me—and thankfully we came to the conclusion together.

Our mother, a one-of-a-kind woman, was extremely talented. Raised by parents who were music teachers, she was an accomplished pianist; she sight-read and also played by ear. She met my dad when she taught band at the high school in his hometown.

Mom was also an accomplished writer, both in verse and music, and always sang in choirs, sometimes directing them.

An artist in many mediums—oil, pencil, watercolor, acrylics, and marker—Mom had a love for nature that emerged in her paintings and drawings. Her creativity emerged in embroidery, event posters, designer cookies, scrumptious pies, and so much more; her work was always detailed and lively!

An excellent seamstress, she made her wedding dress, which eventually became our baby dresses and even doll dresses. Most of our school clothes were her creation.

In my growing years, she also taught tumbling, tap, and ballet lessons in our basement.

In her fifties, after moving with Dad to a big city, she earned a master's degree in library science and worked in the city library.

Though many of these abilities waned as Alzheimer's took over, her ability to play the piano remained. Her love for the outdoors also stayed strong.

But the time had come, and my heart prayed, *Lord, help me find a place for her. I ask for two or three confirmations, and let one be from Mom's own mouth!*

A few weeks later, as I searched for accommodations at dementia-care facilities, a friend recommended that I check out an adult-family home a mile or so from where we had raised our children.

The Little Spokane River valley was woodsy and quaint. We knew the area well—and loved it. Would it suit my nature-loving mom?

I hesitated. Could I really let her go to a place outside our home and my care?

I made the call, reluctantly, but knowing I must.

"We have no openings right now, but why not come to lunch here tomorrow and look at our place? It would be good to see how your mom reacts if we have openings in the future," they suggested.

Hmm, confirmation number one?

I was anxious to visit, knowing her personality would thrive in a smaller place. Still, "no openings" seemed daunting. I knew I was at the end of my abilities to care for her declining health. Still, I grappled with turning this precious life over to someone else, even though I could hear those words—*Share your mom with others*—deep in my soul.

That next morning, I announced, "Mom, today we are going to lunch at a place that may help care for you when I can't."

"That will be nice," she replied with a distant but sweet smile.

Oh, thank You, Lord. Help me in this, please, I silently prayed.

Am I failing in my promise to my parents?

As the lunch hour neared, my stomach churned as much as my mind did. *Am I doing the right thing? What if she feels abandoned? Am I failing in my promise to my parents that my husband and I agreed on? Am I a wimp who just needs to "buck up"?*

The relentless questions tried to discourage me.

No. I know what God said, and He will show me the way, my spirit insisted.

Again, I repeated the reason for our trip to Mom as we drove down the long hill to the place by the river. She didn't respond, caught up in the heart-soothing beauty of the stately ponderosas, vivid blue skies, and winding river. It reminded me of one of her paintings that I loved dearly—one with yellow river irises lining a stream among basalt rocks and tall pines. Heavenly.

We crossed the small bridge over the river and turned downward to the facility situated in the lower level of the caretakers' home. The river sparkled and willow-leaf buds ready to explode trailed into the stream.

Suddenly, Mom exclaimed, "Ooh! Now, *this* is the place for me!"

O me of little faith nearly drove off into the river! Another confirmation—and from her own lips!

Inside the place, tears filled my eyes as we were introduced. We visited with the aides and residents as we ate lunch outside on the picnic table by the river. Two of the residents had commonalities with Mom. Mom looked so at peace. But they had "no openings."

After lunch, the owners whispered to me, "We just got a call that one of our residents must move to the VA hospital. There are four others on the waiting list, but we can see that this is a perfect match for our residents and your mom. We would love to have her here!"

My heart-wrenching decision, made so easy by God, turned out to be perfect! Mom lived there for a year and a half. We could visit every day. She brought her joy, humor, and music to that place. Everyone loved her! It is an answered prayer I will never forget.

Seven hours before my mom stepped into glory, where she no doubt said *again,* "This is the place for me!" she held a newborn—her fourth great-grandchild. One precious life leaving this earth, one coming to bring joy and many of Mom's traits to our family.

An Answer That Ignited Hope

– CAROLYN WAVERLY –

The phone call came on a Sunday night when my husband, Will, was sitting at the dining-room table working on our taxes.

Our daughter had been transported to the hospital for alcohol overdose. Again.

We were fearful and weary of how alcohol controlled her. As we drove to the hospital, I shifted from blaming Rachel to blaming ourselves. *We could have . . . I should have . . . Why didn't I . . .*

"Shame on you!" had been my dad's favorite phrase. While I was growing up, someone in the family was always blaming someone else. Lots of finger pointing. Someone was at the end of that pointed finger.

My brothers blamed me. I blamed myself. No such thing as an accident! Someone spilled the milk! I sang "Amazing grace, how sweet the sound" in our little red brick country church, but the words never followed me home. Two weeks after graduation, I left home.

When I got married, Will and I began to have intense arguments. A patient husband and a counselor helped me navigate them. Moving past blaming others came more easily than not blaming myself.

"Give yourself some grace," I encouraged Will, our kids, and even friends over lunch. Eventually, I could speak the words to myself.

More than twenty years later, when I faced our daughter's addiction, those words from my childhood returned. I should have been able to say something, do something, to stop her.

Rachel, our firstborn, had been compliant, caring, sensitive, and smart. She was a favored babysitter at church, a good student with good friends. At college, she got her dream internship and went for a double major.

"Are you sure it's worth the stress?" we asked. Graduating on schedule, our beaming beauty with multiple cords around her neck, posed for pictures between us and her grandparents.

Rachel's plans always aligned with what she wanted. Until postgraduation.

Rachel's twenties were a blur of binge drinking and alcohol abuse spiraling to out-of-control addiction. Her friends would ring our doorbell at two o'clock in the morning and deliver our intoxicated daughter. We received calls from police officers and had to pay attorney and court fees.

What did we do? Or not do? Why, God? The questions haunted me.

What did we miss? What did we do? Or not do? Why, God? The questions haunted me.

Then Rachel lived in an apartment in a nearby town, and we initiated conversations and dinners and saw her almost every week. On Tuesdays, Will took her to lunch near her office.

I took her shopping, invited her to a cooking class, and bought the occasional extra concert ticket. We worked at the relationship. And it was work!

"You ask too many questions," she told us. She was negative and quiet at best and cagey and lying on the dark days. Almost daily, I texted inspirational quotes, devotions, and prayers to her.

The right words at the right time can turn her life around, I thought.

"You don't know what pressure I'm under at work. My boss expects so much." She always had the same answer.

Shortly before she turned thirty, her department downsized, and she was let go. She went back to Celebrate Recovery, and she accepted our standing offer to pay for a counselor. Without the job, the source of her stress, things were looking up.

I called the counselor's office and asked why the latest check wasn't cashed. Rachel hadn't shown up for her appointment! I had even dropped her off and picked her up at the counseling office.

"I got coffee instead," she said. "And I decided not to go back."

How could I keep on hoping? But on rare occasions, I saw the "old" Rachel, smiling and brimming with kindness and compassion. *How could we reach her?*

I started seeing a counselor. I spoke with an addiction specialist, researched treatment centers, insurance, and costs.

After another phone call from jail, I started attending Al-Anon meetings. Reluctant at first, Will joined me a few weeks later.

Al-Anon was the breakthrough we needed. We couldn't manage or control her drinking. The most freeing lesson I learned was that we didn't *cause* Rachel's addiction. Her addiction was not our fault! It was a disease. *Blame the disease, if you must.*

Other parents struggling with the guilt were moving on with their lives. We could too! I was encouraged. Certainly, we had done more than our share of enabling, possibly postponing her healing, by doing things like paying her rent when we saw an eviction notice.

One Tuesday afternoon in May, I felt an overwhelming need to pray for Rachel's protection. I texted Will. But the urgency to pray increased. *Text your circle!*

Finally, I sent a text to my three praying friends who knew some or most of our family's story.

Why is the anxiety building instead of decreasing? Reluctantly, I dressed up for a dinner for volunteers at the local high school that I would have preferred skipping. *How many events have I canceled because of Rachel?*

Shortly after ten o'clock the phone rang. A man Rachel had met at a bar had given her a choice. Go to the ER, or he was calling her family. A while later, with Rachel sleeping off the effects of her evening in her bedroom in our home, Will and I thanked God for answering our prayer of protection.

I walked into the kitchen and made a cup of decaf.

Pack her bag. Pack her bag. Words from above! She had a few clothes left at our house, so I did a load of laundry at one in the morning and packed her bag.

Upon awakening, my husband and I prayed. Then we walked into our daughter's room and sat. Will said to Rachel, "We think you need to go to rehab this morning."

When she walked downstairs with uncombed hair and wearing clothes from the night before, she carried the pillow from her bed. Just like she was my little girl going to camp. But it wasn't camp.

On the way back home from rehab, Will pulled over to the side of the road. We held each other and wept a decade of tears. Tears of deep gratitude. Pain. Remorse. Relief.

I no longer blamed myself or Rachel; instead, I blamed the disease that stole her twenties. That night, for the first night in years, Will and I slept soundly, knowing she was safe.

In July, she moved to a sober recovery house in Chicago, went to an intensive outpatient program and to AA meetings, and started going back to church. She even got a part-time job cleaning a fitness facility early in the mornings. "I may be cleaning toilets, but I'm not drinking," she said.

A couple of Sundays later, she called. "You'll never guess what happened at church today! A lady said that when she was praying, she felt God whisper, *Ask the girl in the white dress to tea.* She was really nice. She was a missionary."

A year later, she got a full-time job in her field and an apartment with a roommate from the recovery house. Today, she is thirty-four and sober. She still keeps in contact with her missionary mentor. She sends *me* inspirational quotes, and I often get "I love you" texts. Interesting that I seldom got those when we were doing so much—too much—for her.

Sometimes hope quietly comes alongside us to hold our hand, and we are so thankful for a hundred reasons. Sometimes hope comes crashing down, awakening us to His presence before we can catch our breath. Both are sweet in their own way, but the latter changes our hearts, and we are never the same.

A Special Delivery

– JOANIE SHAWHAN –

My eyes darted around the room. I calculated the best escape route should the young woman make a threatening move. The cargo pocket on her baggy garb bulged. I chastised myself for inviting her in. But wait . . . I really didn't invite her in. I had simply answered the doorbell for a voice that announced, "UPS!"

As a shiver raced down my spine, whether from chill or fear, the blustery wind circulating through my sliding glass door reminded me once again why I had ordered the custom blinds she had just delivered.

I hadn't anticipated any danger. A young woman clad in a drab brown uniform, a matching sweatshirt, and heavy laced work boots leaned against the doorframe. Wrapping her arms around the lengthy package, she hoisted it up off the floor. Then she half carried, half dragged the box down the hall and propped it against the wall.

"What's in the package?" she asked. Without waiting for my response, she trudged through the living room and plopped down in my glider rocker.

I stood in the middle of the room and stared at the stranger who had made herself at home in my favorite chair. I didn't know what to do. Should I tell her to leave?

I hesitated, then walked over to the sofa and perched on the edge, stationing myself between her and the door, in case I needed to bolt. I wasn't sure how I should start a conversation, so I asked her name and then told her mine. But she knew my name from the label plastered on the package.

The woman propped her boot-clad feet on the footstool and rocked. "I'm doing seasonal work for UPS," she said. "Christmas is such a busy season for them with all the extra packages, so the UPS truck drops off boxes for the neighborhood in a rented storage room. I load them on a handcart, push it down the sidewalk, and deliver the packages to all the apartment buildings along the street."

As I exhaled, my shoulders relaxed. I wasn't aware I'd been holding my breath. I sensed no malicious intent and concluded I simply provided a place to warm up and rest, one stop along a chilly route, a break from trudging through the ice and snow.

I offered the delivery woman a cup of hot chocolate, which she gratefully accepted. I wasn't sure of proper protocol since I had never experienced a UPS social call.

After she departed, I tore open the box and drew out the blinds. I spent the next hour piecing them together before a broken mechanism disrupted my assembly. I threw up my hands in a huff, packed the blinds back in the box, and reordered.

The following week, the doorbell interrupted my Christmas baking. Powdered sugar dusted the front of my sweatshirt, and green food coloring stained my fingers. The aroma of sugar cookies lingered in the air as the young woman from UPS lugged the package down the hall.

She grinned as she surveyed the rows of cookies spread over my dining room table: Russian teacakes rolled in powdered sugar, pecan-encrusted thumbprints, and green frosted wreaths adorned with red-hots.

The UPS girl walked over to the table, helped herself to several cookies, and took her place in my glider rocker. As she rocked and munched cookies, we chatted about her life, her marriage, her desire for a baby, and her plans for school, as well as our faith in Christ, before she headed out the door.

Over the course of several days, the doorbell rang, though no packages were delivered. My UPS girl, as I fondly called her, grinned, strolled in, plopped in my glider rocker, and nibbled cookies. My suspicion crumbled just like one of my cookies.

I wondered if God had orchestrated some divine plan in these visits.

I wondered if God had orchestrated some divine plan in these visits beyond cookies and shelter from the bitter cold. On one of her visits, we prayed for her marriage, her future, and most importantly, her deepest desire: a baby. That day, I hoped she left filled with a new expectation and not just cookies.

As she lumbered down the icy parking lot, my eyes lingered on her retreating form. I wondered if I would ever see her again. But I had done my part. The rest was up to God.

Over the course of the following year, I wondered about the whereabouts of my UPS girl, especially after Thanksgiving and the upcoming arrival of another Christmas.

One afternoon, I stared blankly at the barren elms casting long shadows across the dirty snow. The doorbell jolted me from the chilly bleakness of the day.

A familiar voice said, "UPS!"

I wasn't expecting any packages. Puzzled, I cracked open the door. My UPS girl!

Her face beamed as she sauntered down the hall. "I'm not working for UPS, but I have thought of you many times this year." With a twinkle in her eye, she said, "I just had to come by and show you my baby."

A car seat dangled from the crook of her arm. Nestled beneath the fleece blankets, a baby girl slumbered.

I hugged my friend. "She's so beautiful!"

I stared at the tiny bundle snuggled in her car seat—the answer to our prayers.

The UPS girl resumed her place in my glider rocker, and we chatted about her life, her plans, and of course her new arrival. I would have loved to offer her cookies, but I hadn't started my Christmas baking.

We hugged goodbye. Once again, my gaze lingered on her retreating form, this year toting a new bundle.

That Christmas, I realized that sometimes it is in the interruptions of the mundane that God delivers His greatest gifts.

The Peace He Promises

– KELLIE JOHNSON –

A yellow ribbon encircled a tree, a red-and-white magnet with a blue star graced the bumper of my car, and an American flag snapped in the wind on my front porch. These were just a few telltale signs that my son was deployed in the US Army.

Our boy had spoken off and on about joining the military after high school. He spent the year after graduation trying to decide and then finally signed the papers, took his oath, and headed to Fort Benning in Georgia for his basic training.

We knew where our son was and could sleep at night with a peaceful spirit and the confidence that God was taking care of him.

But the tide began to turn only two months after basic-training graduation. We received a phone call from him at his new base in New York.

"Mom, guess what? They are sending a unit to Afghanistan for nine months and were short a few guys, so I volunteered! Don't worry about me; I'll be fine!"

Whoa . . . *what*?

Does basic training teach you how to survive a deployment? There were people in Afghanistan who didn't want our troops there. There were dangers and pitfalls, and our son was still so young.

My husband and I knew we had to be supportive, encouraging. And we recognized this would be a test of our own faith as well as his. We sensed the Lord asking, *Do you trust Me? Do you really trust Me with your son?* So we chose to dig in and hand our child back to God with both hands.

Sometimes letting go is key to spiritual peace.

Sometimes letting go is key to spiritual peace.

We wanted peace for ourselves and just as much, or even more, for our son. Who knew that a prayer for peace would become so vital to our survival in our day-to-day lives?

Lord, keep our son close. Help him to feel Your presence at all times, I prayed daily. *And I pray that he turns to You when he is lonely or frightened or sick. Father, You love him more than I do, and so I am trusting You to be his companion on the other side of the planet. Draw him close, strengthen his faith, and give us all the peace that surpasses understanding. Put people in his path that can point him back to You when he needs a reminder that You are omnipresent.*

For nine months, we lived the life of parents with a deployed soldier. Many nights, we were wakened by the ring of our cell phone with a call from another time zone on the other side of the globe. Propping our sleepy heads up, we would video chat with our boy from his bunk. He told us of long shifts with little time to eat or rest. He told us that despite fevers and sickness, you show up for work anyway.

He told us of a head wound that knocked him out cold as he warmed by a night fire, never knowing if it was caused by debris leaping out of the flames or a sniper lurking near camp. He waited days before telling us that news, but he would be coming home with shrapnel buried just under his scalp.

We continued to pray for his safety, and we prayed especially for his spiritual life and a peace that only God could give.

Most people have some sort of an outlet for stress in their lives. Some garden, others run. Our son would pick up a guitar and strum, mimicking whatever he heard.

So how sweet it was of God to make sure that out in the middle of the desert, in a small US Army camp, an acoustic guitar would show up, thanks to an old retired minister of music, in a tiny office outside the entrance to the soldiers' workout room.

That man may have touched many lives while working as an independent contractor in the camp, but I am convinced he was a direct answer to our prayers for my son. The guitar sparked conversations between the two that oozed spiritual wisdom.

What more could we ask for? What more assurance did we need that God had His big hand right on our son's head?

Knowing he now had access to a guitar reminded us that God is in the details of our lives. Putting that retired music minister in the desert at that exact season reminded us that God wants us to grow in our faith, no matter where we are.

Our nerves were rarely an issue during those nine months.

My husband and I clung to Philippians 4:6–7: "Do not be anxious about anything, but in every situation, by prayer and petition, with thanksgiving, present your requests to God. And the peace of God, which transcends all understanding, will guard your hearts and your minds in Christ Jesus" (NIV).

We prayed continually, with thanksgiving, and counted on God to bring us the peace He promises. And He did not disappoint. Like any parent, we had our moments of wondering and wanting to do something more, but we lived with a peace that words cannot describe.

The retired music minister gave that guitar to our son when his tour in Afghanistan ended. It was shipped back to the States and hangs now in his home. My husband and I cut the yellow ribbon off our tree, and we removed the magnet from our car but continued to fly the flag until our son's four-year contract ended.

We are very aware that not all families get to welcome their children home from a deployment with relief and joy—especially those who return with shrapnel in their bodies.

But when we stay close to God, we can rest assured that He does know exactly where our children are and what they're facing—and He will provide peace for their souls, as well as their parents' souls.

God is good. And despite the imperfect world we live in, He does answer our prayers.

A Heavenly Mother's Day

– JOYCE WILLIAMS –

My mama was a very quiet, humble person. She avoided the spotlight like the plague, and you would never find her up front. As a matter of fact, she always sat near the back of the sanctuary when she was in church.

Mama was unstintingly unselfish. I remember when she took my younger sister, Jane, and me shopping. On rare occasions when Daddy had earned some extra money, she would take us to one of the nicest stores in town. At great personal sacrifice, she would buy matching outfits for us, although I do not remember her ever buying anything for herself. That was Mama.

Mama and Daddy worked hard. In the summer, Daddy would go to the farmers' market late in the day and buy bushels of produce. Mama spent many days canning fruits and vegetables to get us through the winter. For years, she provided day care for children in our home. We came to think of them as our little sisters and brothers.

In my early years, Mama did our laundry each Monday on a wringer washing machine. I remember being fascinated by the different galvanized tubs she positioned around that aging relic. One was for cold water, another for hot water, and yet one more for bleach water. It was quite a process.

One of my favorite memories of Mama was watching her read her big black Bible. She loved reading about end times.

One Sunday morning in August, the call came that Mama was gone. I was more than a thousand miles away, and my heart was broken. My husband, Gene, and I could not get a plane out until Monday morning, so I spent the afternoon and evening going through things of Mama's that I had with me. My heart was overwhelmed with sadness that didn't seem to lessen as the months flew by.

The following Mother's Day, I was distraught. My mom was gone, and I was a thousand miles from both of my daughters, Tami and Beth. And word had just come that Uncle Lewis, Mama's brother—our patriarch—was dying of cancer. There was no way I could go to be with any of them. My heart was torn into ribbons of grief.

> As I sorted through a box, I found an envelope that I had never seen before.

As I sorted through a box, I found an envelope that I had never seen before. My mom's spidery handwriting brought fresh tears to my eyes. The words that I read through that misty veil lifted my heart.

Mama had always told us her favorite song was "Beulah Land" as sung by my daughter Bethany. So, I was surprised to read, "My favorite songs are 'It Is Well with My Soul' and 'I'd Rather Have Jesus.' "

My heart was lifted as I thought, *That sums it all up! When our life is over and we have a final testimony to leave as a legacy of our faith, those words say it all.*

As I reflected on the way the Lord had brought such special words of comfort when Mama died, I was assured that somehow He would find a special way to console us once again as we walked back through the valley.

On Friday, I called my cousin Patsy. She said that Uncle Lewis's death was imminent. He had almost died on Wednesday night but had somehow rallied. As a matter of fact, he had been so much better that the doctor had sent the family home to rest around midnight.

Patsy went on to tell me that early Thursday morning his nurse, Debbie, a family friend, heard Uncle Lewis mumbling. She paused for a moment and listened. Then she moved closer to his bed. Leaning toward him, she heard him say, "It's much more beautiful over there than I ever dreamed. Look at all the angels! There's a big river, and I can see lots of people on the other side." He paused, then said, "I see Mary!"

Then he drifted back into unconsciousness. When Patsy finished, I couldn't speak for the tears flowing down my cheeks. He had seen Mary—his sister—Mama! Uncle Lewis had been given a glimpse of heaven and that very special resident. Joy infused me, pushing back the sorrow! What a Mother's Day gift—straight from heaven!

Patsy called early Saturday morning to tell me that Uncle Lewis had joined Mama. Rather than the sorrow I had anticipated, I was comforted picturing Mama welcoming him. Imagine—my humble mother as a heavenly greeter! I visualized brother and sister exploring their new home together, walking on golden streets hand in hand, shouting joyfully. I'm sure Daddy was holding Mama's other hand as they helped to reacquaint Uncle Lewis with so many who had gone ahead—Aunt Ethel and all the rest. Imagine! My humble, meek, back-of-the-crowd mother was right up front—by the portals of heaven!

Now I know that she is experiencing those heavenly vistas and the presence of Jesus firsthand. Thank You, Lord, for a Mother's Day that became a joyous celebration rather than a sad farewell—a Mother's Day glimpse that was out of this world!

Let Him Go

– JULIE PAPIEVIS –

I sat next to my bedridden, seventy-nine-year-old father, gently stroking his arm. His labored breathing the only sound in the room.

The man who had made me feel so loved, protected, and important still appeared to be strong. Maybe it was because he always remained in control of every situation. Now he was determined to be in control even of his own death.

He had decided when to call in hospice. He asked me to accept his decision to forgo further treatment and accept his death.

As I looked at him, it occurred to me that if my father hadn't refused to let me die years earlier, I would not be here with him. Rather, I would be waiting for him to join me.

On May 10, 1993, when I was twenty-nine, my brain stem was nearly severed when a teenage driver, speeding through a red light, hit the driver's side of my car at fifty miles per hour. The odds of my survival were only 4 percent. And many of those who "survived" such an injury spent the rest of their lives in a nursing facility. Life expectancy was greatly shortened by either their injuries or suicide.

Fortunately, the accident took place near a large Chicago-area shopping center. An off-duty paramedic witnessed the accident and provided aid within minutes. An ambulance was dispatched from a nearby fire station immediately. Just fourteen minutes after my accident, I arrived at the local trauma center. Despite the help, I experienced not only death, but life after death.

The doctors waited for my parents' arrival to the trauma center. They needed my parents' permission to turn off the machines that kept my body functioning. All other signs of life were gone. My body had already shut down and released my spirit.

My father told me many times that he knew that each of his children was a gift from God. His responsibility was to take care of them until it was time for them to return to God.

But he refused to believe it was my time. He refused to let me die.

I could not dominate a room as he did with his physical presence. When he entered the trauma center, my mother told me, he remained calm. His calm demeanor, however, did not hide his refusal to admit that his daughter was gone. It did not hide his determination to secure the care his daughter needed. Later, he would refuse to let the hospital move me to a distant nursing home without access to the rehabilitation facilities he believed I needed. He knew if I did not receive the rehab, I would waste away at the nursing home.

A large man at six-foot-six, he arrived at the trauma center to rescue me from death or, at the very least, a shortened lifetime of barely functioning in a skilled nursing facility. Call it intuition, call it a father's hope, but he told me later that he knew I would live.

I spent six weeks in a coma. When I finally woke, my left side was paralyzed, I was incontinent, unable to see out of my left eye, and fed through a G-tube.

During those long six weeks, he considered taking early retirement to care for me when I was out of the hospital.

"Your mom and I didn't know what we would be left with," he told me later, "but we were committed to taking care of you at home."

I moved back home with my parents. The left side of my body was still partially paralyzed. When I tripped and almost fell in front of them, Dad told me he wished he could take the pain and suffering away from me and take it on himself.

I didn't tell my parents about my death experience until several weeks after coming out of the coma. It was difficult to discuss. I had experienced pure joy and peace and had been disappointed to learn I had returned to my body.

How could I explain to my father who refused to let me die, that I did not want to return? When I finally told him, he understood.

My father's chronic obstructive pulmonary disease (COPD) and the cancer that spread to his esophagus had taken their toll on his body. He was tired of the chemo and radiation treatments that could not extend his life and caused an inoperable infection. The treatments might keep him from having a gastrostomy feeding tube inserted but offered little else.

I would not have the same opportunity to rescue my father from death.

He gently asked me to accept his death, to let him go.

Both of us were caregivers of the other. But our roles were different. In 1993, his role had been to refuse to let me die. Years later, my role was to accept his decision to die.

In our discussions about his impending death, our father-daughter language had no words for letting go. In 1993, the words certainly hadn't been there. In a coma, I was unable to say those words to my father. I was unable to say "I found peace and an indescribable joy; let me go. I will wait for you."

> Our father-daughter language had no words for letting go.

And my father, seeing my broken body, did not have the words to say to the physicians "let her go."

Language, I discovered, unlike emotions, has boundaries. Now, we both had to work together to find the words of letting go.

I remained next to my bedridden, seventy-nine-year-old father, gently stroking his arm. His labored breathing remained the only sound. I desperately wanted him to stay. Yet, I knew what awaited him.

And I praised God that Dad would be with Him forever.

A Hard-Won Victory

– VIRGINIA PILLARS –

Help! In early 2005, my prayers sounded more like a desperate plea for rescue from drowning. My situation sucked me into a whirlpool of chaos. As I came up for air, I poured out my heart to God. *Help, Lord. I don't know how to do this. I need You!*

Perhaps the desperation wasn't surprising. In late 2004, schizophrenia manifested in our twenty-four-year-old daughter, Amber. She had come home for a three-day-weekend in early December to rest from the stress she felt at her job. Unaware of the severity of her illness, I thought with a mother's love and care at home, she could get back on her feet and return to her job as a youth minister about an hour from our home.

I took her to my family doctor who prescribed a low-dose antidepressant and a one-week work release. My husband, Roy, and I hoped this would help. However, we had no experience with mental health issues.

Within a week, the insidious symptoms of schizophrenia roared and slashed sharp claws into her ability to separate reality from paranoia.

She became convinced "they" wanted to find her to harm her. "They" used television, movies, radio, newspapers, and magazines to broadcast her life to the world.

One night, she peered out the windows for hours as she searched for "them" lurking outside our home. The day she saw cameras in the bathroom when she showered, I convinced her to enter a hospital as a safe place where "they" couldn't find her. I prayed she'd get help there.

Five days later, after Roy and I paced the halls of the unit beside her while she spewed venom at the staff, she checked herself out against medical advice.

Now, Amber refused any antipsychotic medications that might benefit her.

"They tried to make me take poison!" she shouted at me with clenched fists. "I have depression. I take medicine for that."

My anger raged. *How can God do this to us? We are a family of faith and have tried to serve Him all our lives.*

I felt like I had been kicked in the stomach.

Embarrassed, I kept her troubled mind to myself. Instead, I watched like a rubberneck bystander as schizophrenia stole my daughter's vibrant personality. Fear invaded everything, and voices shouted insults at her through the closed mouths of anyone near her.

Christmas arrived and brought a slew of relatives into our home for the annual party. Concerned about what could happen in her present state of mind, Roy and Amber left after the meal for our son's home. Mitchell, his wife, Melinda, and young son, Carter, stayed at the party with the cousins, aunt, and uncles as I played hostess.

"Where are Amber and Roy?" several guests asked.

"Amber didn't feel well. Roy took her to Mitchell's to rest." I evaded the truth, too ashamed to share the real reason.

When Roy and Amber returned earlier than I expected, I raised my eyebrows as I sought the answer in his eyes. He whispered, "She slept for a while, but when she woke up, she tore through the house. She looked in every closet and behind every door. She got super upset, and I had to get her out of there."

"Where is he?" Amber shouted at her. "What did you do with him?

Before we could stop her, Amber marched into the front room where Melinda sat chatting with cousins.

"Where is he?" Amber shouted at her. "What did you do with him? If you hurt him, you'll pay!"

Melinda stood and squeezed past Amber in silence as the verbal assaults continued. By then, I reached them and slid my arm around Amber's shoulder. I guided her clear.

As Melinda left our home with Carter in her arms, Amber screamed, "You'll pay for this."

Our secret life of horror had emerged into a crowd of relatives. While Amber vomited scrambled words and angry accusations, everyone gathered their things and left our home with downturned eyes.

In spite of my anger and inability to ask God for help, I got it anyway. Mitchell arrived a few days later. He handed me a scrap of paper with a phone number on it. "Mom, I think these people understand. Call them."

"Who is it?"

"It's an organization called NAMI. It stands for National Alliance on Mental Illness. They know what you are going through. Just call them," he implored as he posted the note on my refrigerator with a magnet.

I called. I did find understanding in the form of education and support. At their encouragement, I sent an email to our extended families and friends. After I explained Amber's fragile health, we received phone calls, letters, and messages filled with encouragement and pledges of prayer. One phone call suggested that I read the book *When Bad Things Happen to Good People* by Harold S. Kushner. NAMI people suggested I read books about mental illness.

These two things threw me a lifeline. I came to realize Amber's illness came from our broken world. We hadn't received punishment from God. My anger lifted as I started each morning in prayer and devotion.

While Roy and I learned about Amber's brain disorder, it tightened the grip it had on her. Her delusions and hallucinations increased in frequency and severity until she became convinced of a conspiracy to take her life. When we saw her illness fray the fabric of our tightly woven family, Roy, Mitchell, and I committed her through the court system for forced medication.

I had a glimmer of hope as she received medication through injections. But optimism lasted only a short time. The medicine didn't work. She sank into a world I couldn't reach with alarming speed. Within weeks, I questioned if she knew I sat beside her in the hospital ward.

I reached back out to our families and closest friends. I asked them to pray with us for three things: that the doctors could find the right cocktail of medications to help Amber, that Amber would come to understand her illness and take the medicine, and that I would find the wisdom and strength I needed to face this Goliath.

As her condition worsened, we transferred her to a different hospital. There, the doctor ran tests and started her on an older medication.

"It often helps," he said, "but sometimes has side effects."

We saw glimpses of her personality reemerge. One evening, as we strolled the unit hallway with her, she began to squirm. "Dad, will you rub my neck? It feels stiff."

We slid into the plastic chairs across from the nurses' station. As Roy massaged her neck, she implored, "Harder, Dad. It's worse."

His finger and thumb rotated in small circles on her thin neck. Suddenly, her entire body jerked. Her hands gnarled in an unnatural position while her mouth distorted in a crooked grimace. She cried as she fell across our laps. I grabbed for the waistband of her jeans as Roy gripped her to prevent her from rolling to the hard floor.

"Oh, God! Help us! Help us!" I cried as Roy shouted to the nurses. A team of white soon surrounded us.

"Open your mouth, Amber," one of them instructed. "This medicine will help."

Amber opened her mouth as her eyes rounded in terror. The woman tapped the white paper cup and the small tablet dropped into Amber's mouth.

"I have water for you." Another nurse squeezed into the distraught group and tipped the liquid into Amber's mouth. Amber swallowed.

The team formed a human gurney as they pulled Amber from our arms into theirs. In unison, they whisked her through the hallway as other patients plastered their bodies to the walls. Roy and I scurried behind them. As we entered Amber's room, we shot to the far corner out of the staff's way. We held hands as I prayed in silence.

One nurse held a syringe upright in her hand while another tugged down Amber's jeans. In one swift motion, the plunger pushed the medicine into my thrashing daughter. Amber's muscles released their board-like grip, and she relaxed.

As I watched the shoulders of the staff release the tension, I asked, "What happened?"

"She had a dystonic reaction. It happens in some patients. I know it's scary for her and you, but her life was never in danger. We gave her medicine to counteract it. She'll be tired and sleep now. You should go home. We'll watch her closely all night."

The nurse gave me a warm smile as she massaged the point of injection to soothe Amber.

After all the nurses left, Roy and I stepped up to her bed.

With droopy eyes, Amber spoke softly, "Mom, I need medicine. It helps me. I know I need it," before her eyes slid shut.

In spite of my shaky knees, I felt loved as I realized God had answered my urgent prayers for help. On that frightening night, Amber started the long journey to recovery.

The spectacle of a horrific, physical reaction had produced the answer to prayer. Amber received the grace to understand and accept her illness. Her first step began when she agreed to take the prescribed medicine.

As we drove home, I realized my tears had offered petitions to God. I saw God's love in the people who stepped beside us with education, support, and prayers.

Today, fourteen years later, I live with gratitude and awe. Amber recaptured her life through recovery. She manages her illness, schizophrenia, as she maintains an independent life. This includes an apartment, a full-time job, control of her health and business affairs, and a social life that makes me tired.

And she's a continual reminder to me that God answers even our most desperate prayers.

Nine Bible Blessings to Pray for Those You Love

— BOB HOSTETLER —

A friend shared a touching story. His adult son and daughter-in-law hung over their firstborn's bed a framed representation of the Aaronic blessing from the Bible: "The Lord bless you and keep you; the Lord make His face shine on you and be gracious to you; the Lord turn His face toward you and give you peace."

Each night, they blessed him with those words. Now, when his grandmother or grandfather (my friend) visit and tuck him in, he asks, "Will you bless me?"

Biblical blessings can focus and enhance your prayers even when you don't know what else to pray for someone. Here are nine blessings I like to pray and the Bible verses they're drawn from.

1. May the Lord bless you and keep you; may He smile on you and be gracious to you; may He look your way and give you

peace (Numbers 6:24–26, author's paraphrase of the Aaronic blessing).

2. May God give you the desire of your heart and make all your plans succeed (Psalm 20:4, NIV).
3. May God be gracious to you and bless you and make His face shine upon you (Psalm 67:1, NIV).
4. May you experience the love of Christ, though it is so great you will never fully understand it, and may you be filled with the fullness of life and power that comes from God (Ephesians 3:19, NLT).
5. May Christ make His home in your heart through faith (see Ephesians 3:17, NLT).
6. May you be strengthened with all power, according to God's glorious might (see Colossians 1:11, ESV).
7. May you be filled with joy (Colossians 1:11, NLT).
8. May the Master pour on the love so it fills your life and splashes over on everyone around you (1 Thessalonians 3:12, MSG).
9. "May the Lord of peace himself give you peace at all times and in every way" (2 Thessalonians 3:16, NIV).

6

Forgiveness and Reconciliation

When you can't forgive someone, pray for them. It may or may not change them, but it will always change you.

ANONYMOUS

"To err is human . . ." Alexander Pope wrote more than three hundred years ago. Unfortunately, it is oh, so true. And we humans err so frequently, especially if our hearts get out of sync with our Father's heart.

So often when we err, what we do affects other people. We may hurt them with our thoughts, words, and actions. And on the flip side of the coin, to be human is also to, sooner or later, be the recipient of pain or bad behavior inflicted by someone else.

Jacob was certainly a poster child for treating his brother, Esau, badly. Perhaps you remember the story of sibling rivalry to the extreme degree.

Isaac, the son of the famous Israelite patriarch, Abraham, had two sons—twins, born only minutes apart. Esau, the older twin, was a hunter. Jacob, the younger, stuck closer to home and was his mother's favorite. One day when Esau came home from hunting, he was hungry, and Jacob had some food ready. However, Jacob wouldn't share without a price. In exchange for the stew he had prepared, he expected Esau to give up his birthright. The birthright was the oldest son's right to benefits including inheriting family leadership and a double paternal inheritance.

Esau was rather carefree about the birthright and agreed. Later, Isaac, nearing death, was ready to bestow the family blessing upon Esau. First, Isaac sent him out hunting and told him to prepare a special meal. Meanwhile, Jacob and his mom, Rebekah, disguised Jacob so that the nearly blind father would mistake him for Esau. They went to the extreme of Jacob wearing his brother's clothes and placing extra animal hair on his arms so he would feel and smell like Esau.

The trick worked. Isaac bestowed the main family blessing—including a wish for fertility and dominion—on Jacob instead of his older brother.

When Esau got home and learned what Jacob had done, he vowed to kill his brother, so Jacob ran away to live with his maternal uncle. In his exile, Jacob had his own lessons to learn and had his own encounters with God, and God's hand ended up being on Jacob.

But then, twenty years later, God told Jacob to return to his homeland—where Esau still lived. Jacob sent a message and gifts ahead to try to warm up his brother's heart. Could the trickster find forgiveness from his brother? When Jacob learned his brother was approaching with a large group of people, he wondered if there was forgiveness. Scripture tells us that Jacob turned to God in prayer, asking God to be with him as he faced his twin brother, Esau. And the two men made peace. (See Genesis 27, 32–33.)

Romans 12:18 tells us, "If it is possible, as far as it depends on you, live at peace with everyone" (NIV).

Living in peace with others is not possible without forgiveness. And forgiveness is usually not a one-time affair. In fact, there will be people who offend us and hurt us repeatedly. Peter asked Jesus how many times we have to forgive someone else, and Jesus replied, "seventy times seven" (Matthew 18:22, NKJV) . . . or pretty much as many times as the person needs forgiving. We can certainly set up boundaries in our lives so that a chronic pain inflicter has less chance of hurting us, but we are to be reconciled with others.

And that's not always easy to do, no matter if we're the one receiving or inflicting the pain. Sometimes forgiving is one of those things we can do only through God's power and strength. We have to call upon Him to give us the grace we need.

As you read the stories in the chapter ahead, reflect on your own relationships and let the Holy Spirit touch your heart. Commit those messages to the Lord, asking Him to give you wisdom and work through you . . . and you can be sure He will!

Put That Bottle Down!

– RAMELLE T. LEE –

When I was young, our family underwent the most earth-shattering time of our lives. My dad announced to our family that he had purchased a lottery ticket.

"I've got the winning ticket for ten thousand dollars!" he announced. However, somehow Dad's winning lottery ticket couldn't be found.

Dad searched through every drawer, through the pockets of our clothes and coats, and throughout the entire house looking for that lottery ticket. He was obsessed! And he began to question my mother and me, as well as my twin brother, Lovell, about where we'd hidden his ticket.

Initially, we assured Dad that we had never seen the ticket that he had purchased. For a while, he believed us and dropped the questioning. But then Dad continued to blame us for his not being able to find his lottery ticket.

In our peaceful home in southwestern Detroit near the beautiful Detroit River and the grand historic Ford River Rouge plant, our lives changed.

The tension escalated every weekend because Dad would start drinking and be consumed with looking for his lottery ticket. He was headstrong and persistent. That meant every time he thought about the ticket, he brought it to our attention too. He angrily accused us, "You're not fooling me! You all know where my winning ticket is! I'll get it from you."

Nothing we said or did ever changed his mind.

As time went by, Lovell and I moved out of our parents' home into our own apartments. However, every time we visited their house, Dad accused us of having his lottery ticket.

My mother was a quiet, godly woman who always did everything she could to keep peace. She didn't like to fuss or argue with Dad. But Dad's compulsive drinking caused all our lives to be turned upside down.

Dad was a skilled tradesman and a master cement finisher, and he always achieved outstanding performance on the job. He never allowed anyone to take advantage of him. If he didn't like something you were doing or saying, he would tell you.

Dad had no fear of anyone. He demanded respect from everyone he came in contact with and always tried to be fair with people who employed him.

When Dad was not drinking or thinking about his lottery ticket, he was extremely productive. He was known as "Mr. Fix It" in the neighborhood. Often neighbors came to Dad for advice. He would do everything he could to help them with their household projects. Even if he didn't know how to fix a problem, he would spend time trying to figure it out.

Dad had a lot of good characteristics. He was a strong and caring man. But the alcohol kept taking him to a place of anger, rage, and fault finding.

Dad never did find that lottery ticket. But he kept looking for it. He even threatened to come over to my apartment to search and threatened my life and my brother's life. Things got so bad, my brother Lovell stopped coming to see Dad at our family home.

One night, Lovell called me at midnight and said, "God told me to go and see Dad and tell him if he doesn't stop threatening his family about that lottery ticket and stop drinking, he will burst hell wide open."

Lovell was an ordained minister. Dad didn't appreciate receiving these remarks from him, but one thing was for sure—he feared God and even stopped attempting to harm his family.

Despite the warning message, Dad started drinking heavily again the following weekend and threatened all of us about that lottery ticket.

"Yeah! I'm going to do something to all of you!" he said. "I mean it!"

Mother was sitting on the couch in the den. All of a sudden, Dad started cursing and picked up the bottle of alcohol to take another drink. Then he stopped, looked at Mother with the glass in his hand, and said, "Barbara, did you hear that?"

"Hear what?" Mother responded.

"Did you hear that? Someone said to me, 'Put that bottle down!'"

Mother calmly replied, "It was not me."

Dad looked at the bottle of alcohol and twisted the cap back on it. He put the drinking glass back on the table and started crying uncontrollably.

Mother was shocked. She didn't know exactly what to say to Dad.

Dad stood up with the bottle in his hand—he walked straight without stumbling—and placed it on a dining room shelf. After that, he poured the unfinished drink down the kitchen sink and went back to the den.

> Tears were streaming down his face as he sat next to her.

Tears were streaming down his face as he sat next to her. Finally, Dad admitted that he was completely out of control, and he apologized to Mother for the way he had acted.

The next day, Dad told me what happened. He wanted me to call Lovell and let him know what happened.

I firmly said, "Dad, please talk to Lovell yourself." Surprisingly, he did.

He asked us to come over. We didn't know what to expect when we entered my parents' house. Dad apologized to me and Lovell in person. Dad never picked up a liquor bottle again. He never again threatened us, his family, about that lottery ticket.

God intervened miraculously in the heart and life of my dad. Dad heard the voice of the Lord, and it changed his life! He kept that liquor bottle in the garage for a few more years. He used it to show people as he told them about his earth-shattering experience.

Dad never took another alcoholic drink in his life.

God answered the prayers of our family. No matter how many obstacles we faced with this situation, we stood on the Word of God. We believed and prayed that He would turn this situation around.

It was extremely difficult to deal with all the challenges we faced as a family. But God was faithful to rescue all of us from our distress. He will do the same for you when you pray and put your trust in the Lord.

No, or Not Yet?

– CINDY RICHARDSON –

Shock and disbelief kept me paralyzed as my teenage daughter packed her possessions in plastic trash bags. Her recent rebellion culminated in her decision to move in with her boyfriend's family. No yelling, no big fight, just a quiet determination to change her life.

No amount of conversing, cajoling, or crying could stop her. I wailed from the depth of my being. I remember thinking, *If I don't get a grip, I am going to crack my sternum.* A picture of Jesus praying in the garden of Gethsemane came to mind, and suddenly I knew how His anguish could produce sweat like drops of blood.

In no way did I think my grief comparable to Christ's, but I felt certain that He understood my grief.

The boyfriend pulled into our driveway. I went outside to plead with him not to take her. "I want you to know that you are breaking my heart. This is the worst day of my life," I choked out before heading back to the house.

Almost to the door, I felt the Holy Spirit prompt me to turn around, and I returned to his car. He rolled down the window and through sobs I declared, "I want you to know that I believe in God. I believe He is still good and one day He will get much glory from this."

Then I did the only thing I could: I cried out to God. My faith journey with the Lord had yielded many answers to prayer, and I expected He would bring my daughter home quickly. Thinking I had enough faith for God to answer my pleas, I prayed without ceasing.

Yet God was strangely silent as days turned into weeks and months, with still no return. Though I continued to knock on heaven's door, I began to question my faith. If mustard-seed-size faith can move mountains, I concluded mine must be pitifully small.

Journaling my prayers helped me keep focused. I felt the Lord speak to my spirit, giving me His promise of hope. At first, I had more bad days than good.

Continuing to teach kindergarten was a struggle. I was concerned that my students would suffer because I was consumed with grief. I asked God how they would know and feel His love since I had so little to offer them.

A few days later, I received a note from a student. In large blue crayoned letters, it read, "I love my teacher, and I know she loves me. And that's the truth."

I was overcome by this direct answer to my prayer. Receiving love notes from my kindergartners is a joy I'd experienced many times, yet I'd never before (and haven't since) received one that declared she *knew* I loved her. My favorite part came with the added "and that's the truth."

I continued wrestling with my faith as I explored what hope had to offer me. Teaching at the Christian school my daughter had attended made my pain more intense. Daily I partnered with parents to train their children so that one day they wouldn't depart from God's path. Yet my own child was straying far from God's best for her.

Since I had come to faith in Christ later in life, this daughter was the only one of my three children to have a Christian upbringing. She was the only one to start her school career with a biblical worldview. She had been a camp counselor and had gone on a mission trip before meeting her boyfriend at work. I trained her in the way she should go, but now that she was older, she was departing from it.

One day, a friend gave me a handmade, heart-shaped book entitled *Promises from God's Heart to Yours*. She apologized for not getting it to me sooner, but it had taken her longer than expected to finish. Through tears, I assured her the timing was perfect.

God was throwing me a cord of hope.

God was throwing me a cord of hope. When I couldn't find a promise for my particular circumstance, He was providing eternal promises for every circumstance from His Word. He was encouraging me with truth and assuring me that He would never leave or forsake me.

Promises from God's Heart to Yours sustained me during the five months my daughter lived with her boyfriend's family. When she first left, I just wanted her home. Later I wanted her to have an encounter with the God who loved her and answered prayer with plans to give her hope and a future. The promises in that book sustained me when she finally returned home and I discovered I would join the grandparents' club.

Learning to trust God with the unknown and the unwanted circumstances of my life proved to be answers to prayers I'd forgotten I had even prayed. Learning to praise God despite my unfulfilled desires taught me to find my delight in my relationship with God.

My daughter's boyfriend wanted to get married, but he was an unbeliever, and she was only seventeen. I prayed for his salvation and that decisions made regarding the precious life forming in my daughter's womb would be wise.

Together my daughter and her boyfriend attended sessions at the local pregnancy resource clinic where I had been a volunteer counselor. I asked God to help me love and support my daughter through her unplanned pregnancy, just as I'd done for dozens of strangers-turned-daughters at the clinic.

A few months later, God answered my prayer after my sister was tragically killed in a car accident. Watching the body of Christ comfort our family and listening as I shared stories of my sister's life and faith, my daughter's boyfriend knew he wanted that same peace, comfort, faith, and hope, and he surrendered his life to the Lord.

Shortly after the funeral, we began to plan their wedding. Life hasn't always been easy, but time and again God answered prayers with a cord of hope to help me stay afloat as my daughter and her new husband navigated through the waters of parenting, financial challenges, and relational issues.

I've learned that every prayer we utter is answered when offered in faith and hope. However, *yes* isn't the only answer to prayer. *No* and *not yet* are also answers, and I have learned that they often turn into the best answers, if we're willing to hope.

When God Closed the Door

– DIANA LEAGH MATTHEWS –

Everywhere I turned, my mind was on a man I'll call John. I stared out the large bay windows from my workplace looking for his truck.

Is he here yet? When will he be here?

John was a client who visited our office almost daily. Over time, we built a friendship. Our work-based communications would lead to much longer conversations about a myriad of topics. We never ran out of things to talk about, and he seemed to enjoy my company as much as I enjoyed his.

However, now he seemed to be seeping into my heart. And I couldn't stop focusing on him.

One evening at a Bible study, I talked about John with a friend.

"Is he good for you?" she asked.

My heart wanted to scream Yes! but my mind screamed No!

"I'm not sure."

For the first time, I was being truthful with myself.

"Seek the Lord's will on this," she said. Then she took a deep breath before continuing. "Years ago, I was in the same boat. I was so in love with this man, but I knew he was wrong for me. Our lives were meshed together. Eventually, I prayed for the Lord to remove him from my life if this was not the man He had for me. A week later, the man announced he was moving to the other side of the country. I knew the Lord answered my prayers."

I couldn't forget my friend's story. Every evening as I took a walk, I asked the Lord if John was the man for me. Yet in my heart, I knew he wasn't. We were too different.

Nevertheless, I returned to my drug of choice—John. I could not get enough of him. When he wasn't there, I looked for him. And when he arrived for his daily visit, I wanted to be near him and didn't pay attention to my work.

John constantly showed me that he wasn't an appropriate choice for a relationship, but I didn't want to see or hear it or believe it. Through the stories he shared, he revealed his need for revenge and to not let anyone close to him. He frequently made it clear that he had no interest in marrying. To make matters worse, he was old enough to be my father.

However, we both loved his parents, who were my coworkers. We both enjoyed music, history, and trivia. I thought we both loved the Lord, but one afternoon when discussing our relationships with Christ, he shrugged it off.

> I was sinking down the rabbit hole, and fast.

I was sinking down the rabbit hole, and fast. I could not get enough of this man, and it affected every portion of my life. Finally, one evening, I asked the Lord, *If he's not the man you have for me, then please take him out of my life.*

One week passed into two and then three. I wondered if the Lord had heard me, but I knew He had. My previously friendly banter with John was now strained and forced. Where had this come from? Had I done something wrong? Had he always been this way, and I refused to see it?

One day at lunch, I was talking with a coworker about my feelings for John. I felt a whisper in my soul: *Stop talking. Be quiet.*

Ignoring the silent command, I kept talking and a heaviness spread over my heart. I wondered why I could find no peace.

That very afternoon, I was called into the owner's office. My feelings about John were exposed. Even little kindnesses I'd done were taken out of context and presented as evidence against me. Instantly, I knew my coworker had betrayed me. What hurt most was to know John was demanding that I be fired.

Even as the owner told me I was no longer needed, my heart whispered, *I forgive you, John.* Forgiving my coworker and the owner was not as easy or instantaneous.

I felt dazed as I left the building and mindlessly drove around. *This is how you answer my prayer, God? By taking my job?*

Then I reminded myself that I'd asked the Lord to remove John from my life. This was how He chose to answer my prayer.

The next few months were difficult as I struggled to move on. John continued to fill my heart and thoughts. Each time he came to mind, I prayed to God. *You know his heart and needs. Draw John closer to you.*

I'd never prayed for someone's soul the way I prayed for John's over the following months.

The Lord was good. He provided me with a temporary assignment and eventually opened doors to a better position. Moving on from John wasn't easy, but I kept reminding myself he was never mine. I'd seen all the warning signs and knew we didn't belong together.

The Lord made me a stronger person and demonstrated how much He cared about me during this difficult time.

In Matthew 21:22, Jesus tells us, "If you believe, you will receive whatever you ask for in prayer." The Lord heard my prayer and answered—just not the way I expected. However, He knew best and worked it all out to His honor and glory.

Five Steps to Forgiveness

– PABLO DIAZ –

Forgiving others can be hard to do. Most of us even struggle to forgive those who are close to our heart. Author Sonja Lyubomirsky says, "Forgiveness is a strategy that takes a great deal of effort, willpower, and motivation. It must be practiced."

When we feel as if we have been hurt, betrayed, and deeply wounded, our pain is real and healing takes time. Though we know and read in Scripture, "Vengeance is mine, I will repay, says the Lord," we are still driven by our anger to inflict revenge upon those who have hurt us. And too often we chose to try and forget what has happened, but this will not solve anything.

How do we proceed? It takes lots of prayer, strategy, time, and effort. Author and psychologist Martin Seligman offers a five step process called REACH in his book, *Authentic Happiness: Using the New Positive Psychology to Realize Your Potential for Lasting Fulfillment*. In this acrostic, he offers us a positive and helpful process:

1. **R**ecall: Begin to forgive by objectively recalling the hurt you experience.
2. **E**mpathize: Attempt to understand the person who hurt you from their perspective.
3. **A**ltruistic: Seek to rise above your anger and desire for vengeance and choose to be altruistic and forgiving.
4. **C**ommit: Forgive the person publicly. Try writing a "certificate of forgiveness."
5. **H**old: Continue to hold on to your forgiveness of the person, even when memories of the painful event recur.

These steps are worth taking, and research shows they have worked for many.

Lord, lead me through the process of forgiveness, and give me the courage to do so.

7

In the Nick of Time

God is never late and rarely early. He is always exactly right on time—His time.

Dillon Burroughs

Timing is everything in life, right?

The timing of prayers is no exception.

The danger and fear are imminent and real. And even as our conscious mind begins to grasp what is going on, our heart automatically reaches out to connect with the One who knows us best.

"O God, help!"

There's no time for theological dither. The prayers are short. They are intense. They are real.

Perhaps our favorite scriptural illustration of this one is Peter. Jesus sent His disciples to the other side of the sea while He went off alone to pray. The boat was far from land when the disciples saw Jesus approaching, walking on the water. Peter jumped out of the boat to take a watery walk with the Lord.

But then Peter felt the wind on the waves, became afraid, and began to sink, and he asked Jesus to save him. And *immediately* Jesus reached out his hand and caught Peter (see Matthew 14:28–32).

Our Lord does not stand on ceremony or respond only if we get the narrative exactly right. His children are in trouble and He moves. As instantly as our cry for help, He is there.

In other situations, God seems to delay. The cancer gets worse. The finances don't appear to be coming through. The loved one continues to make bad decisions.

We continue to call upon God, holding on to the faith we have. But God seems a little hard of hearing at the moment or at least distracted from paying attention to our problems.

Imagine how Mary and Martha felt. Their brother Lazarus was ill. When it looked like Lazarus may not make it, they called for their friend Jesus, probably with full expectancy that Jesus would dash to their side and solve the problem. When you're best buds with the Son of God, it's bound to be taken care of, right?

Instead, Jesus poked around two more days before He went to His friends in Bethany. Two days is a long time when someone's dying, and as Jesus knew, Lazarus was gone when He arrived.

Martha said to Jesus upon his arrival, "Lord, if only you had been here, my brother would not have died" (John 11:21, NLT). She expected more from her friend and perhaps wanted Him to feel guilty.

But the story ended happily. Jesus raised Lazarus from the dead. As a result, all the family, friends, neighbors, and others saw the glory of God in real time, more than they would have if Jesus had arrived when Lazarus was sick or had just died.

Author and pastor Rick Warren says, "Delays are as much a part of God's plan as answered prayers. God wants you to trust Him."

It's all a matter of timing. Sometimes our prayers are answered before the words fly through our lips. At other times, for reasons that only God knows, He delays. Maybe to help us grow. Maybe to strengthen our faith. Maybe to give us something better than what we're praying for. Maybe so the glory of God will be revealed.

In the pages ahead, you will read stories about God's perfect timing. Let the words encourage you that God hears your prayers and He answers. Maybe right away, maybe after a while, but always at the perfect time. Of that, we can be certain!

A One-Word Prayer

– DAVID MICHAEL SMITH –

I'm not sure if I whispered the word, or if it was merely a desperate thought. But that word was all time allowed.

It was a cold and starry night in early December. I was sixteen, and after watching the hometown Christmas parade complete with marching bands and holiday floats, I was running the roads with my best friend, Bruce. Not only did he have his driver's license, but he was also the proud owner of a newly painted Chevy Malibu with mag wheels, raised-white-letter Goodyear tires, and an engine that purred like a leopard. It was a car that made most of our classmates envious . . . and Bruce knew this as he squealed the tires at every intersection.

I had just started to think about attending college to pursue a criminal justice degree so I could be a Delaware state trooper. No one in my family had ever attended—let alone graduated from—any college. I would be the first. Someday, I'd also get married, have kids, and be somebody. I had my whole life in front of me. And as the song lyrics go, the future was so bright I had to wear shades.

Bruce and I exited town and headed out onto the country roads lined with farm fields and forests, simple illuminated homes dotting the landscape. Bruce pushed the accelerator to the floor and turned up the music. Neither one of us wore a seat belt.

"You think you should slow down a little, Bruce?" I inquired nervously. He just laughed. He was young and confident about his driving abilities—but inexperienced.

After a few more turns, we were on the darkest roads, mostly abandoned in the quiet winter countryside. In the distance, traveling west to east, we saw headlights that seemed to be moving quickly.

"I'm going to catch up to that guy," Bruce proclaimed, "and I know the perfect shortcut."

Dread hovered over me and then settled upon my shoulders.

Our car accelerated on the dark asphalt then suddenly braked as Bruce approached a bumpy dirt road that dissected through a wheat field. He swerved onto the gritty lane, fishtailed, then regained control and beelined toward the target vehicle.

"Let's see if I can get 'er up to seventy-five on this old road," Bruce said. Just as he reached his goal, the back of the car started to violently swerve. We seemed to be hydroplaning—not on water but on gravel.

Bruce's face was pale. He fought to regain control of his car, but he overcorrected, and the car threatened to go completely sideways. With our momentum, we surely would have tumbled over and over.

I've heard that when you face death up close, the event seems to go in slow motion. Everything was muted in silence, and I did, in fact, see several brief flashbacks: my parents, siblings, friends from school, my pets, and the pew we always sat in at church.

The second thought? *We're going to hit that tree.*

We were approaching the intersection where Bruce had hoped to catch up to the other car. Next to a stop sign was a huge oak tree, immovable, even to a speeding metal machine weighing several thousand pounds—not including the two fragile humans inside the passenger cabin without airbags.

I'm too young to die, I thought. The tree, illuminated by the car's headlights, seemed to be rushing toward us head-on, a hungry monster ready to devour its prey.

Then I uttered a desperate prayer.

Please . . .

At once, the car veered left. It seemed like an angel swooshed in and pushed the car's front bumper away from the massive tree.

We hit with the sound of thunder. A hailstorm of glass rained into the car. The passenger door was ripped from its hinges. The smell of leaking oil filled the night air. The engine was dead. Everything was still, instantly—except for my thumping heart.

Everything was still, instantly—except for my thumping heart.

"Are you okay, Bruce?" I asked with a shaky voice.

"Yeah, you?" He was in tears, frozen in shock.

I suddenly realized I was indeed okay, not a single major abrasion or bruise.

A miracle.

Bruce had only a small bruise on his thigh where his leg rammed the steering column. We could have easily died.

When I eventually got home that evening, the event replayed continually in my mind. And I realized God can hear our simplest, earnest prayer—anytime, anyplace. Even if it's one whispered plea.

God in the Classifieds

– MARY KAY MOODY –

You really should consider it," Bill said as I served him a Reuben and french-dip sandwich.

"I know. Good money, flexible hours." I filled his coffee cup.

"Office across the street." He chuckled. "Really short commute."

During at least three lunches a week, Bill, owner of a real estate company, tried convincing me to switch careers.

My manager approached, whispering, "Deuce at table seven," to let me know I had new customers waiting.

I nodded. "I'm thinking about it, Bill."

"Free training," he called as I walked away.

At two thirty, I clocked out and hopped into my banana-colored Nova. I'd bought it used because it was reliable and simply designed so I could do my own tune-ups, which was a comforting thought as I stopped for groceries.

Fifteen minutes later, I parked at our small trailer with the postage-stamp-size yard. Not much room for an active seven-year-old. My son,

Karl, and I had painted the tire we used as a planter, trying to spruce things up, and planted a tiny garden. Though I was still paying for the trailer, I wished I could afford a real house *with a yard.*

Life had been an adventure since we moved from Virginia. Karl and I had explored the Outer Banks and rode a Mississippi River paddleboat on our cross-country camping trip. Now we were plunked in a working-class suburb of Chicago, near my parents.

I grabbed my grocery sack and greeted Karl, his mop of light-brown hair blowing about as he walked from the school bus.

After dinner, homework, and playing checkers, I hugged him before he climbed the ladder to his loft bed, which we constructed from plywood and four-by-four posts. It was the only way to get play space in his seven-by-nine-foot bedroom. The floor became his raceway, circus, or open range for toy horses.

"Mom?" He leaned on one elbow and peered over the side rail, frowning.

"What's the matter?"

"I'm mad."

"About what?"

"We'll never get our farm. You spend all our money on food!"

Ouch! He so often heard, "Sorry, buddy, we can't afford that toy." And though chili and peanut butter weren't gourmet, I was doing my best.

"I know, honey. Right now, that's all the money we have." I shrugged. "I'm trying to earn more so we can buy a farm someday."

"While we wait, can I get a dog?"

Double ouch! "Sorry, not yet."

His lower lip shot out. "I know. We can't afford it."

"And allergies. On the farm, a dog can live in the barn, and it won't bother my allergies." I mussed his hair. "Thanks for being patient."

He sighed and then smiled feebly. "It's not easy."

"I know." I kissed my fingertip and planted it on his cheek. "Good night, honey. I love you."

"Love you too."

Over tea, I pondered Bill's job offer and assurances that commission far surpassed tips, an important consideration for a single mom. Still, tips came in daily. How could I go weeks with no income?

I decided to do both and enrolled in the real estate licensing class. A red-letter day came on June 21: I accepted Christ as my Savior in the morning and passed the state exam that night, though notification didn't come until mid-August.

Late summer, a visiting preacher at church spoke on Habakkuk 2:15. Strong fist pumps accompanied his booming voice, "Woe to him who gives drink to his neighbors" (NIV).

My waitress job came with directions to push alcohol. During afternoon hours, waitresses ran the bar in addition to waiting tables. That Sunday, I heard the "woe" and prayed.

Leave that place, God told me.

So I quit on Monday—going from steady-income-waitress to commission-only real estate agent.

But the real estate market had ground to a virtual halt. Mortgage rates soared to 15 percent. Despite the more experienced agents in the office offering good information, contacts, and a rationale on why people should still buy homes, I called people, answered phones, showed wide-eyed young couples homes, and sold . . . nothing.

Rates eventually skyrocketed beyond 20 percent. I was able to list a house, but until it sold, I would earn nothing.

So I added working at a deli back into my schedule. Then I tried one restaurant after another in the surrounding suburbs, but my earnings were never enough. I had other skills, but two things restricted my job search: waitressing put money in my hand daily, and I wanted to be home with Karl after school.

Repeatedly, I begged God for a job that didn't require me to drive congested freeways to downtown Chicago.

By the time winter blew in, I had to juggle funds between food, gasoline, and heating fuel. One January night after putting Karl to bed, as I sipped orange-spice tea, I pondered the ways God had provided for us: friends invited us for dinner, one bought fifty dollars of heating oil, and the township office gave a fifty-dollar credit for groceries, which allowed us to eat *and* bake cookies for Christmas gifts.

God took care of us in many remarkable ways, but as winter moved into spring, houses were rarely selling, and my tips still didn't cover expenses.

I pleaded with God to show me what to do. Gradually, He nudged me to check the Chicago classifieds and hinted I might have to return to suits and long commutes on crowded buses to provide for my son. A friend from church offered to have Karl stay with her family after school.

So I bought a Chicago newspaper and checked the classifieds.

One ad appealed to me. The Theraplay Institute sought people who liked working with young children. *That's me.* Preschool education had been my college major.

Training provided. *Yes!* I gulped as I read the location: Michigan Avenue. The Chicago Loop. I sighed and then scheduled an interview. After it concluded, I had to return for five days of unpaid training, at the end of which the institute would hire five people.

Each step of my search had been bathed in prayer. Buy the paper. Call. Take an afternoon off for the interview. Spend precious dollars on gas and parking. But this last bit—a week off work without pay *or* a guarantee—appeared to slam the door.

> I begged God to make things clear: I wanted skywriting!

But I felt the urge, against all common sense, to continue. I begged God to make things clear: I wanted skywriting! None appeared. But He nudged me to go on.

So with faith a smidgen greater than my uncertainty, I continued. The training ended Friday afternoon. We were to receive phone calls the following week. More waiting. More uncertainty.

I dragged through the Sunday shift at the restaurant, hoping I hadn't made a huge mistake and that the day's tips would be enough to pay the rest of my rent.

Late Monday morning, the phone rang.

"Mary, it's Ernestine."

I gulped. The large lady with the electric smile had livened our training sessions. But I wondered why the doctor who interviewed me wasn't calling. Maybe she called only those hired.

"Grab a pen. I've got the address of a school I want you to meet me at Wednesday morning."

I snatched a pencil. *More unpaid training?*

She gave me the address and told me to meet her in the principal's office.

Ugh. Way north. It'll take me an hour if *I can miss rush hour.* But that was a future worry. My more immediate thought, *Should I even take another day off work?* This was one costly job interview. "Ernestine, it sounds very interesting. But is this another part of the interview?"

Her lilting laughter bubbled. "No. You're hired. This is prep for going solo."

My jaw dropped, then I stammered.

She giggled. "Does that mean you'll take the job?"

"Oh, yeah."

The next weeks were filled with hours of driving to schools all over Chicago, celebrating successes with timid or acting-out little ones, and enjoying coaching discussions with Ernestine over lunch. A memorable one took place in mid-July.

Munching burgers and fries, Ernestine and I discussed my caseload and then chatted about our families. I told the story of my desperate job search. How a week of training without pay was a gigantic step of faith, that I had long refused to consider a job in downtown Chicago, and how glad I was the institute was still hiring by the time I abandoned my resistance and checked out a Chicago newspaper.

Ernestine said, "I prayed you would stick it out."

"You did?"

She grinned in her delightful, impish way. "Of course. I knew you would be good at this."

I shook my head. "Thank you. I appreciate your confidence—and your prayers."

"Now I see why God urged me to pray for you. During training, I could tell you were burdened, but until now I didn't know how badly you needed the job."

"God's timing is amazing. That last week before training started is the only time I checked Chicago papers. This job is a delightful answer to prayer."

"Oh, Mary, a bigger answer than you realize."

I stopped mid-sip of my cola. "How so?"

"You didn't nearly miss *weeks* of advertising for the job. We ran the ad only once."

"Only one week? That's incredible."

She leaned forward and appeared to have popped diamonds into her eyes as her grin grew. "Not one week, Mary. One day." She giggled. "God really wanted you to have this job."

Later, as I drove home, tears pricked my eyes as I grasped the depth of love God had shown me. I realized that He was totally reliable—and I was no longer a *single* parent.

Trust and Obey—Fearlessly!

– J. WESLEY EBY –

You can't mean it, God. You really don't expect me to do that!

As I prayed, my reaction to the impression I'd just received was immediate and strong. But as I sought the Lord in earnest, the thought would not leave.

I had moved our family of four to the Navajo Nation in northeast Arizona three weeks before. I had accepted an opportunity to work for the Bureau of Indian Affairs as a civil-service teacher and left my education job in Alabama. My first assignment was at Lukachukai, a small, isolated community 150 miles from the nearest off-reservation city. Frequent trips to a supermarket or the corner drugstore were impossible.

When we left the Deep South for the Southwest, we decided to put our three-bedroom house on the market. Paying the mortgage and maintaining a house that was two thousand miles away seemed impractical. We asked a real estate agent to handle the property when the house did not sell before we moved.

After a few weeks and no buyer, I became concerned—so concerned that I began to pray *and fast.* I entered my prayer closet each day during my lunch hour.

After several days of intercession, the troubling thought filled my mind that shook me to the core: *Write to the real estate agent, and tell him you believe the house has sold.*

I cringed. I sweated.

This cannot be from the Lord, I reasoned. *God, You don't mean it, do You? How can You expect me to write such a letter? How silly I'll look!*

But the thought would not go away. Daily, the disturbing idea returned. Instead of looking forward to my quiet times with God, I wanted to avoid the confrontation and was uncomfortable.

I knew the real estate agent was a Christian and a devoted churchman and scripture reader for his congregation. Yet, this did not relieve the turmoil that stormed within my heart.

God, how will the agent react to such a letter? I debated. *It doesn't make any sense.*

My heavenly Father patiently dealt with my doubt. *My child, won't you trust Me?*

Trust? Such an illogical command, I countered. *How can you be so . . . ?* The word I wanted to say remained in my mind, unuttered. But He knew.

Another week went by, then two. I became more and more discouraged. I drove to Kennedy's Trading Post, which also served as the local post office for thrice-weekly mail deliveries. Each time, I anxiously looked for the all-important letter informing me that someone had purchased our Alabama home. Each time, I went away disappointed.

My encounters with God became shorter and shorter. I began to sense a spirit of rebellion welling up within me.

But, God, what am I to do? I questioned. *You've backed me in a corner.*

Trust Me, Wes, the Lord whispered. *Just trust Me.*

Trust. There it was again. The word planted itself in my soul, daring me to evict it. As I pondered its meaning, the lyrics to a familiar gospel song "Trust and Obey" came to mind.

Obey. The word plopped down beside *trust* and refused to leave. *Trust and obey.* The phrase played over and over, like a phonograph needle stuck in a scarred groove on an old record.

But still I balked. *Why are You doing this to me, God? Why are You teasing me?*

Yet deep in my heart, I somehow knew I was in a no-win battle with the sovereign God.

In the meantime, our financial situation did not improve.... We needed a miracle.

In the meantime, our financial situation did not improve. We were paying rent on our government housing while also paying the mortgage on our unsold home. We could not continue to support both properties for long. We needed a miracle.

So back to prayer and fasting. What God wanted me to do did not go away; it only intensified. *Trust and obey*. The simple expression lingered, probed, and tormented.

Days turned into weeks. The struggle within raged, and I was becoming desperate.

Just trust Me, Wes, the Spirit nudged. *All you have to do is obey.*

One day during my noontime devotions, I finally acknowledged that my pride and stubbornness were blocking the answer to my petition. I confessed my sin and asked for forgiveness. And though I did not understand the why of His baffling directive, I promised the Lord that I would accept His plan.

I wrote the letter and sent it via the US Postal Service. I was still uneasy, but the conflict was over, or so I thought.

As the waiting began, the devil began to play with my mind and heart. *You haven't heard about your house yet, have you? What's the real estate agent going to think? That you're one of those fanatical Christians, one of those radical types? How could you have believed this idea came from God? You're not very smart, are you?*

Each time I drove to the trading post, the hoped-for mail was missing. The enemy's taunting dogged me; his questions hounded me day and night. *When are you going to give up, Wes? Haven't you learned your lesson yet?*

Then the Holy Spirit reminded me, *Remember, you obeyed. Now, trust.*

Two weeks later, the "it-couldn't-get-here-soon-enough" letter arrived. I ripped open the envelope and pulled out the letter. As I began to read, tears clouded my vision, making it hard to see the words: "I received your letter today, and it surprised me, to say the least. I was planning to write you and inform you that your house has just sold. God *does* work in strange ways sometimes, doesn't He? . . . By the way, did you have window screens. If so, where did you store them? Please let me know as soon as you can."

I rejoiced. I praised the Lord. What a lesson I had learned! Even though God's ways are perplexing at times, my obedience is all He requires.

I now have a new understanding of and appreciation for the old song, "Trust and Obey." And I sing it with gusto.

A Still, Small Voice

– ANNA M. GREGORY –

My oldest son came home from the US Navy for a few days. We loved having him home before his transfer to Iceland for a year or so.

He and his brothers enjoyed driving around, checking out what others were doing. Of course, they had to go camping before he left. Yet it seemed the time he was home was short. Soon he was getting in his rented car to head back to his base in Virginia.

I watched as he drove away. It seemed just a while ago he was a young boy, playing and laughing and bugging his four brothers.

I knew it was a long drive to Virginia, so I said a quick prayer for his safety. Other drivers were not always careful, and I knew my son could become distracted changing the channel on the radio or checking some other thing in the car.

Late that afternoon, I was cleaning house when I felt a compulsion to pray. Not only was I supposed to pray, but I heard this clear but small voice in my mind. *Pray for your son.*

The feeling was so urgent that I knelt to pray immediately for about ten minutes. I wasn't sure exactly how to direct my prayers, so I simply asked for my child's safety.

The feeling was so urgent that I knelt to pray immediately.

After a while, I felt God's hand lift from my heart, and I stood. I wondered if I had listened carefully enough. Ten minutes later, my phone rang.

My son spoke quietly, "Mom, I wrecked the car. I was trying to change the channel on the radio and looked up. I thought I had the green light and started through the intersection. But the light turned red, and I didn't see the truck come flying through the intersection. It totaled my little rental car."

"Are you hurt? Is anyone else hurt?"

I could almost hear him shake his head.

"No, no one was hurt," he replied. "But, Mom, that car is folded up and dented, completely destroyed. But I have only a couple of scratches on my arm. I can't believe it. I should have been killed, but I wasn't. It's like God was watching over me right then."

I laughed. "My dear son, God was watching over you. God told me to pray, so I did. I thank God for keeping you safe."

I danced around the kitchen after he hung up. I thanked God over and over again for protecting my child.

Another day, I was feeling pretty bad. My allergies were overwhelming me, so I lay on the bed to take a short nap.

A voice whispered in my mind, *Your children are on the lake.*

I knew that. Two of my sons, the oldest one and next to the youngest one, their wives, and their children had taken my younger son's boat to a lake farther from home.

I was still groggy, but the voice whispered again. *Your children are on the lake.*

I sat up and stared. I knew it was God's voice, and I wondered what He was trying to tell me. I dropped to my knees and asked God to care for everyone who was in that boat, to keep them safe and secure. Again, I sensed God's hand lift from my heart, leaving a great sense of peace. He was assuring me things were fine.

Later, my younger son stopped by. I asked him how his day had been and watched as he shook his head.

"That bonehead brother of mine. You won't believe what he did. We were getting close to shore, and I didn't notice he had taken off his life jacket. The engine on the boat stalled and quit. Close to shore, there was a tree hanging over the water. He reached for it to pull us closer in. I shouted, Mom. I told him not to do that, but it was too late. He fell over the edge of the boat into the water. Mom, that lake has an awful undertow. I looked over the edge and couldn't see him. I tried to start the engine, but it wouldn't start. I saw him pop up about a quarter of a mile away. The boat still wouldn't start. We threw him everything we could think of that he might grab on to, but everything sailed the wrong way."

My son took a deep breath before continuing.

"Mom, I finally dived into the water with a buoy and swam underwater toward him. I knew he was panicked. As I came close, I shoved the buoy to him hoping he would grab hold. After a few tries, he grabbed hold, and I towed him to a tree stump that stuck out of the water. I then swam back to the boat, climbed back in, and prayed the thing would start."

He laughed.

"It finally did so we drove to the stump, picked up my brother, and everything we threw out."

My son sat silent for a moment. He told me his wife had shielded the children so none of them would see my other son drown.

"That would have been awful, but I felt like someone was out there with us, watching over us. Do you think that was possible? I mean, my brother would have drowned if I hadn't been able to do the things I did to rescue him. Mom, I am not that good a swimmer to do what I did."

I looked at him and smiled. "Now," I said, "let me tell you about my day."

From Panic to Prayer

– VERONICA L. ASAY –

Please, God, please!

I've lost count of the number of times I whimpered that litany while in bed as I pulled the covers over my head, curled my legs to my torso, and wrapped my arms around my knees. Erratic thoughts ricocheted through my anxious mind. The room spun, my heart palpitated, and my body broke into a cold sweat. Tears stung my eyes.

I'm dying! This is it. I'm really dying!

The thoughts thrust me into a full-blown anxiety attack. I couldn't stop it and would be at its mercy until it subsided naturally.

Ten or fifteen minutes later, my mind wandered enough for my body to unwind. The tension began to leave, though my limbs were now heavy with fatigue and I was still on edge. I pushed down the covers. It was time to start a new day.

This was part of my routine, day in and day out, for more than a decade. The panic struck at various points in my day, but the panic attacks in my own bed were possibly the worst. I should have felt safe, but I seemed to be at my most vulnerable when I was there.

What began as nervousness at fifteen morphed into chronic anxiety and depression, which led to severe agoraphobia. At one point in my early twenties, I was diagnosed with generalized anxiety disorder. Most of my youth was eaten by one illogical fear or another.

I made the best of a dark situation, reminding myself that no matter how bad things seemed or how miserable I was, God had a plan. Whenever I felt like He had forgotten about me, God would whisper in my ear, *Never will I leave thee; never will I forsake thee.*

Each morning, I dragged myself out of bed, dressed in comfortable clothes, and muddled through the day. I lived with my parents and sister, who must have been at a loss as to what to do with me. My parents were edging toward retirement while I was having difficulties moving past the threshold of the front door. They more or less accepted me as I was, never questioning my quirks or pressuring me to do more.

By my midtwenties, my depression lifted and things started to improve. Life wasn't so dark anymore.

Then, suddenly, my dad died. Once more, I was thrust into a tailspin of anxiety and depression, the worst I had ever experienced. There seemed to be no end in sight.

One morning, months after Dad's death, I was lying on the couch, in too much pain to move a muscle, when I realized I couldn't go on like this.

This isn't fair. Not to my mom, not to my sister, not to Dad's memory, and not even to myself. Dad wouldn't want to see me like this.

I deserved better than this.

Dear Lord, give me strength, I whispered as I rolled off the couch.

I put on my coat and hooked the leash to my dog, Grace. I took a deep breath and left the house. In my anxiety, I moved slowly, shuffling my feet like an old woman rather than strolling like a girl in her midtwenties.

After our walk, I led Grace to the backyard, and we stood there for a few minutes. The sun was beginning to rise, golden hues stretching across the sky. Once more, I heard God murmur in my ear: *It will be all right. There is hope. I have a plan for you.*

> The dark cloud that hung over me for so long began to recede.

After living in a self-constructed prison for ten years, the idea that I would be all right seemed crazy. I had long accepted the fact that I would never have the life or experiences normal people had. Yet, the dark cloud that hung over me for so long began to recede. My depression lifted.

The ten-year prayer I had been praying—that my anxiety and depression would let up—was slowly being answered. I began to work part time. I formed new friendships. I actually developed hobbies outside the home. No matter what I did—how big or how small—God's hand was in it all.

Then the opportunity of a lifetime presented itself for me to travel to Poland to tour Auschwitz-Birkenau and the old city of Kraków. During the nights leading up to the trip, I would lie in bed and ask God, *Can I really do this?*

What if I back out? What if I freeze up? What if I have a meltdown on the plane or in Kraków or in Auschwitz?

I would practice my breathing exercises and ask the Lord to give me peace.

My grace is sufficient for thee, He'd respond.

Instead of panicking, I basked in His presence.

On the day of my departure, though I was nervous to leave the States for the first time, God whispered in my ear that everything would be all right. Taking it one step at a time, I was able to travel via bus and two different planes without a hiccup. No anxiety attacks and no meltdowns, only excitement for the adventure of my dreams.

When I reached my room in the Radisson Blu Hotel in Kraków, I marveled at the miracle God had performed. I—who at one time couldn't leave the house or walk around the block—was on my own, on the other side of the world. My week in Poland was extraordinary as I toured the streets of Kraków, sampled cuisine, shopped in the main market square, explored the infamous death camp of Auschwitz-Birkenau, and visited Oskar Schindler's factory.

On the final day of my trip, I shopped for souvenirs for my loved ones and went on a horse-drawn carriage ride through the city.

My departure from Poland was bittersweet. I had experienced the adventure of my dreams, and I was at peace. Those special memories will live in my heart forever.

I have since asked God why it took so long for Him to answer my prayer—a prayer that began when I was fifteen and wasn't answered until my late twenties. Only now do I realize that God was working in my life all along. The years of suffering made my triumph much sweeter, and my adventure and my life far more enjoyable.

God always answers our prayers. The answer may not come today or tomorrow—it may take ten years or more. But He is always listening, and His response is always worth the wait.

Prayers of Desperation

– ILEA BOUSE –

"Broken neck?"

My heart sank as I heard my husband talk to the person on the phone.

I lifted my one-year-old daughter from the floor where she played with her toys. I cradled her in my arms as I watched my husband pace the room.

"Yes, yes, okay, okay," he repeated over and over, the phone pressed against his head.

My heart pounded harder in my chest. Whose neck had broken?

My mind raced to all the people I know and love: father-in-law, mother-in-law, mother, sisters, brothers, friends.

When each face flashed through my mind, I quickly prayed, *No, Lord, not him. Not her.*

My husband hung up the phone, looking at it with his back toward me for endless moments. I wanted to give him some time to compose himself, but my heart demanded answers.

"Who? Who broke their neck?"

He turned with pain etched into his face. "Dad."

Then he sat and leaned against the table with both hands on his head.

My eyes filled with tears, and my knees shook as I sat next to him. My daughter grabbed a spoon from the table and began pounding it gently. Between beats, she put it in her mouth, creating a rhythm of pounding and tasting.

Normally, I would correct this behavior, but the gentle taps grounded me to the present, tempering the current storm.

"Is he alive?" I whispered, losing my breath as the words tumbled out.

"Yes, but in critical condition. He's being rushed to Portland," he answered as he relaxed his hands and looked at me. He gently pulled our daughter from my lap and kissed her head. He held her tightly against his chest as he looked vacantly into the room.

Frozen, I waited. I wanted the details, the plan, and the reassurance of "it will be all right." But all I got was silence.

"I need to go," he finally said.

"We'll all go," I said as I lifted our daughter from his lap. I grabbed the diaper bag and began stuffing it with clothes, diapers, and everything needed for a week. I then stuffed an overnight bag for myself.

Outside, a fresh coating of February snow remained on the ground. Portland was more than an hour away, and the trip would be treacherous. It probably would be better if I stayed home with the baby, but I wanted to be there for my husband. I wanted to be there for the family. I wanted to be there for me.

"I'll go get Mom," he said.

"How did it happen?" I finally asked. Mom was usually with Dad.

"He was in a car accident with a friend. The friend's okay, but Dad broke his neck," my husband said woodenly. Then he grabbed an overnight bag for himself before we left to pick up his mom.

While he drove, I prayed. It was late, so the pastor and church secretary wouldn't be at the church, and it was also too late for me to call anyone else.

We arrived at the hospital near midnight. We were told to wait in an intensive care unit lobby or to return in the morning. We chose to stay. My daughter slept peacefully in her car seat, tucked gently in her snowsuit and favorite blankie.

Sometime during the night, the doctors said Dad was not breathing on his own. He needed a surgery that would take several hours and include risks such as paralysis and death.

We waited. Morning brought more anxiety. Dad was still in surgery. I needed a release from the tension. I wanted Jesus to show up and make everything right.

Lord, please heal him, I prayed. *And, Lord, please send Pastor John.*

I realized my prayer for our pastor to come was unrealistic, but I longed for someone to insert some peace and faith into the pain and uncertainty of the situation. Unfortunately, I had no way to get a message to Pastor John.

I rubbed my eyes in disbelief.

I had barely uttered my unrealistic prayer when Pastor John walked through the door. I rubbed my eyes in disbelief. Was the waiting room vigil playing tricks on my mind and eyes?

He came over to the family, and everyone embraced him. He prayed with my mother-in-law and her sisters as I watched in awe.

"How did you know we were here?" I asked.

"I was driving on the highway and felt the need to pull over at a rest stop," he said. "While I was there, I ran into your husband's uncle. He told me about the accident and that your father-in-law was brought to Portland, but he didn't know where. I guessed it might be this hospital. I felt prompted to turn around and come. It's a miracle, really, that I found you here."

Tears poured down my face.

"God answered my prayer for you to come," I blurted out. "Thank you."

After the surgery and several months of rehab, Dad survived his neck injury without any signs of paralysis. God answered that prayer too.

My heart lifts even now as I reflect: God answers even unrealistic, desperate prayers.

How God Answers Desperate Prayers

– BOB HOSTETLER –

Preacher and author Leonard Ravenhill said, "God does not answer prayer. God answers desperate prayer."

Many years ago, I had grown extremely unhappy with my prayer life. I had repeatedly resolved to rise early enough in the morning to pray, only to turn off the alarm and go back to bed—day after day. I was desperate to change. So I asked a friend who lived just down the street (and apparently had no trouble rising early) to be a prayer partner.

I asked him to arrive at my house early in the morning (he had small children in his home so we always met at mine) and walk in the front door without knocking. I told him I would have the front door unlocked, the coffee on, and would be waiting in the living room. There we would pray together. I also asked him never to tell me when he couldn't make it; that way, when he didn't show, I would go ahead and pray alone since I was up and at it anyway. Marlin's faithfulness fueled my faithfulness. Or forced it. But it worked. I became regular in prayer, and though he has long since moved away, I think of him every time I pass where he used to live.

When my son was a teenager, my wife and I were terribly concerned for him. He was struggling in so many ways, and all of our efforts to help him had been ineffective. I was so desperate for him—for his mind, his soul, his life—that I decided to go somewhere and spend three days doing little besides praying for him.

I found a retreat center not far from home where I could be alone, walk, and pray. It was my first prayer retreat, and it was so helpful that I've scheduled an annual (sometimes twice a year) silent prayer retreat for more than twenty years since then. I can't say that my prayers on that retreat were answered immediately, or even quickly, but they were answered. Abundantly, in fact.

Soon after my daughter had given birth to her firstborn, a beautiful girl, we knew that something was wrong. Calleigh was a month old when she was diagnosed with cystic fibrosis, a life-threatening condition we knew nothing about at the time.

We all prayed desperately and constantly for her healing (and later, for Calleigh's brother, Ryder, who was also born with the disease). But today the two of them, now nine and seven, still cope daily with their condition, and we still pray daily and desperately for healing.

And while a miraculous healing hasn't yet appeared, we do believe that God is using many means (including our grandkids' amazing parents) to make and keep them healthy. We still pray desperately, though, in the fervent hope that God will answer our prayers for them as vividly and richly as He has answered many other prayers.

Sometimes I have been desperate *to* pray. Other times I have been desperate *in* prayer. Always, however, desperation has been the soil and seed that bears the fruit of answered prayer—for me, at least. Maybe it will do the same for you.

8

Unexpected Answers

Beware in your prayers, above everything else, of limiting God, not only by unbelief, but by fancying that you know what He can do. Expect unexpected things "above all that we ask or think."

Andrew Murray

Surprise!

Who among us doesn't like to get some special little treat? And those of us who are parents, even those with fur babies, know the look of joy when we give our children something they longed for but didn't expect or something that we knew was perfect for them! That is the joy and the grace of a loving parent!

And that is the joy, the grace, and the desire of our loving God. Scripture is full of the promises of God's good intentions toward us. He loves to share His wisdom and knowledge with us.

Solomon was a man who understood what it meant to have God's grace lavished on him. As the son of the great king David, he followed in his father's footsteps when he became ruler. Solomon loved the Lord, and God was so pleased that in a vision God offered to fulfill anything Solomon asked for.

Did Solomon ask for riches or more kingdoms? No, instead he said, "Give me an understanding heart so that I can govern your people well and know the difference between right and wrong" (1 Kings 3:9, NLT).

This pleased God even more. He not only gave Solomon a wise and understanding heart, He also gave Solomon riches and fame. God gave above and beyond what Solomon asked for or expected.

Sometimes we pray for one thing and receive another, but we can be sure that God, who knows the universe and knew us before we were born, will always give us the right thing.

When we ask, God answers. Sometimes His answers are unexpected. Sometimes we may even think that God did not understand us. But that's where faith comes in. We can trust a loving Father to answer our prayers in the right way . . . the way that's best for us. As Jesus said in Luke 11:11–13, "You fathers—if your children ask for a fish, do you give them a snake instead? If they ask for an egg, do you give them a scorpion? Of course not! So if you sinful people know how to give good gifts to your children, how much more will your heavenly Father give the Holy Spirit to those who ask him?" (NLT).

That's what the authors in the next pages found: their heavenly Father knows best. Because God has such a great love for us, we can trust Him to answer our prayers in the perfect way. Then we can cry out with the apostle Paul, "Now all glory to God, who is able, through his mighty power at work within us, to accomplish infinitely more than we might ask or think" (Ephesians 3:20, NLT).

A God-Sized Surprise

– ANITA ESTES –

"I'm sorry, but we cannot offer you the position you interviewed for. We decided to hire someone else. Thank you for your interest." *Click.*

I was stunned. They told me I had the teaching job, and I had already met some of the students and the teachers. I felt like such a failure. Later, I discovered they had to hire back the person they fired, but that didn't help matters when I still wasn't working in December.

I turned to taking care of my family of three children, two cats, and a husband, while I continued to fill out applications and pray. *Dear God, I've been asking, seeking, and knocking for almost two years. Don't You have anything for me, or do I need to forget about ever teaching again?*

January rolled around, bleak and dismal. One day when I walked into the house from grocery shopping, my daughter, Mara, excitedly told me someone had called and had left a message. As I listened to the answering machine, I couldn't place the rich, deep voice of the man named Theodore nor the school he referenced, Circle of Courage.

I had never applied there, so I was perplexed. I listened again and discovered it was in a nearby city, Poughkeepsie, where I had no connections.

But maybe God was at work. I called the number, and Theodore explained, "We found your application online."

"What kind of school are you?"

"We're a public, special education school," he explained.

"What kind of employment is available?" I had recently taught special education since my master's degree was in that area. My undergraduate degree was in art, but I hadn't taught the subject in fifteen years.

"We are looking for an art teacher, and we'd like you to come in for an interview."

> It would be a long shot for me to get this job.

What a surprise! Art teaching jobs were hard to find, and a number of local colleges churned out young art education majors. It would be a long shot for me to get this job and an answer to my prayers.

At first, I felt a little nervous as I sat before the four men interviewing me, but then I warmed up and easily answered their questions about educating students with special needs and emotional problems.

They smiled when I described my vision, "I believe art can open up a new world to these students to explore creativity, express their emotions, learn positive ways to channel their energy, and do something constructive of their own."

When asked about classroom behavior issues, I responded that I would consult with administration first before implementing a behavior plan that involved positive reinforcement for good behavior.

Then we began to chat about different ideas and what the Circle of Courage philosophy entailed. The lead interviewer said he sometimes had the students write positive affirmations and words of wisdom from the Bible, such as "Love your enemies, do good to those who hate you, bless those who curse you, pray for those who mistreat you" (Luke 6:27–28, NIV). I was impressed to hear him quoting Scripture.

Then the head of the committee asked me to step outside, just when I thought everything was humming along nicely. *Did I say something wrong? Dear God, please let them know if I'm the right candidate for the job.*

After about five minutes, the committee head called me back and told me, "We've had almost two hundred applicants for this position, but it appears you are a good match for the school. You fit our vision and might even become a lead teacher."

I was so surprised. I felt honored to be chosen from so many applicants and tried not to sound overenthusiastic when I said yes to the job.

I left the interview walking on cloud nine. I couldn't believe I got an art teaching job in a special needs school. I don't remember the car ride home because I was so excited. I rushed into the house to tell my husband the good news.

"It's a special needs school for both young children and teens who are in need of supervision. It will be tough, but I feel good about it. I'll get to use my special education training. I know the job is from God."

My husband gave me a quizzical look. "How so?"

"I never directly applied, but they saw my application online. I didn't realize it would be available for other schools to see. God sure has a sense of humor, getting me a job I didn't even know about. His timing is perfect!"

That night in bed, I thought more about the situation. The winter before, I had been disappointed because I had prayed to go on a mission trip to Africa with our church, but the timing and money didn't work out. Then I sponsored children from Ethiopia, Brazil, and India in order to make an international difference. And now, with this new position, God was bringing the children of the world to me.

While I was at Circle of Courage, I taught art to elementary students who began life in homes spread from Mexico to the Middle East, from the island of Jamaica to Haiti, from countries in Africa to South America. I worked with all types of schoolchildren—refugees and native born, students with English as a second language, and students proficient in English.

And every day I prayed, *Dear Lord, help me to love the children and have patience with them, and give me wisdom to deal with the difficult students and make a difference.*

At times, I encountered some very challenging students. I tried to show them God's love and how to respect one another, enjoy learning, and be creative to the measure God gave them.

As the years progressed and my energy levels dipped, God surprised me again. When I had to work two years longer than anticipated, I asked God to renew my strength so I could run and not grow tired, walk and not faint. And God faithfully gave me what I needed.

God had provided just the right job at the right time, and He sustained me in it until it was time for me to go. Isn't He surprising!

Expanding Our Horizon

– BARBARA HOLLACE –

For twenty-three years, my husband and I navigated life without owning a car, but life had changed. My business was moving at a snail's pace. Why? I had to turn down opportunities because I lacked readily available transportation. Public transportation is great but has its limitations. And you can tap your friends for a ride only so often.

You can tap your friends for a ride only so often.

The solution to our problem remained elusive because we didn't have the money to buy a car. Unlike Cinderella, we did not have a fairy godmother who could turn a pumpkin into a carriage or, in our case, a car.

We ran to the Lord in prayer, knowing that nothing was too hard for Him, and He was our Provider. Meanwhile, we would wait, pray, and praise the Lord for what we had. Our heavenly Father always seemed to stretch our resources to cover our needs.

In January 2016, I was working with a business coach who was trying to help me move my business from just surviving to thriving!

"You need a car!" she repeatedly told me.

Honestly, I wasn't convinced. After years of making life work without a vehicle, you adjust your expectations and accept your limitations. My husband and I had no complaints. We had learned the lesson of Philippians 4:11–12, "I have learned to be content whatever the circumstances. I know what it is to be in need, and I know what it is to have plenty. I have learned the secret of being content in any and every situation, whether well fed or hungry, whether living in plenty or in want" (NIV).

Each month besides discussing strategy, my coach and I prayed for our specific needs—business and personal. In January we started praying for a car, and each month she asked for a progress report.

Initially, I was going along with the prayer request for a car halfheartedly. But the Bible says all we need is a mustard-seed amount of faith. I probably had that much faith.

It wasn't that I thought God was too small, but a car didn't seem to be a necessity, and it seemed to me that God had far greater things to tend to in the world. Even when I was growing up, public transportation or my own two feet were all I needed.

I had not shared my prayer request with others. I think I was embarrassed to ask for prayer for such a thing. I was still struggling with the magnitude of such a request.

However, one March Sunday after church, I saw a new car in the parking lot. "I need one of those. I need a car!" I exclaimed.

Finally, my heart and head understood the need to be more sincere in my request.

A couple of weeks into April, a fairly new friend I'd quickly grown close to asked me to go to breakfast with her. But the specific time and location she suggested did not work with the bus schedule and the distance from the bus stop to the restaurant. Instead, she offered to pick me up.

Over breakfast, we shared some laughs and talked about what God was doing in our lives. Then the conversation took a different turn. My friend asked if we had a car. I thought it was a silly question because she had picked me up, but I replied, "No, we do not."

My friend said God had been speaking to her about buying a second car. It didn't make sense to her because her car worked fine. She had no need for a second car. But even so, she had found a great deal on a used car and had purchased it.

And then came the really big shock: "I want to give you the car to use indefinitely."

Tears rolled down my cheeks.

There was only one thing to say, "Yes! Thank you so much."

My mind grew foggy. How would I explain to my husband that I went to breakfast with a friend and returned with a car? I could barely grasp the idea myself.

My friend explained the logistics of picking up the car and some paperwork that needed to be done.

"And I will also cover the insurance on the car."

What? Not only the car, but insurance too!

Since we hadn't been insured for twenty-three years, it would have taken some maneuvering to get car insurance at a decent price. Thankfully, I had a good driving record—and my driver's license was current.

What started as a halfhearted prayer on my part had come to fruition. It wasn't because of my bushel full of faith but because of God and those He tapped on the shoulder to be a part of this miracle. These two women in my life—my business coach and my friend—both stepped out in faith and obeyed, and my husband and I received this love gift from God.

My business coach was correct. The vehicle opened up more business opportunities. My husband and I were also able to drive to see family. God had opened up a door into our future, expanding our horizons. And just two years later, this gift from God met a critical need during my husband's health crisis. Getting him to doctors would have been far more difficult if we'd had to rely on public transportation or family and friends.

Through our car miracle, I learned that nothing is impossible with God. God made a way because He saw our need—not just in 2016, but also on the horizon.

Prayers of faith open doors, even when those prayers are prayed by our friends. That miracle opened up my eyes and my heart to the wonder-working power of our heavenly Father.

Two Prayers and One Answer

– MELISSA HENDERSON –

A visit to the local animal shelter was a gift from my daddy. I was eleven years old and excited about the possibility of owning a dog. Mama wasn't sure about our family having a new pet given the history.

The cottontail rabbit I had received as an Easter present decided to live under the neighbor's home. After crawling many times under there to fetch the wayward pet, Daddy gave the rabbit to his coworker. Goldfish in bowls never lived long enough for me to enjoy their company. I wasn't sure if I fed the fish too much or not enough. A black-and-white newborn kitten my babysitter had given to me constantly scratched my arms and legs. I could not understand why the kitten didn't want me to dress it in baby-doll clothes and push it in my toy stroller.

As we stepped inside the local shelter, Daddy and I heard howling dogs. I had never seen so many dogs. Big ones, little ones, loud ones, quiet ones. Puppies and older dogs. Black, white, brown, spotted, and of all varieties.

A volunteer led us down the hallways as we peered into cages and wished we could take all the animals home with us. We realized we had a small backyard and should probably look for a dog that was already housebroken and trained.

After thoroughly gazing at each dog, Daddy and I found a long-haired black dachshund. This dog quietly leaned against the wall. No barking, no howling. Beautiful dark brown eyes and soft fur.

"Who is this?" I asked.

The attendant said, "This is Susie. She's new here. Just came in."

Daddy and I both fell in love with Susie. "This is the one, Daddy."

"Are you sure? Do you want to look some more?"

"No, this is her. Susie."

As the volunteer opened the gate and scooped sweet, gentle Susie into her arms, Daddy and I knew she was perfect for our family. We walked to the front of the shelter. Daddy filled out paperwork as I listened to instructions about caring for a new pet.

With documents filed, food obtained, and a new leash hooked onto her collar, we were ready to take Susie home. She sat peacefully in my lap on the drive home. We couldn't wait to show her to Mama.

As I walked in the front door with Susie on the leash, Mama looked up from her book and smiled.

"Well, I see you found a friend."

"Yes, Mama, this is Susie. She is housebroken and trained. I love her already."

I took Susie to every room in the house, pointing out special things like her water and food bowls, my room, and a special rug for her to sleep on.

Later in the day, we loaded up the car and went to our local drive-in, which offered the most delicious hamburgers and french fries. Susie rode in the back seat, snuggled next to me.

With the driver-side window rolled down, we waited for our curbside waitress to come and take our order. A slight breeze made the summer evening enjoyable, and we listened to music coming from other cars in the parking lot.

"Hey, how are y'all today? What can I get you?" our usual waitress asked. Daddy started giving the order. The waitress looked inside to the back seat where Susie and I sat. Her face became pale, and her eyes pooled with moisture.

"Where did you get that dog?" she stuttered through tears.

"Excuse me, where did you get that dog?" she stuttered through tears.

Daddy explained how we had been to the local shelter and brought home this new family member.

Susie stood up on her front legs and leaned against the window. Her tail wagged.

"Is this Susie?" she could barely speak.

"Yes, this is Susie. How did you know?" Daddy asked.

Our waitress stopped crying and answered. "Susie was my dog for a few years. When I moved, I couldn't take her with me. And I couldn't find anyone who wanted her, so I had to take her to the shelter. I asked God to give Susie a wonderful family and to maybe let me see her again one day."

She continued. "Now, I see God has answered me. I will know where Susie lives and that she is loved. Thank You, God. And thank you all for taking her home. My prayers have been answered."

By this time, we were all crying happy tears. Happy that Susie had a new home with us. Happy that her previous owner could be comforted, knowing where Susie lived now. Happy to remember God answers our prayers in His timing.

Finding Susie was an answer to our friend's prayers. And to ours. God provided answers to all of us and we are thankful.

A Cat I Couldn't Refuse

– NATALIE GIDNEY –

Heartbroken. Once again, the allergist had diagnosed our three little girls with asthma and allergies to fur and feathers and dashed their hopes to bits.

We had hoped that maybe this would be the year things would change. For the past few years, we were told our daughters could not have pets with fur or feathers, but they could have fish, lizards, or snakes. But our girls didn't consider any of those creatures as pets. Their hearts longed for a cat or a dog.

People talked to us about hypoallergenic dogs—they don't have dander and won't cause allergic reactions. But our daughters' doctor had told us that their asthma and allergies were so bad that it wasn't worth the risk. Plus, I felt getting a pet and having to get rid of it if they had a reaction seemed cruel. It seemed better for them not to have one at all than to have to pry one out of their hands and hearts after they were attached.

We wanted to keep our kids as healthy as possible, so we told them that cats and dogs were definitely out of the question.

As time went by, they stopped asking us about having a pet. We thought they had accepted the diagnosis, not knowing that they were all praying that God would send them a pet.

One day, a big orange-and-white male cat appeared in our yard. He'd been spending time at our next-door neighbor's home but got a bit too brazen and snuck into their house, disrupting the delicate balance of their two Siamese kitties. Then he decided to kill a bird and throw it at their window. They sent him away. Away was our home.

Every time I saw the cat, I tried to shoo him out of the yard. But he wasn't going anywhere. My husband and I didn't want to be harsh, but we had decided that we weren't going to have any pets, period. End of discussion.

Then one day, our oldest daughter saw the big orange kitty in our yard. She called for her sisters. Then she asked me if she could feed him. She headed toward the cat with an open can of tuna, her sisters following. When the cat smelled the fish, he moved closer to her. Then she threw the can at him and ran for cover.

The excitement and wonder on my daughters' faces couldn't have been any sweeter. I savored it for a few moments then returned to reality. How I hated to deliver the news they already knew. My heart sank as I put on my stiff upper lip and spoke those heartbreaking words. "Girls, you know we cannot have a cat. Go back in the house."

"Mom, how can you send away what God sent us?"

Then those little faces looked at me with betrayal and hurt. At that moment, one of them said, "Mom, how can you send away what God sent us?"

"How do you know God sent you this cat?"

"We've been praying for a pet, Mom, and God sent us this cat," our middle daughter announced, with hands on her hips.

How does a mom who believes God—and teaches her children to believe God—argue?

I was in a corner. We were at a tender place in their faith and my own. If I sent the cat away, I was telling them God made a mistake. If I agreed to keep him, they might get sick.

I told them we would pray about it. They left excited—knowing God had answered their prayers and certain He would show us what they already knew. They knew God had answered their prayers. God sent them a pet. Not just any pet, either. It was a cat, the pet of their dreams.

As we prayed about what to do, my husband and I both came to the same answer. God had answered our children's prayer in a powerful way, but we needed to set some ground rules for our daughters to follow. They agreed, and we now had our precious gift from God—Sammy.

Sammy did not like to be inside, which was perfect. He was definitely an outdoor cat that happily lived in our barn. We made him a little house with a bed in it. Because the girls had allergies and asthma, they couldn't hold him. So they would pet him with a stick.

What kind of cat would sit still to be petted with a stick? One that God sent to us. It was precious to see them light up when their Sammy would come to meet them, greet them, and be patient with the affection they showed him.

As time passed, they got braver and (unbeknownst to me) began to pick him up and cuddle him. They would take their allergy meds and puffers as needed. But I still didn't realize what was happening until I recently saw the pictures they had taken with him.

Sammy was certainly a patient boy who loved each of us individually. He loved it when we spent time outdoors. When he was lonesome, he would jump up on the veranda rail and drag his paws down the window until someone talked to him.

Unfortunately, on New Year's Eve 2018, our beloved Sammy died during the night. He was such a part of our family that we miss him tremendously. As we remembered and talked about our cat, we all realized that this kitty knew all our secrets. Sammy loved each of us unconditionally, and each of us shared many things with him. We joked that we were glad he couldn't talk.

Almost eleven years ago, God answered the precious prayers of our girls and sent us a pet, even though we were told that we couldn't have one. We thank God for our precious Sammy boy, who will be forever remembered as an impossible prayer. When we couldn't see a way, God saw it and provided miraculously.

Paid in Full

– BARBARA TODD –

The dreaded day arrived: the first medical bill from my emergency surgery appeared in the stack of items I grabbed out of the mailbox. We expected the bills but hoped to have more time to save some money before they started rolling in.

Timing can be so important on the path of life. My emergency surgery came about a month after my husband started a new job, which meant no insurance until he was employed ninety days. I worked part time as a preschool teacher, so I had no insurance, nor did I receive any wages while out of work for the month, recuperating.

Discouragement knocked on our door several times, but we decided to ignore the loud banging and pray instead, asking the Lord for help and direction. We did not know how or when we could dig ourselves out of this financial hole.

Our cupboards were bare, which our three young teenagers didn't appreciate but understood. The situation bordered on desperate. We continued to pray and trust in God.

> My husband did not get paid for another week, and our bank accounts were squeezed dry.

My husband did not get paid for another week, and our bank accounts were squeezed dry. He decided to talk to his parents who lived next door to us. They lent us fifty dollars. We made our list of the most needed items and decided to go grocery shopping after church the next day.

On that Sunday, a children's choir from Africa sang at church, and the children told their heart-breaking stories of losing parents and siblings. They were touring the United States to raise funds for their education and for more orphanages.

In the middle of the choral program, my husband leaned over and whispered that he felt led to donate twenty of the fifty dollars we had just borrowed from his parents. I agreed so I scratched some grocery items off our list.

This was my first day out since the surgery, so by the time we got home, I was emotionally and physically drained. Shortly after I lay down to rest, the phone rang.

My close friend asked if she could stop by for a few minutes. Fifteen minutes later, she walked in with a grocery bag in her arms and told me someone had put it in her car and asked if she would deliver it to us.

How kind, I thought.

As I began pulling items from the bag, I gasped. I pulled out many of the items we scratched off our list. Starting to cry, I called my husband into the kitchen. I told my friend about scratching off some of our grocery items when we donated to the children's choir group.

Just then, she remembered that someone else had given her an envelope for us. She pulled it out of her purse and handed it to me. Inside was a twenty-dollar bill—the exact amount we had donated!

We were all in tears at that point, thanking the Lord for the miracle of unexpected provision. The people who anonymously provided the gifts knew nothing of our situation.

What a miracle! Our faith and gratefulness to the Lord soared high that day. It was the encouragement we needed for what we were to face next.

The following day, I received the first of many medical bills. I dreaded even opening it to see the cost of the surgery. I remembered God's faithfulness to us the day before. I knew we could trust Him during this financial issue too.

I debated as to whether I should open the bill right away or wait for my husband, but curiosity stirred within me.

As I opened the doctor's bill, I gasped. Stamped on the front of the bill from surgery were the words PAID IN FULL.

How could this happen? I noticed some additional writing at the bottom of the bill. I read the typed statement: "This bill has been paid by someone who wishes to remain anonymous."

What in the world? I wondered. *Who would do this for us?*

I couldn't wait for my husband to come home so I could share the great news with him and our children. Together we thanked the Lord for His continual provision. We felt blessed beyond measure—grateful to a living God who is fully aware of our every need.

Following that first bill we received, *all* the other surgery-related bills were marked in the same manner: "This bill has been paid by someone who wishes to remain anonymous."

We never did find out who paid the bills, but we had a sneaking suspicion that my husband's new employer paid them. He was a gracious and generous man.

This life lesson remained imprinted on my heart. It has been my strength when we've been challenged with other issues in our lives requiring us to cry out to the Lord in prayer. He has always provided for our needs, even if not in the way we requested. Ever since the day that first dreaded bill arrived, I've come to trust that God provides in His way and in His time!

It's All in God's Hands

— JENNIFER LYNN CARY —

I stared at the envelope, undecided. Was it a come-on? Was help really available? Well, certainly I wouldn't know if I just stared and didn't open the silly thing. I held in my hand a letter from the US Social Security Administration.

Nearly two years before, we had applied for Social Security Insurance (SSI) for our son, Ian, who had been diagnosed with cystic fibrosis. We were turned down. Ian didn't meet the criteria. In the meantime, his treatments and hospitalizations were becoming more expensive, and the insurance didn't cover all his bills.

So for two years, we knocked on every agency door we could find and prayed for God to open the right one. Every agency was sympathetic to our plight but offered no help.

But now it seemed that God had opened a very big door.

Someone had not liked being turned down for SSI and had fought the decision all the way to the Supreme Court. The result was a victory not only for that person, but also for everyone who had been rejected in the past ten years.

We were able, even encouraged, to reapply, and if we qualified this time, we would get paid for the two years in between applications.

Oh, what we could do with that kind of money! I had gone back to school in hopes of training for a job to bring in more income while my husband worked from sunup to sundown with his own lawn service. Instead of renting in an undesirable area, we could put a down payment on a house in a good neighborhood. We would be able to purchase a reliable vehicle for my husband's business, since the truck was on its last engine.

However, we needed to go through the application process—again—to obtain any money.

Prayer partners joined us, and God's favor poured out. We were approved and given approximately twenty thousand dollars with two stipulations: the money had to directly benefit Ian. (Well, a vehicle to get him to doctor appointments would surely count, as would a roof over his head.) And the money had to be used within one year.

You might think that spending that kind of money in one year would be simple. It's not. We prayed over every dime.

First and foremost, I told our SSI agent that we were believers and would have to tithe. He didn't argue. Apparently, it was allowed as long as it was the normal 10 percent.

You might think that spending that kind of money in one year would be simple.

Then we needed to find a good vehicle for a great price. I'd never negotiated a car deal before, but again God's favor was apparent. We were able to buy a Mazda, with low mileage for only four thousand dollars, which included the tax.

The next part was the house.

Even though I had talked with an agent, I could feel the time running out. So I asked for prayer in our Sunday school class. A friend dropped her card on my lap. "If you want to give me a call, I think I can help you."

I had forgotten that Carol Ann was a Realtor!

My husband and I called her. She asked what three things we had to have and what three things we wanted to have. The next Sunday, she gave me a printout of about a hundred possibilities. I narrowed it down to twenty and drove past each one. Then I narrowed it to five and gave those to my husband. He picked two, and Carol Ann arranged for us to go through the houses. The first one was perfect! We made the offer.

I had just earned my BS degree in elementary education. My first job was a part-time hourly position with at-risk kids in a room that was the teachers' workroom. It was the only room, besides the office and lounge, with a phone. This was before I had a cell phone.

The inconvenience of people walking in and out of my class to use tools was overshadowed by this one God-ordained thing. When the mortgage company was trying to negotiate a rate, they could contact me. Interest rates made a sudden drop, and since I had a phone handy, I was able to say "lock it in."

One other thing came about through timing. Had we been approved when we first applied, not only would we not have received that chunk of money, I wouldn't have been a recent graduate. That diploma and teaching certificate gave us better standing to buy the house, even though I was in an hourly wage position, because of my "potential earnings."

And the house we bought was in the neighborhood where the kids could continue going to their school. I could walk to work if I wanted. But even though we'd put all our ducks in a row, dotted every *i* and crossed every *t*, we remained in waiting mode.

I knew this was all in God's timing. But a part of me was afraid it might take too long and we'd forfeit the down payment money we'd set aside.

So I began taking walks in what we hoped would be our neighborhood, praying the whole time. I thanked God for every step of the journey. I prayed, knowing this was all in God's hands, and that was where I put my trust. Each time I passed the house we wanted to move into, I knew God was working it out, and I returned to our family with more peace.

One week later, we signed the papers and received the keys. The mortgage payment, with taxes and insurance included, was a hundred dollars less per month than we were already spending on rent.

Since then, we've seen the housing market skyrocket and crash. We've seen our Ian relocate to heaven, and we've watched our daughters graduate, marry, and move on. We've played with our grandchildren in this house. In fact, in four more years, the house will be fully bought and paid for.

I cannot begin to count all the blessings God has poured out on us at this address. But it had to be God's timing. And I've learned God's timing is best.

I Hear You, God

– HEATHER SPIVA –

What's that rumbling sound?" I yelled to my son, who was downstairs.

I was upstairs in my office and could hear the sounds of a video game and the clicking of a game controller. My twelve-year-old was obviously engrossed in one of his favorite video games. But that wasn't the rumbling I heard.

"What rumbling sound?" he said.

"You know, the one that sounds like a truck is idling outside of our home. Can't you hear it? It's so loud."

My son stopped his game and came to see me standing at the top of the stairway. "There is no rumbling sound, Mom."

Okay, this was odd. Truthfully, I had amazing hearing . . . to a fault. This "amazing hearing" made me a light sleeper, it made me jumpy over random sounds, and it could annoy me to no end. A simple sound outside or around the house would compel me to search until I found its source or else it would keep me up all night.

And now there was a rumbling in my right ear . . . that wasn't really there?

I mentally checked through our activities of earlier that morning. My two boys, my husband, and I had spent the morning in California's Sierra Nevada foothills, having a great time in the snow on a sunny day. In the early afternoon, we headed back home.

I hadn't noticed any unusual loud sounds when I went up to the mountains; there were no crazy noises, no earsplitting events that would have caused my eardrum to act like it was throwing a temper tantrum. The morning had been peaceful and fun, full of laughter and snacks, as well as familial snow shenanigans, such as hiking and sledding.

True, I was getting over a cold that had migrated to my ears and managed to partially block my hearing in the healing process. But this was normal. I had dealt with this many times before, and every time the colds went away fine!

Except for now.

I assumed this was a lingering part of the cold and that in a matter of hours or a day or two, I would be back to normal.

Little did I know this was the beginning of a battle with something called stress-induced tinnitus, a ringing in the ears. It can appear with the onset of loud noises and then disappear. Or the ringing can stay and be a part of your hearing—whether you want it or not—for the rest of your life.

In truth, Googling illnesses was the very thing I should not do.

I became desperate for an answer.

So I did what many people do: I went to the internet. In truth, Googling illnesses was the very thing I should not do. Instead of focusing on getting well, I became focused on my illness. Instead of focusing on God to help me through it, I focused on what doctors and others said and on what I read in articles just to get me through the day.

Months after contracting tinnitus, I spent hours researching what tinnitus was, how I could have contracted it—particularly without being near loud noises that would have injured my ears—and how I could make it go away.

It was staggering to find out how common it is, how debilitating it is, and how little help there is for those with this condition.

Many times, I felt like I was going to lose my mind because of the incessant rumbling sound (for many patients, the sound can be high pitched or buzzing; it can even be a hissing or whistling sound) and because the rumbling seemed like it would *never* go away.

I even went to an audiologist who had wonderful news (much to my dismay), reporting that I not only had perfect hearing but had better than perfect hearing (great). She explained that my tinnitus was stress induced (Awesome. So, *how* do I get rid of stress as a wife, mom, and business owner?) and that I should learn to relax, get a massage, and spa my life up . . . basically de-stress my mind, which has succumbed to playing tricks on my hearing.

Perfect.

Actually, it was perfect. I just wasn't listening to what the audiologist was saying.

So I needed to de-stress? That meant laying this burden of tinnitus on God's shoulders—not mine, not the audiologist's, and especially not Dr. Google's. And the only way that would happen was through prayer and patience.

Months went by, and the tinnitus persisted. I switched my diet, tried many different vitamins, read study after study, and still nothing.

I prayed for God to take away this stupid condition that I didn't want and hadn't asked for.

But one day, I recall praying a prayer of desperation. I felt God wasn't listening to me, that our line of communication had closed, and I couldn't understand why He was doing this. And do you know what I did? I gave up.

I didn't give up praying, but I gave up the *want* of tinnitus alleviation. I remember saying to God, *I don't know how to fix this. I've tried it all. I'm doing my best to give it to You, but obviously I'm not doing a good job with that, either. You can have it, this tinnitus! Whether You take it from me or leave it, so be it. If it's a thorn in my side—one that You've given me—obviously You think I can handle it. I want what You want. Even if I don't understand why You want me to be in pain.*

That day felt good. The prayer made me feel better.

Yes, the rumbling was there, and there were moments when I forgot about it. But every night, I had to sleep with a fan in order to drown out the rumbling, which was a daily reminder that the tinnitus was still there.

One night, a few days after the relinquishing prayer and before I drifted off to sleep, I thanked God for healing me (even though I was still waiting for the healing). I thanked Him for letting me draw closer to Him because of this condition. And as I fell asleep, I remember thinking, *But if there is something I'm not hearing, something I'm not listening to rightly, tell me what to do to fix it. I'm willing.*

Right then, I had an image of shiny black vitamins being poured from a bottle into my hand. I had never taken this vitamin before, and I didn't know what it was. But it was in my mind as I fell asleep and engrained in my memory.

The next day, I went to purchase a new supply of a vitamin I'd run out of that had nothing to do with my condition. As I was perusing the aisle, I picked up a vitamin I hadn't tried before and took it home.

I opened it and held it over my hand. Out poured shiny black vitamins—vitamins I'd seen in my momentary vision the night before.

I took one, and in a matter of hours, the rumbling in my ear stopped.

The tinnitus was gone!

It happened so quickly, and I felt so normal, that I hadn't even realized my hearing was back to normal and the rumbling had stopped until hours later. I was healed. After six long months, my hearing was back to normal!

Prayer is a way for us to be close to the One who made us. It is a gift, a fantastic and glorious gift. I often wonder if my condition was a way God chose to draw me closer to Him. I wonder if I hadn't persisted in prayer, would the answer have come? I wonder if I hadn't relinquished my desire, would I have envisioned the shiny black vitamins? How did I know what vitamins to pick, having never seen them before?

I don't know the answers to those questions. But as the quote often attributed to Albert Einstein says, "There are only two ways to live your life. One is as though nothing is a miracle. The other is as though everything is."

I think everything I went through was a miracle—even contracting an illness that I shouldn't have gotten. Because of it, I drew closer to God through prayer. And by taking the problem off my shoulders, laying it at His feet, and focusing on the One who has all the power *instead of on the condition*, I got to see a miracle unfold right before my eyes . . . and ears.

God was listening to me the whole time; the real lesson was my learning to listen to Him, even when my ears were playing tricks on me. And because of this miracle, my hearing will never be the same.

Unexpected Answers

— BOB HOSTETLER —

We read the Bible and wonder why our prayers don't get answered like the prayers of the people we read about in Scripture. But not every prayer was answered. The Bible itself makes that clear. Here are four questions to ask yourself if your prayers aren't being answered.

1. **Have I asked—or just wished?** A wish isn't a prayer. James wrote to early Christians, "You do not have because you do not ask God" (James 4:2, NIV). How often have I wanted God to do something but haven't really made that "something" a subject of prayer?
2. **Have I asked according to God's will?** Even Jesus submitted His requests to the Father's will (see Matthew 26:39, 42). So it's worth asking myself whether I'm praying according to my agenda—or God's.
3. **Have I asked from selfish motives?** James wrote, "When you ask, you do not receive, because you ask with wrong motives, that you may spend what you get on your pleasures" (James 4:3, NIV). What percentage of my prayers are motivated by my own desire

for pleasure and comfort? Chances are, the higher that percentage, the less my experience of answered prayer is likely to be.

4. **Have I considered that God may have something better in mind?** Elijah—the great champion of God, the great man of faith, the great prophet of Israel, prayed, "Take my life" (1 Kings 19:4, NIV). Mary and Martha, grieving the recent death of their brother, Lazarus, each said to Jesus, "Lord, if you had been here, my brother would not have died" (John 11:21, 32, NIV). In each case, the petitioner was disappointed—for a time, at least. Elijah eventually went to heaven in a chariot of fire, and Mary and Martha saw God's resurrection power displayed before their very eyes.

God's ways are not our ways, He says (see Isaiah 55:8–9), so it shouldn't surprise us too much if our prayers sometimes go unanswered because He has a better idea.

9

Change and Challenge

"Help" is a prayer that is always answered.

Anne Lamott

The dependable thing about life is its lack of dependability. Just when we think we have it figured out or when things are going smoothly or we can begin to relax in the mundane, *boom!* Something changes.

In fact, centuries before Christ was even born, Heraclitus of Ephesus, a Greek philosopher, first made popular the thought that change is the only constant in life.

As our lives move on and change, we face so many things. We lose people we love—sometimes without warning; sometimes we watch their bodies diminish. Our children leave home, changing our relationships with them forever, and while the changed relationships are not necessarily bad, the difference can be uncomfortable. We transition to new jobs or new locations. We face health issues and aging. And we encounter adversities as we walk along life's path.

Paul was one of those who faced adversity, and he described some of the challenges he faced after committing His life to preach the good news of Christ. And Paul knew who to turn to when adversity came and when it seemed unlikely to go away. Scripture never specifies exactly what Paul's problem was, but Paul implored God three times to take it away.

Did God remove this distress and challenge from Paul's life? No. Each time Paul asked God to take away his problem, God replied, "My grace is all you need. My power works best in weakness" (2 Corinthians 12:9, NLT).

Many times when we pray over the challenges and difficulties we face, God will send in the cavalry and rescue us. He will bring the healing, solve the problem, and answer our prayers, making us shout our praise for His deliverance—whether in great situations or small ones.

At other times, He provides grace. In this sense, grace is really sort of nebulous or fluid. It is the enabling power and hope God gives us so we can make it through any situation as we face challenges and difficulties. God gives us the grace to overcome fear and difficulties and keep our eyes on His victory, on His omnipresence, and His omnipotence.

So how do we pray when we go through the changes and challenges of life? Oswald Chambers advised, "We have to pray with our eyes on God, not on our difficulties."

That's the example you'll find in the stories in this chapter. You'll see the very real struggles people faced, and you will see them turn to a very real God who sometimes answers our situations by changing problems and sometimes answers our prayers by changing us. You can find, as they have, that challenges and changes don't have to threaten us because we can call upon the one who is the same yesterday and today and forever. We can know the truth of James 1:17, which reminds us, "Every good and perfect gift is from above, coming from the Father of the heavenly lights, who does not change like shifting shadows" (NIV).

Out of My Control and into His

– DIANNE E. BUTTS –

The sun floated bright in the eastern Colorado sky that June morning in 2013. I pressed the starter on my burgundy Kawasaki Vulcan. The motor idled—the familiar voice of a friend. I zipped my black leather coat, buckled my full-face helmet, and tugged on leather gloves.

My husband Hal's pearl-white Harley-Davidson Ultra Classic rumbled to life. We both had decades of experience riding. A few years earlier, Hal had retired as a major with the Colorado State Patrol, and he made sure we always wore helmets.

I swung my leg over the seat and heaved the big 1500-cc motorcycle off its kickstand. I squeezed the clutch and stepped down on the shifter into first gear. Hal rode out of the driveway and I followed, the morning air chilling my face.

Soon we pulled into a parking lot to meet Margi on her red Yamaha V Star. All of us wore the back patch of the Christian Motorcyclists Association, an organization that works to share Jesus with bikers and everyone we meet. That day, we planned to join an annual ride that benefits fallen police officers.

The three of us joined leather-gloved hands as Hal offered his prayer. "Keep everyone on the ride safe."

"Give us opportunities to talk with people about You, Jesus," Margi added.

"Keep our motorcycles mechanically sound," I petitioned. I'd noticed a spot on the garage floor under my motorcycle, so I'd tucked a quart of oil into my saddlebag as a precaution.

We hopped on our machines and headed north from Pueblo, Colorado, toward Colorado Springs on the interstate, riding in our usual staggered formation: Hal led in the left-wheel track, I was behind him in the right-wheel track, and Margi last in the left-wheel track.

An hour later, we met up with the ride. At the first stop, volunteers set out water bottles and doughnuts. Hal asked the volunteers to join us in prayer. Surprisingly, most of them did. "Bless all these people working hard for this ride, Lord," Hal prayed. "Keep all the riders safe."

We climbed back on our bikes and rode on smaller highways through the Black Forest into Castle Rock, where I had grown up. We stopped there for lunch.

When we planned this ride, I asked Hal and Margi if they would mind making one stop near the restaurant. After lunch, I led them to nearby Cedar Hill Cemetery.

I gazed up toward the hill to the east. Though the town had grown, I could still see the high school I graduated from among the new houses. Memories surfaced.

A month after my high school graduation, my brother, Fred, who was four years older, came home on leave from the Marine Corps just in time for my eighteenth birthday. We celebrated my birthday, then went riding motorcycles. The next day, he rode his Harley to visit friends.

On his way home, a drunk driver pulled out right in front of him. Fred swerved but could not avoid a collision. He died at the scene. His headstone lay here, next to Dad's grave. It was a good opportunity to visit.

We rode the next leg on back roads through beautiful country before the route swung back to the interstate highway. We stopped for fuel. In the hot afternoon sun, I shed my coat and long-sleeved shirt, stuffed them into a saddlebag, and snapped my leather vest over my tank top. I tugged on short-fingered gloves.

We rode south through Colorado Springs, passing the familiar sign indicating thirty-five miles to Pueblo and home. The speed limit increased to seventy-five miles per hour. Hal sped up to the posted limit. I rolled on the throttle.

My bike felt sluggish, as if we were riding into a headwind. I glanced at the passing trees, trying to see if they were blowing.

Hal pulled farther ahead. Strangely, I was having trouble keeping up. I pushed my motorcycle against that "wind," but the gap between me and Hal widened.

I glanced at my speedometer: only sixty-five miles per hour. Margi, close behind, no doubt wondered why I was slowing down.

A pickup truck behind us pulled out to pass.

I twisted the throttle and glanced in my rearview mirror. The pickup truck was passing Margi, pulling a camper behind it. My bike drifted left as I tried to move right.

> Suddenly, I knew exactly what was happening: my front tire was going flat.

The truck began passing me and my motorcycle drifted farther left.

Then the camper came alongside as I drifted dangerously close to the passing vehicle. My handlebars started to shimmy. Suddenly, I knew exactly what was happening: my front tire was losing air, going flat.

Where was Margi? How close? I was in trouble, and I didn't want to take her out.

Everything happened in moments. Fractions of seconds. I hoped to swerve left behind the camper into a dirt median. But I couldn't hold it and veered left into the camper.

All of a sudden, my left shoulder hit the camper hard, knocking me off my motorcycle. Then I tumbled down the highway sideways as the asphalt and highway spun before my eyes.

Over and over again as I tumbled, I uttered, "O Jesus!" His precious name was my ultimate prayer, my everything prayer, encapsulating all I could possibly pray if I had the time.

I stopped rolling, facing down the highway. Hal was out of sight.

Would someone hit me at seventy-five miles per hour? I planted my right elbow on the asphalt and pulled past the white line onto the shoulder. Conscious. Alive.

Beneath ripped short-finger gloves, my hands already were swelling and turning purple. I hugged them to my chest. Margi ran to me.

With emergency medical training years ago, I knew what to do: Don't move. I wiggled my toes. No paralysis. I could breathe. I could think.

How far down the highway was Hal? When did he notice I wasn't behind him?

A woman knelt on my left, a man on my right. They applied pressure to my bleeding bare arms. Someone called 9-1-1. The man and woman helped for what seemed like a long time. Finally, sirens sounded in the distance.

I'd caused quite a traffic jam on both sides of the four-lane highway. Cars crawled past.

I lifted my head. At that precise moment, when I could see across the highway between two passing cars, I saw Hal ride north!

Paramedics arrived and soon after, Hal. "I had a flat tire," I told him. "How's my bike?" I learned later it was totaled.

The ambulance carried me south to a hospital in Pueblo. A paramedic gave me pain meds and treated large patches of road rash on my bare arms. Though I tried to tell him how Jesus saved me, the meds made my mind fuzzy. Instead, he told me how Jesus had saved him.

When the ambulance arrived at the emergency room, the ER doctor asked, "Where do you hurt?"

"My hands."

"How fast were you going when you crashed?"

"Sixty-five miles per hour."

She ordered a full body scan and wouldn't let me move until that was done. Nurses cleaned the asphalt burns with a painkilling disinfectant.

Hal and Margi arrived later.

"I tried to let that camper pass so I could crash in the dirt median."

Hal shook his head. "The median's really steep there. Besides, behind the camper he pulled a Jeep on a tow bar."

What might have happened had I tangled with that?

The doctor stitched up my elbow. My beat-up full-face helmet sat on a counter. "Without that helmet," the doctor said, "she wouldn't have a face." That moment, I believed my helmet saved my life.

The body scan revealed no internal injuries. I had a chipped bone in my foot, a few stitches in one elbow, and three large patches of road rash. Within hours, I went home.

Tumbling down the highway at sixty-five miles per hour out of control, I was completely helpless and dependent on God. When you get right down to it, isn't that pretty much where we each live every day?

Lad's Rescue

– ELAINE McALLISTER –

That early March day held great promise as sunshine brought warmth to the frozen earth, but within the hour my husband, son, and neighbors would be faced with a life-and-death struggle.

This hint of springtime in Kansas prompted our church friends, the Beckers, to invite my guys over after church. It was a perfect day for a trail ride in the remote area not far from our country homes.

Our son had recently adopted a young, spirited wild mustang named Cherokee, and the Beckers loved sharing their knowledge about horsemanship with Travis. He was working hard to train Cherokee and seemed to have a natural ability with horses. They responded well to his efforts, and this rancher's daughter was thrilled with my son's newfound interest. I had grown up with horses and both loved and respected these creatures of strength and beauty.

My husband, Jim, was a city kid when we met, so he was definitely a novice on horseback, but he enjoyed a good trail ride. Bruce Becker saddled his favorite—and oldest—horse for Jim. Lad was a large horse, rather tall and fairly stocky, but very mild mannered and trustworthy. He was a great choice for my husband.

The four horses headed down the hill to the beginning of that familiar trail. The horses knew the way as they meandered along a winding creek, in and out of brush and heavily wooded areas, and across narrow dirt roads that led to nowhere.

Spring thaws and heavy rains would send water rushing down creek beds and over the concrete slabs on the roads where vehicles could cross the creeks. During rainy seasons, the roads were impassable as the dirt turned into a muddy mess, but in the heat of the summer both the roads and the creek beds were bone dry. In these times, farmers ventured out on these roads only when they had to and forded the creeks on those concrete slabs, but most of the time local traffic is nonexistent. It was perfect for a Sunday afternoon ride.

Birds chirped, a light breeze rustled through the leaves of the trees along the trail, and the creek ran full following a recent snow melt. In fact, the water level was nearly high enough to cover the concrete slab, and recent runoff caused erosion of the creek bank.

Such a scenic and peaceful trail. It was a favorite one, as riders would often startle deer nestled in the underbrush and enjoy the chatter of squirrels scampering overhead from tree to tree. It was a narrow, one-way trail. There was no riding side by side through the creek.

Lad and Jim were bringing up the rear, leisurely following the others and enjoying the surroundings. Lad knew the trail well, but wasn't expecting the erosion, made worse by the other horses just ahead. Just as Lad's front feet reached the concrete, his back legs slipped off that muddy, eroded bank and into the creek. Lad went down, and he went down hard.

Jim quickly scrambled out of the saddle and hollered at the others for help. Lad's chest and belly rested on the slab, his front legs were skinned and extended straight in front. With his rump wedged tightly against the muddy creek bank, his back legs dangled precariously in the cold, murky water. This was not a good position for any horse—especially a large one that was up in years.

All the coaxing in the world didn't help. Bruce tried, but Lad was stuck and unable to move. Lad's breathing was shallow and labored, the weight of his body resting fully on his chest and belly. He wouldn't last much longer, and there was no time to go for help.

A strategically placed steel post prevented the guys from pushing Lad's front end into the water so they could lead the large horse across the creek and up the other bank. Now, they would have to get his back legs out of the water and onto that concrete slab. His eyes were glassy, and he was in grave danger.

"Oh God, please help us!" my husband, son, and neighbors prayed frantically. God was listening, but the work would be up to them.

Bruce was an amputee with an electronic prosthetic leg, so as much as he wanted to save his beloved horse, he couldn't even get in the water. Bev, his wife, was a tiny gal without the strength to move Lad. Jim would do anything he could but wasn't real comfortable working with horses. It was up to Travis. And . . . God!

Travis jumped in the thigh-high frigid water determined to free this much-loved giant of a horse. The rescue was intense, and if Lad thrashed about at all, it could be very dangerous. Travis had to trust Lad, but Lad also had to trust Travis as he reached down through the murky water to find and grasp Lad's slippery, wet hoof. Then Travis would try to get Lad to relax his leg enough so his hoof could be lifted to the safety of the concrete slab.

A farrier has to learn to maneuver a horse's leg into position to trim hooves and put on horseshoes—it's not always an easy feat. Maneuvering the leg of a big horse in trauma and underwater added to the difficulties.

> Minutes passed. Prayers went up. Hearts raced. Tension mounted.

Minutes passed. Prayers went up. Hearts raced. Tension mounted.

At last, one leg was up. Now, if only Lad would remain calm as Travis repositioned himself in that cold, muddy water to retrieve his other hoof while steering clear of the steel post. A few minutes went by as my son struggled for a grip. Finally, both legs were safely on the slab, and Lad was resting on his side and catching his breath. The big horse was cold, wet, and thoroughly exhausted but no longer in imminent danger.

Travis was in much the same condition, as the thankful onlookers realized just how close they had come to disaster. "Thank You, Lord!"

After allowing Lad to rest a while, the four set out for the barn. Bruce climbed back on his horse, but Bev, Jim, and Travis led their horses on a shortcut across the pasture. Lad seemed to be okay except for being scraped up and traumatized a bit, but Bruce was eager to check him out more extensively and coddle him. What a miracle!

Pain eventually forced Travis to climb back in the saddle and let Cherokee do the work of carrying him back home. Thoroughly soaked from the neck down from this underwater rescue, he just couldn't take another step with his frozen feet encased in soggy, muddy socks and boots. The adrenaline that had kicked in when needed was gone, and Travis was exhausted.

The relaxing trail ride hadn't gone as planned that day, but everyone was thankful for the determination of a young teen and the divine assistance of a loving God.

Lad got some extra pampering back at the barn. When Travis got home and dropped his muddy, wet clothes at the door, he did too!

Answering the Prayer I Forgot

– PAM ZOLLMAN –

"You're home early," I said, smiling, as my husband, Bill, walked through our front door a few days after Thanksgiving. My smile disappeared as I noticed his worried face.

I had been reading a book on the couch while our two-and-a-half-year-old son, Keith, took his nap. Normally, I would have jumped up to greet him, but now that I was seven months pregnant, I had a hard time just standing up.

His shoulders slumped as he sat beside me. "I've been laid off."

I sucked in my breath at the devastating news. "What happened?"

"The company can't pay everyone anymore, so last hired is first fired." Bill sighed. "But I wasn't the only one. They let half the employees go."

My husband had been worried this might happen. He had noticed that the engineering firm he worked for had lost clients and not gained new ones. The economy in Houston, Texas, was built on oil, and when oil prices declined, as they had recently, it affected everything.

Smaller oil companies were closing their doors, and the laid-off employees no longer could afford their homes. People had begun to walk away from their houses, abandoning them to the banks, as they started over somewhere else.

With the glut of cheap homes on the market, there wasn't a need for new houses. As a civil engineer, Bill worked on developing new subdivisions, designing the streets and the water and sewage lines. But now there wasn't a need for civil engineers in the Houston area.

"I don't know if I can even get another job like mine," he said. "And our insurance runs out at the end of the year."

That was bad news. Our second child was due January 16—two weeks too late to be covered.

As we sat next to each other, Bill grieved the loss of his job, and I silently prayed. The future didn't look good. Besides having a toddler and another child on the way, we also had to think about a mortgage, a pantry that needed constant filling, and a never-ending supply of diapers.

And Christmas was only a month away.

I hadn't been in the work force for three years, and it would be close to February before I could look for a job after the baby was born. Could we hang on until then? Could I get a job that would cover our expenses until Bill got another job?

I needed to do the only thing possible: trust God.

I placed my hand in my husband's, closed my eyes, and began soundlessly praying. *Lord, please help us find a way to pay our bills and feed our family. Help Bill find another job. You are our refuge in times of trouble.*

Psalm 46:1 came to mind: "God is our refuge and strength, an ever-present help in times of trouble" (NIV).

And then I remembered Philippians 4:19: "My God will meet all your needs according to the riches of his glory in Christ Jesus" (NIV).

That was when I realized that God was speaking to me through those Bible verses.

"God will provide," I said aloud, feeling strangely peaceful.

Bill glared at me and said, "Don't give me that religious nonsense." Then he stormed into our bedroom and slammed the door.

My husband was not a Christian. I had been praying for him for years to accept Christ, but it seemed as if his heart was harder than ever toward Jesus. It had recently gotten so bad that he didn't want me reading the Bible or praying in front of him. So, of course, my saying anything about God would upset him.

Later, when Bill had calmed down, he came out of our bedroom and said, "We need to talk seriously about how we're going to survive."

I sighed and sat at the kitchen table with him.

"My unemployment money doesn't kick in for a couple of weeks," he explained, "so it will be extremely tight. When I do get it, it will be only a little more than half my old salary."

"Your mother and my grandmother won't let us starve," I said.

He avoided my eyes. "We're not going to ask them for help. It's our problem, our responsibility."

He and his mother didn't always get along. And when she helped, sometimes there were strings attached.

"Okay," I said, "we won't ask our families for help."

But I continued to talk with my heavenly Father. I knew that God had a plan for us.

For the rest of that week, I helped Bill polish his résumé. While he scoured the newspaper listings for jobs, I went through our kitchen cupboards, planning cheap meals. Keith was almost potty trained, so we wouldn't need many diapers until after the baby was born.

Several days into the job hunt, Bill threw his pen down in frustration. "I'm never going to find anything."

"Yes, you will," I said. "God will provide."

Bill's face clouded with anger. "You don't know that!"

"I do," I said. "I really do."

"No, you don't. All that religious stuff is garbage." He picked up his pen and notebook and walked to our bedroom.

At week's end, he had found five civil engineering positions and sent his résumé to those companies. I smiled, knowing God had provided those opportunities.

Two weeks later, in the middle of December, I was eight months pregnant. Bill was worried sick about finances because his unemployment paperwork was still being processed and we wouldn't have any money to buy Christmas presents.

Bill stopped pacing and stared at me. "I just don't understand how you can be so positive."

"Why haven't I heard back yet from those companies?" He paced in the kitchen as I cooked dinner.

"You will." I stirred the onions and garlic in the skillet.

"Yeah, if I hear back, it'll most likely be a rejection. Probably a hundred people are applying for those jobs," he said as he walked around the kitchen table again.

"No, I know you'll get one of those positions." I added the hamburger to the pan.

Bill stopped pacing and stared at me. "I just don't understand how you can be so positive."

I turned away from the stove "I have total faith that God will provide." I braced myself for his angry retort.

Instead, he stared at me and then walked out of the kitchen.

That week the first of God's provisions came, and it was amazing. Bill heard back from the five companies, and they *all* wanted to hire him. But then a sixth company called him and offered him a position. And that was the job he picked. He would start work on January 2, after the Christmas holidays.

We were watching a basketball game on television when Bill said, "You were right. I think God did provide for us."

I smiled. "Yes, He did."

"But," he continued, "we still have a problem. They told me that my insurance plan won't go into effect until February."

"That is worrisome," I admitted, "but I know that God will provide."

Bill said, "I sometimes wish I could be so positive like you."

Christmas came on Saturday that year, and our families gathered, exchanging presents and good cheer.

On Tuesday, December 28, 1982, I went to my weekly doctor's appointment. It was about two weeks until our baby girl would be born. The ultrasound picture had been hard to make out, but my doctor had assured us that Elizabeth would be around six pounds. I was feeling very bloated as the doctor examined me.

"Elizabeth is coming early," Dr. Morgan said. "You're already five centimeters dilated."

"How early?"

"Hard to tell, but she'll definitely be here before her due date."

Lord, how early will she be here? I prayed on my way home. *If she comes before January 1, is that too early?*

That was when I felt the tiniest breath of air tickle my ear and I heard, *Don't worry. I'll provide.*

Was it real? Was it imagined? Did I hear it with my ears? Or with my heart?

Did it really matter? I truly believed that God had just reassured me, and I felt wonderful.

Early the next morning, on December 29, Bill rushed me to the hospital. And eight hours later, Bryan was born. Yes, God had a surprise for us. The doctor had predicted a six-pound girl, but I delivered a ten-pound boy!

Bill was amazed. "How did you know the baby would come early?"

"I told you," I said. "God said He would provide for us, and He did."

"Yes," my husband said, smiling widely, "yes, He did." Then he looked at me seriously. "As soon as you go back to church, would it be okay if I go with you?"

Now I was totally amazed. God had answered all my prayers in the past four weeks, including the one I had forgotten. I had been so focused on our current situation that I had neglected to pray for Bill's salvation. But God hadn't forgotten.

God provided.

From Punishment to Privilege

– SANDI BANKS –

Prayer changes things.

I knew that. But I must have needed a refresher course that unforgettable day when an old sweater brought me up close and personal with a holding cell, a squad car, and a cop.

If sweaters could talk, what a tale this one could tell.

I recall the very day, a year earlier, when this one-of-a-kind hand-knit sweater called my name from its residence on a mannequin in a classy little boutique on the East Coast. And of course, I just had to have it. I mean, who wouldn't love to own a wooly, warm creamy-beige number with colorful autumn leaves appliquéd on front, back, and arms?

My sweater and I became besties that next year, and I wore the pants off of it, so to speak—until the "cop" episode questioned its heritage. And mine.

The episode began early on a crisp, springtime-in-the-Rockies kind of day. The sun had just peeked over the horizon, casting a glorious lavender hue on the snowcapped tip of Pikes Peak.

Ordinarily, I would have embraced such a gorgeous morning, but everything on my to-do list seemed to outrank anything on my wish list. And already I was exhausted.

My job of hosting our ministry's conferences kept me running, and I loved it. Having just bade farewell to a hundred of our finest conferees, I had to quickly shift gears, with less than twenty-four hours to prepare for the next hundred people. I ran through my checklist:

- Drive 15-passenger van from mountains to Denver airport—3 hours. Check.
- Deliver conferees with luggage to respective flights. Check.
- Return to Manitou Springs—2 hours. Check.
- Drive to Colorado Springs to buy week's groceries for next 100 people. Load van.
- Drive back to Denver, set up, prepare, host evening reception at hotel.
- Get up early, check out, help load vans: books, equipment, food, luggage.
- Drive new conferees to mountains for next conference—3 hours.

Reviewing the list, I figured I'd have just enough time, between the third and fourth tasks, to run by the air base for a quick errand. My Plan A. Not God's.

Snatching my shopping list, purse, and sweater from the car, I raced into the military base store, grabbed a few items, checked out, and put my sweater on before heading out the door.

When I reached the parking lot, a military policeman nabbed me.

"Come with me, ma'am," he gruffly insisted as he ushered me back into the store. He confiscated my sweater, purse, and purchases, then placed me in a "holding tank" and left.

There I remained planted for more than an hour, bewildered.

"What did I do?" I asked anyone passing. Everyone either ignored me or grimaced, but no one would talk. Time crept along like a desert tortoise.

I have to be honest—I felt every range of emotion imaginable: anger, fear, frustration, self-pity, anxiety, disbelief, annoyance, hurt, exasperation . . . and more. No one told me why I was detained or what they planned to do with me or when they would let me go. Nobody seemed to care that I had things to do, places to go, people to feed.

Finally, a uniformed man entered the room.

"What did I do wrong?" I half demanded, half pleaded.

"We believe you stole the sweater."

"What? You have got to be kidding! That old ratty thing?" My tirade began. "Look at the cuffs, it's obviously not new! I carried it in here! Your store doesn't even sell anything remotely resembling that sweater! Check your inventory!"

I was on a frenetic roll now. "It's *my* sweater, handmade, one of a kind. I bought it in a boutique back East, I can prove it! I have a receipt, and—"

I took a breath just long enough for him to get a word in. "Receipt?"

"Yes, I have the receipt, at home in—"

"Good. You'll need it for court!"

With that, he put me into a squad car, drove me across the base, and deposited me in another holding tank, my belongings still impounded.

In the corner of the room, several airmen tried to get the surveillance cassette tape working to play it for the police officer. They talked about this man as if he were royalty. Or a superhero. He certainly had respect and status. Maybe even a golden scepter. The cop would review the tape, interrogate me, and pronounce sentence.

So I waited for what seemed an eternity, growing more angry and humiliated. I felt helpless. I kept glancing at my watch. No cop. I wanted to scream, "Let me go! I have stuff to do!"

In desperation, I finally cried out to God, "Lord, I don't understand this, but You do. Please help!"

As the hour hand turned, so did my heart and my attitude. My get-me-out-of-here! prayers became show-me! prayers, followed by something quite uncharacteristic for me: I kept silent.

As I allowed God's Spirit to speak to my heart, a strange calm came over me. I became reflective, focused.

Bible characters who had been treated unjustly began appearing on the canvas of my mind. First, our Lord Jesus Christ—the ultimate injustice—sinless, condemned without cause. Then I pictured others who'd been unfairly treated, unjustly accused, humiliated, or imprisoned: Joseph, Noah, Job, Stephen. The prophets, John the Baptist, the apostle Paul. On and on, they paraded until God had my total attention.

Then it hit me. Hadn't their unjust treatment served a divine purpose? Wasn't God there? And here? Didn't He know about, even sometimes orchestrate, such events?

Almost giddy, I dared to wonder—could this minor pause in my day, this slightly untidy situation, possibly be used for His purposes?

A sense of anticipation replaced my sense of wrong. A wide smile emerged on my face for the first time all day—as if that glorious hue on Pikes Peak had made its way onto my countenance. What was God's plan in all this?

As I praised and prayed, humbly listening for His voice, eagerly awaiting His next step, without warning, a shadowy figure appeared in the doorway—the police officer.

He was big. He was burly. And I almost expected him to be wearing a crown or a cape.

He strutted in and pulled up a chair. Dispensing with formalities, he got right down to the business of interrogation. *Who was I? What was I doing on base? Where had I been? Where was I headed?*

My answers were straightforward as I told him about the Christian conferences.

"So! You're a Christian?"

"Yes, sir, I am."

With that, he took a deep breath, looked me in the eye, removed his hat, set it on the table, and said, "I want to talk to you, not as a cop, but as a concerned dad. Is that okay?"

I listened as he told of his young son—the light of his life—whose mother and her new husband had put him in a Christian school. This was one livid dad!

I listened to his feelings of anger and frustration, fear and confusion. An hour earlier, I might have retorted, "I hear you, brother. Join the club!"

I listened with a heart of compassion, and our roles reversed.

But instead, I listened with a heart of compassion, and our roles reversed. I started asking *him* the questions, and when he told me the name of the school, I beamed. It "just so happened" I was well acquainted with that particular Christian school and several of its teachers and administrators.

"That's a great place—and they love those kids!" I began sharing all the positive things I knew about the school, the teaching staff, and the curriculum—encouraging him to look at it objectively.

"Have you seen any schoolwork he's brought home?"

He thought a moment. "Well, actually, I was really impressed with a paper he showed me last week." He brightened. "It was really good!"

"Have you ever sat in on his classes?"

"No."

"I'm sure they would be more than happy to have you visit. I can put you in touch with the headmaster, if you would like. I think it would be an important first step."

He smiled and agreed. About that time, one of the airmen approached. "Sir, we have the surveillance tape ready for you now."

The concerned dad stood, put his hat back on, resumed his cop role, and snapped, "Forget the tape; this woman is innocent. Give her back her belongings. I'm going to personally escort her back to her car." And he did.

On the way, we talked nonstop about the Christian school, his son, and all the good things in store for him there. I even seized an opportunity for a brief word from my sponsor—how God and *His* Son had made a difference in my life—before arriving at the parking lot and bidding farewell.

I stepped out of the squad car and received my sweater and other personal items back, along with a profuse apology and a grateful grin.

What I thought was a punishment turned out to be a privilege.

I've often wondered what became of that cop and concerned dad. Did he get involved with his son's school and become a Christian? Only the Lord knows. Maybe one day I will too.

In the meantime, I've tucked away that antique leaf-laden sweater, along with the memories, but have the lessons close at hand, to remind me:

When we pray, things change—sometimes the change is not in our circumstances but in our attitude toward them. When we pray, even angry, bewildered, hurting hearts can become compassionate, forgiving, and hopeful.

Not only did God work wonders in the life of a concerned dad and in the heart of a suspected sweater snatcher, but He even redeemed the time that day. He worked out every detail of the grocery run, hotel reception, three-hour drive, and ministry to our lively new crop of conferees.

If sweaters could talk, this one would have plenty to say. "There I was in detention. There she was in a tizzy. Thankfully, she finally prayed!"

When others accuse us, God may use us, so "pray without ceasing" (1 Thessalonians 5:17, ESV).

Invisible Love Letters

– PEGGY EASTMAN –

The newborn was full term and beautifully formed, with a sweet face. But his skin was yellow, and he was listless and unresponsive. As she listened to the doctor, my niece Alice—a first-time mother who was almost never flustered—tried to concentrate without crying.

Little Jack had a skyrocketing level of bilirubin, a pigment formed in the liver by the breakdown of red blood cells. He was severely jaundiced, and the doctor said that for this type of bilirubin, the phototherapy with a special lamp, which was often used on jaundiced newborns, would not work.

Exhausted from labor, my niece tried to process what the doctor was saying: "Possible blocked bile ducts, liver transplant . . ."

Liver transplant? She was allowed to nurse little Jack briefly, and then the baby was whisked away to the neonatal intensive care unit (NICU), where the doctors put him on a special formula designed to lower his bilirubin level. She could no longer hold him, let alone nurse him.

Alice's husband, David, put his strong, well-muscled arm around her. A master at cracking wry jokes, David could usually make her laugh—but he had no jokes now.

Our extended family had convened in Dallas, Texas, for Christmas to celebrate this little boy's birth. We had experienced many losses of adults, including the death of Alice's father, Jack, whom the baby was named after, but we were looking to this newborn to bring us the hope of a brand-new generation. The elder Jack was my only brother. The two of us had been very close, and I was devastated when he died.

All of us had been so thrilled when we learned Alice was expecting; I had no children of my own and looked forward to cuddling little Jack, buying him toys, reading *Winnie the Pooh* to him, and being a loving great-aunt.

But now . . .

Liver transplant? In a newborn?

I shuddered. Could a parent donate part of a liver to an infant? Or . . . did another baby have to die for little Jack to get a new liver? If so, how long would it take to find a liver that was a right match?

I shuddered again. A little red heart on my driver's license marked me as an organ donor; I believed strongly in the lifesaving potential of donated organs. But I could not pray for little Jack to get a liver transplant from another baby; I just couldn't. Surely, this was not the right prayer, and God would never want one infant's life ended to heal another's. God, always merciful, would surely find another way to heal this little boy.

Lord, You gave this baby life and sent him into our family as a precious gift when we were still grieving the losses of adults we loved, I prayed. *Please surround little Jack with Your love, bring his bilirubin level down, cure his jaundice, and give his liver the power to heal itself.*

I asked my pastor and my women's Bible study group back home in Maryland to pray for little Jack's total healing, nearly breaking into tears when I let them know about a possible liver transplant. I felt better knowing an army of prayer warriors, including our extended family members, was praying constantly that this baby's liver would heal completely on its own.

Finally, after he had spent a week in intensive care, the doctors agreed that little Jack could go home. But he was discharged with a thin tube threaded through his tiny nostril and down to his stomach. The new parents were supposed to feed him following a strict, frequent schedule with a special prescription formula they mixed at home and hung in a bag from a pole. The formula then dripped into the baby's feeding tube.

One doctor who had seen little Jack in the hospital, a renowned pediatric liver specialist, wanted to see if just maybe his bilirubin level would drop without major medical intervention. The other doctors who saw him were much more skeptical.

The frequent tube feedings exhausted my niece and her husband, and sometimes their baby threw up shortly after a feeding. We worried that he wasn't getting enough nourishment.

Sometimes little Jack cried because the tube was uncomfortable. He even waved his tiny fingers and pulled the tube out, and Alice had to insert it in again. It was tricky and she struggled, but she became an expert at getting the feeding tube back in place.

Tests showed that very gradually, the baby's bilirubin level was coming down. As his skin slowly lost its yellow tint, little Jack became more responsive and active, waving his tiny arms and kicking his little feet.

Then he began to smile occasionally. When we saw that smile, our hearts melted. Little Jack was acting more like a normal newborn. We dared to hope that just maybe there would be no more talk of blocked bile ducts or a liver transplant.

We family members were all tired, as much from our worry and emotional strain as from our lack of sleep. On Christmas Day, Alice's mother, Jill, and I worshipped at The Chapel of the Cross, a small church near where we were staying.

I thought of that other tiny baby who was born on Christmas Day in a humble stable.

As we knelt in the sanctuary, beautifully decorated with red poinsettias and greens, I thought of that other tiny baby who was born on Christmas Day in a humble stable—the one who grew up to bring hope to so many. I thought of God's boundless generosity in sending His only Son as a vulnerable infant to save all humanity. Such a generous God hears and responds to the prayers of His people.

I read from a brochure given out at the chapel, which contained the comforting words of Matthew 11:28: "Come unto me, all ye that labour and are heavy laden, and I will give you rest" (KJV).

Another chapel brochure proclaimed that those who believe in Christ "will say their prayers daily, in the morning and evening." We were certainly doing that and more.

After the service, we asked the chapel pastor to pray for little Jack. I thought of all the prayers lifted by us and by others our family members had talked to, emailed, and texted. Hundreds of faithful people contacted other faithful people, so hundreds more were also praying for our baby. The prayers were like powerful, invisible love letters winging their way to God because we all cared so much about this tiny newborn.

I hated to leave little Jack and travel home to Maryland after Christmas. But he was improving daily, and I knew I could keep praying for him wherever I was. As I held him before I left, I prayed, *Lord, I know You hear me, and I know You want to heal Jack. Please, please, let his liver heal on its own. Please save this baby from surgery. And most of all, please spare him a liver transplant.*

Before long, I learned that the feeding tube had been removed and that little Jack could now eagerly breastfeed. His bilirubin level was near normal and then dropped further.

My prayers now overflowed with gratitude to a merciful God. There was no medical explanation for why such a severely jaundiced infant had healed without medical intervention. As the liver expert talked to Alice, she said, "He is one of my mystery babies."

No medical explanation existed, maybe. But God had made sure that this world-renowned expert had been there to encourage the other doctors to wait. And those of us who had prayed so hard were convinced that little Jack's complete recovery was part of the biggest mystery of all: the unlimited power of faithful, fervent prayer.

No Chance of Survival?

– KRISTI EDINGTON –

As I listened to the speaker, I wondered if this would be the last women's conference I would ever attend.

I had been on IV antibiotics for a month with no end in sight. The five layers of mesh in my abdomen were seeded with infection and would have to be removed. The surgeon wasn't sure he could do that and keep me alive.

During the previous nine years, I had been through nearly fifty surgeries—all with complications—and had survived a coma that had lasted three months. But lately, I just didn't have the energy to fight anymore.

The conference fulfilled my soul, and I longed to go down front to be prayed over by the staff. I just couldn't go down the two floors of steps.

As tears built in my eyes, my Bible study leader asked what was wrong.

"I want so badly to go down to the front for prayers, but I physically can't," I said. "I am so tired of being sick. I just don't know how much longer I can endure this."

Without pause, my group surrounded me and held me in their arms as they prayed for God to intervene and be with me through any more trials ahead.

I felt uplifted after we prayed. During the entire trip home, I sat quietly in the van, just letting all that I had heard over the last two days sink in. I felt an inner peace that night, something I hadn't ever felt before.

Two days later, I was back in the hospital. A clot had formed in my vein from the Peripherally Inserted Central Catheter (PICC) line. The staff added some medicine to dissolve the clot, but it unexpectedly persisted and became infected. And it was so large, I would need surgery to dissolve it. However, after three surgeries, the medical staff was unable to destroy the clot, and the stents they inserted to help the blood flow clotted within twenty-four hours.

As the clot continued to spread, my heart began racing with the slightest movement. Lifting my hand to answer the phone made my pulse soar well above two hundred beats per minute. My breathing was strained during these episodes and talking was nearly impossible. I felt as if my heart were going to explode at any time.

> I felt as if my heart were going to explode at any time.

I was so scared.

Then some of my Sunday school class came to visit. Again, they held me and prayed for God to intervene, to give me peace and comfort. After they left, I felt so much better. I was no healthier; I just felt a relief in my soul.

I know that no matter what happens, God will use it for good, I thought.

From that point on, every time someone prayed for me, I felt a gentle hug. I could actually feel the arms of our Savior around me, and I knew that someone had said a prayer for me.

Eight days later, I was jetted to a hospital four states away. I prayed during the entire flight that I would get the help I needed to live for my three-month-old granddaughter and my youngest daughter who was still in high school.

When I arrived in the new hospital, my medical team identified the problem and proceeded with surgery to remove all five layers of mesh, scheduling replacement of the mesh three months later.

On the drive home, my husband pulled in at a rest stop. I thought I was strong enough to not to use the walker, but I was wrong. I hit uneven concrete and crashed to the ground. My husband quickly picked me up. I examined the damage from the fall: only one scraped knee and two scraped hands.

I went straight to bed after our twelve-hour journey. I was exhausted.

The next morning, when the nurse came to check me out, she noticed that my entire left side was black. The fall had caused internal bleeding.

We rushed to the hospital. I was in critical condition. The massive bleeding was causing clots to form throughout my blood vessels. This made treatment extremely difficult.

The doctors couldn't stop the bleeding because of the clotting and couldn't treat the clots because of the bleeding. The hospital began infusing me with blood and blood products to make up for the large amount of blood I was losing. If by some miracle I survived, I would likely lose both arms and legs. The outlook was dismal.

I continued to feel God's arms around me and could still feel prayers. I felt the pain of my injuries, but my soul felt a greater peace than words can describe. There was no fear of death, no worry. I knew that God had this and His will would be done. He didn't cause the pain and suffering, but I knew that great good would come from it—even if I was no longer on this earth to witness it.

The next days were filled with blood transfusions and pain medication. My family sat by me, frequently crying for fear of losing me. The specialist assured them that even with all they were doing, I was losing the battle.

The doctor begged me to sign a "Do Not Resuscitate" form. I refused. I assured him that whatever happened, God was in charge. "Christ has a plan for me. I don't know if that means death soon or if I will survive this, but I do know that He will be the one determining if I live or die, not a piece of paper."

Before long, I was close to death again, not once but three different times. But I felt overwhelming calm even as the injected medicines caused violent reactions in my body. Each time, I was comforted in a way that I cannot explain.

Eventually, my body began to heal, and I was able to leave the hospital.

One morning, I woke up feeling empty. With all I had been through, I was never depressed. Why now?

I realized that God had let me go, but He remained close. And I knew I was ready to be watched from afar.

Even in hopeless situations, prayer works. I don't know why I survived and others don't, but I know that all things do work together for good for those who love God.

I also know I would not have survived without the prayers of others.

I await the time when I feel the presence of God like that again. That peace and comfort goes far beyond anything in this world. There are people I would miss, but the overwhelming joy of heaven holds even greater power over death. Until my time to go, I will continue to follow His words and commands, as God watches.

Perfect Timing

– SALLY WILLARD BURBANK –

"Y'all need to come for lunch this Sunday. I'm fixing to cook up country ham, grits, and peach cobbler."

When I heard the deacon's wife speak, I felt as if I'd landed in a different country. My husband and I had moved fourteen hundred miles from northern Vermont for me to begin a rigorous internal-medicine internship in Nashville, Tennessee. I didn't know a soul and was anxious to make friends. But would I ever fit in with a world of sweet tea, heavy makeup, and southern drawls?

Thankfully, I soon met Tonya, who shared my love of health care, hiking, and gardening. We attended a weekly Bible study together and enjoyed hoofing around the Vanderbilt track in our mutually *un*successful attempt to lose weight.

Unlike me, however, Tonya desperately wanted to be a mother. For five frustrating years, she had sought pregnancy, using monthly ovulation kits, fertility shots, and endometrial surgery.

A year into our friendship, I rejoiced when she announced she was two months pregnant. But a month later, she miscarried. We wept at the loss of her precious baby . . . and her hope.

The discouraging saga continued for five more years. Every month started with hope. *Maybe Tonya will conceive this month!* But every month ended in bitter disappointment. All our church friends were having babies, and I knew each glowing announcement of "We're expecting" rubbed salt in Tonya's wounds. Since she and Phillip would make ideal parents, I prayed regularly for them.

Unlike Tonya, I was ambivalent about motherhood. Did I really want to surrender my free time, money, and sleep? Did I want to put up with nasty diapers, spit-up, and whining? And what if I turned into a cranky, inept mother? Worse, what if my children became selfish, mouthy brats, heroin addicts, or lazy bums? In short, I was afraid to rock the boat—or in this case, the cradle.

My husband, Nathan, wanted children almost as much as Tonya did, and I knew he'd make a firm, loving father. He had been patient with me all through medical school and residency. But on my thirty-first birthday, he tossed out a gentle reminder. "You've completed all your schooling, and we're not getting any younger."

As a doctor, I knew birth defects increased after age thirty-five. Plus, knowing Tonya's frustrating battle with infertility, I realized conceiving a baby might take months—even years. Alas, if we were going to have a baby, I shouldn't dawdle.

Conflicted, I told my husband, "We won't *try* to get pregnant, but I won't do anything to prevent it, either. We'll let nature take its course, and if it's meant to happen, it will happen."

I figured with my stressful job and hectic schedule, it would take months, maybe even years to conceive. I'd have plenty of time to get used to the idea of parenthood, right?

Wrong! Try one month! One measly month.

I couldn't believe it when I immediately became pregnant. Morning sickness attacked with a vengeance, and the toilet became my new best friend. Meanwhile, my husband bounced around like Tigger on Ritalin, proudly announcing, "I'm going to be a father!"

Once my dreadful first trimester of nausea ceased, I warmed up to the idea of motherhood—except for the overwhelming guilt consuming me every time I walked the track with Tonya.

Why me and not her? She wants it so badly. It's not fair!

I dreaded telling Tonya so much that I put it off for five months, hoping she would get pregnant before I had to break the news. I beseeched God every day, "Let Tonya conceive before I share my news. I don't want to hurt her."

By my sixth month, my baby bulge became so obvious I could delay no longer. With a pounding heart and sweaty palms, I gently shared my news with Tonya. Shocked, wounded eyes stared back at me. She burst into tears. "I didn't know you even wanted a baby."

Memories of Tonya's crushed expression compelled me to petition God even more fervently. First, I wrote scripture verses on index cards to carry with me until I had them memorized. Then I researched Old Testament stories about infertile women who eventually conceived: Sarah, Rebekah, Rachel, and Leah. As I prayed, I begged God to bless Tonya, just as He had blessed those biblical matriarchs. I also added

I begged God to bless Tonya, just as He had blessed those biblical matriarchs.

a caveat: "Please, Lord, make it happen before my baby is born." I didn't want my new baby to ruin our friendship or dump acid on her hurting heart.

Morning, noon, and night I uttered the same prayer: "Please, God, bless Tonya with a baby, and let her conceive before my baby is born."

Eight months into my pregnancy, I went into labor, and nine hours later, at 7:59 a.m. on October 4, my wonderful son, Steven Nathan, made his grand debut into the world. Love poured through me as I gazed into the eyes of my tiny blessing from God. How could I have ever doubted wanting this sweet bundle?

Once Steven was asleep, Nathan and I began calling our friends and relatives with our good news. How I dreaded calling Tonya. I was disappointed with God. Never had I prayed with as much faith, consistency, and fervor as I had when I prayed for Tonya. But what did I have to show for it?

When I had notified everyone on our list *except* Tonya, I knew I could procrastinate no longer. I didn't want her to get the news through the grapevine. I sucked in a deep breath and called.

Surprisingly, she sounded upbeat and promised to visit later that day.

After "oohing and ahhing" and insisting that, yes, Steven *was* the cutest baby on the planet, Tonya said, "I'm dying to tell you something. I found out at seven o'clock this morning that I'm pregnant!"

My mouth dropped. *Tonya is pregnant?* Tears of joy pooled in my eyes.

Wow! God not only answered my prayer—He timed it to the very hour!

I knew I wasn't the only one who had prayed for Tonya, of course. Her husband, family, friends, Bible study group, and even a missionary in Japan were all lifting her in prayer daily. Many had fasted on her behalf. But God's timing—*to the very hour*—was God's special gift to me. It was God's reminder that He listens to those who pray without ceasing and answers if the prayers are in line with His purposes.

Nine months later, Tonya delivered a healthy, beautiful baby girl she named Michelle.

Both our children are now in their twenties. Michelle has grown into a lovely woman with a baby of her own! Tonya is now a grandmother!

I may not always understand God's ways, but this experience taught me I can trust God. If I pray with consistency and faith, He does answer prayer.

A Cat with a Lot of Moxie

– KIM McGUIRE –

"One quick peek," I promised myself as I drove to the shelter. Though two months had passed, I still reeled from the death of my best buddy, Clouseau. The male silver tabby Persian had succumbed to cardiomyopathy. His heart was just too big . . . in more ways than one.

Losing him had knocked the emotional wind out of me after a brutal divorce. I was living solo for the first time ever. The lunch-hour jaunt to the SPCA shelter was just a diversion, a bit of wistful kitty window shopping. I wasn't ready for a new friend yet.

I quickly toured the kitten room, watching the tiny fur balls romp and wrestle, climbing and leaping to and fro. Adorable, but not one of them truly touched my heart.

It was just a bit of wistful kitty window shopping. I wasn't ready for a new friend yet.

I wandered into the adult cat area and paused in front of a cage holding two felines. The fluffy tabby with big ears, white boots, and a plush tail came to the front of the cage and locked eyes with me. When I opened the door and scooped him up, he kissed me on the nose. My fate was sealed.

Good thing my boss loves animals as much as I do, I thought. I wouldn't have too much trouble justifying my extended lunch hour. I filled out the necessary forms and placed the kitty on hold, and then sped to the pet store to purchase supplies. Back in the office, I made a halfhearted stab at working for a few hours until my boss laughingly urged, "Go on, get out of here!"

When I returned to the shelter, I found the adolescent cat posed calmly near the front of the cage as if to say, "I'm still here. What took you so long?"

I christened him Moxie.

As I stumbled through the next few months, trying my unfamiliar single life on for size, Moxie showered me with rainbows of kitty love. When I parked at the computer, he curled up on my lap. When loneliness struck, he would snuggle and purr it away. At night, he crept onto the bed and planted reassuring kisses on my face. Outdoors, Moxie amused me by racing up trees and leaping at butterflies. He put his whole heart into whatever he did.

One day, I was out shopping when my cell phone rang. A neighbor had found Moxie lying in the road. He had been hit by a car and was severely injured. My friend had rushed him to the nearest vet before calling.

The familiar feeling of grief grabbed at my chest and threatened to overwhelm me. "Please, God, not Moxie!"

I hurried to the veterinarian's office and found Moxie listless in a cage, unable to move from the waist down. His pelvis had been broken. His sad, puzzled look ripped through me. I couldn't bear to end his sweet life. Instead, I went home to mourn what I would have to face the following day. I jumped on my bike and went on a long, tearful ride, praying for guidance and bracing myself.

The next day, I dragged myself into the vet's office to share my terrible decision. This time, a different doctor greeted me. He had a different point of view.

"I've seen young cats like Moxie make a full recovery from a broken pelvis," he said kindly, sending hope zinging through my veins. "Because of his youth, the bones may mend themselves by growing back together."

If I was willing, he would keep Moxie for a week to give him a chance to heal. The staff would administer any necessary meds and help him use a litter box. When the week was up, we would see if a miracle had occurred.

I visited Moxie almost every day. My prayers were soon answered. After seven days, it was clear he could feel sensation in his lovely white boots as he tottered like a newborn colt. The X-ray showed a healed pelvis—I could take him home! The added hitch in his gait just increased his cuteness factor.

We celebrated our reunion with furry fake mice and extra cuddles. Moxie also resumed his mission of helping me cope with change. We substituted a cat tree for the real thing and augmented his playtime with lasers, feathers, shoelaces, and other crazy items he hauled into the living room.

Over time, Moxie's resilience induced me to embrace my single status. If he could make such a remarkable recovery with God's assistance, then so could I.

That was a number of years ago. Now, I am remarried to a wonderful man, and I have taught him to love cats almost as much as I do. And when my memory lingers on Moxie, I can't help but smile. He was a survivor, and I got to enjoy him while he purred and kissed his way through his eight remaining lives.

I'll always thank him for showing me the true meaning of *moxie*.

A Prayer on the Stair

– BETH GOOCH –

Lord, you know I don't have the courage to walk out of here myself. If you want me to quit, you'll have to slap me up 'side my head.

I prayed as I climbed the stairs to the third floor of the building where I had worked for nearly forty years. The concrete steps were stained with coffee, sloshed by generations of reporters, editors, photographers, and page designers slugging caffeine late into the night as they cranked out the morning paper.

How many times had I trod those stairs? I had started working there as a college journalism student, fortunate to have a career in my chosen profession. But changes in the industry led to repeated job cuts. Each layoff brought fresh sadness, as well as guilt that I had survived the cut and annoyance at being asked to absorb the duties of former coworkers.

The newsroom looked like a ghost town, with rows of empty desks. Our once-robust staff of 220 had dwindled to fewer than 40.

A large, national chain had recently bought our publication as well as the daily paper in a nearby town. They had fired the entire copydesk at the other newspaper, so we had picked up that work in addition to our already heavy loads.

Reading stories for a publication in another city was not a problem, at least not technically. They used the same computer software we did, so that aspect of the change had been easy. But the staff at the other paper didn't like having strangers in another city edit their copy. They were often rude, and their hostility worsened a difficult situation.

Newspaper folks have a reputation for being crusty, but we'd always had camaraderie in our office. Even through tough times, we were a team. Producing a daily paper is a 365-day job, including holidays. I'd spent almost every Christmas Day of my adult life with my coworkers. We were sort of a family.

Now most of those friends had been laid off and the ones who remained were tired and cranky from the extra work and the jabs of the staff in the neighboring city.

The job I had long enjoyed was no longer fun, and I was desperate.

Surely, God didn't want me to remain in that unhappy situation. But how could I quit? With so many out-of-work journalists in our area, finding a job would be tough. And what would I do about health insurance? The thought of being jobless scared me, but I couldn't believe this was what God wanted for me.

I had already experienced two glitches that morning. My security badge didn't unlock the gate like usual. I had to use another door that didn't require me using my badge. And when I tried to log into the computer in the newsroom, my password wouldn't work. I called the information technology department, and a man promised to look into it.

While I waited for the computer issue to be resolved, a fellow copyeditor walked over to my desk and said, "I've been called to HR."

We all knew that being called to the human resources department meant only one thing: layoff.

He looked so dejected that I offered to walk to the human resources office with him. As we walked down to the first floor, I encouraged him to keep a clear head.

"Make sure they give you credit for all the vacation time you've accrued," I advised. "And ask them how long they will extend your health insurance."

He nodded sadly.

We entered the human resources office and recognized our managing editor seated with the publisher's attorney. Their grim expressions turned to confusion when they saw me.

"Beth," the managing editor said, "what are you doing here? We hadn't called for you yet."

Yet?

"Am I being laid off too?" I asked.

"Yes."

So that's why my security badge and computer log on didn't work. They'd already locked me out of the system!

They'd already locked me out of the system!

"If you're going to do it, I'd like to get it over now," I said.

I pulled out a chair next to my coworker. We sat at a table across from our former boss and the attorney, who assured us we were being laid off due to financial reasons, not for any fault of our own.

We asked about vacation time and health insurance, as we'd discussed on the way to the meeting. We had to sign some papers to receive our final paychecks, and then we were released.

I walked out of the building into the late-March sunshine. I started my car and drove home, feeling lighter and more relaxed than I'd been in a long time.

Later, I learned that I was one of twenty-three people cut that day.

A few weeks after the layoff, we all gathered for a farewell party at a friend's house.

I told them about praying for a clear message from God about whether He wanted me to remain in that job.

"I'm sorry," I joked, "that you all were collateral damage in God's plan for my life."

We always hear that God works in his own time, and there's no point in trying to rush Him. Psalm 27:14 says, "Wait on the LORD: be of good courage, and he shall strengthen thine heart: wait, I say, on the LORD" (KJV).

But on that particular spring day, God chose to answer my plea in less than two hours. Talking to Him about my work problems and then receiving a clear, unequivocal response, just as I'd asked, gave me confidence as I learned to navigate the world of the unemployed.

As I moved forward, I claimed a scripture, Revelation 3:7: "When I open a door, no one can close it. And when I close a door, no one can open it" (CEV).

I don't want to waste time fretting over whether a job is wrong or right, I told God. *I'm just going to apply for every position I hear about and trust You to close the door if it's wrong and open the door if it's right.*

Each time I applied for a job and faced rejection, I was disappointed but confident that no matter how good the job had seemed, God had something even better in mind for me.

Six months after the layoff—the very week my unemployment benefits ran out—I was offered a job. It was a position for which I had not applied, in a place I wouldn't have thought to seek employment—a church. My dear heavenly Father, after months of slamming doors I wasn't meant to open, opened a door to the perfect position where I could use my skills while trying some different things.

It all happened in His timing, and it all started with a prayer on the stair.

Breathe, Sister, Breathe!

– BEATRICE FISHBACK –

Breathe. Inhale. Exhale.

Generally, that is an easy thing to do for the average person walking the streets, going to work, doing her shopping, or rocking a baby. We don't usually think about our lungs and how much we need them. That is until we no longer can breathe.

Ten years ago, I was with my husband at his West Point reunion. The football game was drawing thousands to the stadium to cheer the Army team. It was a family affair that year with my sister, Mary, with her husband and their children joining the grand occasion.

Mary had been having health issues, but climbing the stadium stairs that day seemed to knock the wind out of her sails as she struggled to take one step at a time.

Shortly after the weekend, Mary went to see a specialist and was diagnosed with pulmonary fibrosis. This disease happens when scarring occurs in the lungs, which causes reduced oxygen in the blood. There are no known causes or cures. More recent treatments include lung transplants, which are risky and have long-term consequences.

Not all siblings have good relationships, but my sister and I have been through thick and thin together. Sure, we fought like most, but we also coped with our father's alcoholism and the trauma that war had left in his soul. Our mother "forced" us to play together by insisting we would have no other friends until we could get along. Perhaps she was so adamant because her own sister—my aunt—had died when our mother was a teenager. Mom never got over the loss and recognized the importance of loving a sister.

So my sister and I argued, loved, joked, sang together, and fell in love with some of the same boys. I always knew she had my back. She took the fall for me when we got into trouble, talked to me through the wee hours of the night, told me tales when I couldn't sleep, and consoled me when my heart was broken. We didn't always get along but she was, and always has been, there when I needed her most.

News of Mary's diagnosis sent everyone reeling: her husband, children, grandchildren, and me. After all, she was only fifty-six at the time. Young. She had a lot of life still ahead of her.

Breathe, dear sister, breathe.

The prognosis wasn't good. Mary was eventually referred to a pulmonary specialist in New York City. She went through a slew of tests and attended a variety of courses with her husband to prepare for the worst-case scenario—a lung transplant. Emotionally, she went into a downward spiral . . . and fast. Who wouldn't, given such news?

I was living in England at the time and flew back to the States to visit. One day, I found Mary in a fetal position in her bedroom in tears. We had cuddled and cried together as children. Now we cried together as adults, as if we were children again. Our mother had passed away several years before, but the love she insisted my sister and I share lived on.

I wish I could say that a miracle happened and her lungs were restored as we prayed for healing. But other answers to prayers happened along the way.

As Mary came to terms with her disease, getting medical help to stem the tide of her illness and speaking to a counselor, she learned several things. First and foremost, she recognized God's hand on her life and how He answers prayers—not always how we would like, but even in the worst of days, He has the best for us.

> At that moment, she realized God was giving her another chance at life.

One day, while lying in her bed, she distinctly heard God say, *Mary, you can either wallow here or you can get up and live.*

At that moment, she realized God was giving her another chance at life. People loved and needed her, including me. She also learned how essential it was to be an advocate for herself. She kept a three-ring binder with the details of everything that was said, medicines that she was prescribed, the variety of doctors' advice, and others' input. She joined an online support group and learned how to deal with the disease.

The pulmonary fibrosis didn't go away, but Mary was becoming a new woman. She began to pray more diligently, no longer taking loved ones for granted, and started taking back her life—with God now in the control room of her heart.

Since Mary's diagnosis, I have watched her struggle, give up on occasion, and curse the oxygen that she has to live with twenty-four hours a day. Yet I've also seen her determination and unflappable desire to strengthen her body, mind, and spirit. She joined a church, became a member of a gym, and began doing aerobic exercises at a local center. Mary has also become an advocate for others. In learning to live with this illness, she has helped countless others—both in person and in the online support group.

Mary's internal scarring is still there, and she carries oxygen wherever she goes, but answers to our prayers were happening that she wasn't even aware of. Her spirit, her attitude, her love, and her faith had grown stronger than ever before.

When Mary visited the specialist in New York City recently, he was stunned. Mary's lungs are exactly the way they were ten years ago. They haven't gotten better, but they have not worsened as anticipated. These days, she walks more than five miles a day, loves to travel to the beach, and spends as much time as she can with her family.

Breathe, dear sister, breathe. You still have a whole lot of living to do.

A Cardinal's Wing and a Prayer

– MARILYN NOLL, AS TOLD TO RONICA STROMBERG –

The phrase "on a wing and a prayer" became popular during World War II when John Wayne's *Flying Tigers* movie showed two characters discussing the plight of a returning pilot and his plane. When John Wayne asked about the plane, the other character said, "She's coming in on one wing and a prayer."

The phrase has come to mean getting through a tough situation by relying on divine help or luck.

I have lived that phrase throughout much of my life but have come to think of the "wing" as belonging not to a plane but to a bird—specifically, a cardinal.

My mother died from stomach cancer when I was ten years old. And in one of my last memories of her, she was standing at the back window of our house, whistling to cardinals in the yard.

Whenever I saw a cardinal after that, I was reminded of her. The bright-red bird became a symbol to me that my mother's spirit was still with me. I drew comfort from each sighting.

Years later, when I was a mother with three grown children, my husband, Dick, became ill with mouth-and-throat cancer. The doctors tried to arrest the cancer with surgeries, chemotherapy, and radiation, but the disease soon spread throughout Dick's body.

Still, every time Dick and I took a trip to the doctor's office or a hospital, we would spy a cardinal along the way. Dick would have an all-right checkup and would continue living with the cancer. We began to see the cardinals as a sign of hope.

During the year when Dick was being treated with surgeries, he and I traveled several times from our home in southeastern Iowa to the university hospital in Iowa City. On our final trip to that hospital, a male cardinal flew right in front of our Thunderbird, about a yard from the hood ornament. Later, when the doctor saw us, he told Dick, "I can no longer do anything for you. You've had all the surgeries you can possibly have."

We left, discouraged but still searching for hope.

We prayed for divine healing, but as a pastor's daughter who had lost her mother, I knew God's will might be different. Dick and I ended our prayers with this acknowledgment and the words "Thy will be done."

Dick received radiation and began having checkups and chemotherapy at a hospital in a town a half hour from home. On a drab November day, as we drove to one of these checkups, we looked for cardinals but failed to see any. Once we arrived at the hospital, the doctor discovered Dick had contracted pneumonia.

Because the illness was so hard to treat and Dick was already stricken with cancer, the doctor admitted him to the hospital. We were told the pneumonia would likely be fatal.

I drove home alone through a chilling gray mist, no cardinals to be seen anywhere. Alone at night, I slept fitfully and prayed throughout the night, "God, please be merciful to Dick."

As a schoolteacher, I had to work the next day, so I reported for duty but cannot tell you what I said or did to stop myself from unburdening my cares on the children. I was fortunate to have many years of teaching experience. I felt as though I was on autopilot.

While I was teaching, a nurse from the hospital called and said Dick was in intensive care. I called our children, and we all went to his bedside. Dick's condition continued to deteriorate, and he passed away two days later.

> I stared out the window, searching for anything that might have life to it.

The next morning, grief weighed me down to the bed. I struggled to get up. Tears blurred my vision and fell uncontrollably to my cheeks. I swiped at them and, still in my nightgown, staggered to the kitchen window. I stared out, my eyes searching for anything that might have life to it.

"Oh, Lord," I prayed aloud, "how will I get along without Dick? How can I live the rest of my life without him?"

As if in answer, a bright-red male cardinal flew through the dreary view and landed on the ground right below the window. The bird faced west, the direction Dick and I had always gone when we wanted to put our troubles behind us and get away on a vacation.

Thank You, God, I prayed. *You let me know that Dick's spirit is still with me.*

About two minutes passed, and a female cardinal alighted on the neighbor's ground, east of the male. The two birds stood facing each other, separated by a chain-link fence.

This is just like Dick and me, I thought. *He's on the other side of eternity, and I'm on this side. Time and years—who knows how many—are all that separate us now.*

I thanked God for this comforting thought, which seemed yet another message of hope delivered by cardinals in my life.

Now I'm in my seventies, and cardinals continue to signify hope, comfort, and peace to me, which I want to pass on to others. Every year when I send Christmas cards, the recipients can count on finding a red bird in the artwork. People have responded to my tradition by sending me cardinal-decorated items as gifts. I display my cardinal collectibles throughout my home year round. Everywhere I look, I find hope renewed.

Six Short and Simple Prayers for Coping with Stress

– BOB HOSTETLER –

Maybe your life is all sunshine and cotton candy. No shadows, no sadness, no stress.

Well, good for you. Feel free to move along, because the rest of us are dealing with stress—lots of it for some of us. And at times we feel like we're about to buckle under.

But that's why I'm so happy that I can turn to God in prayer, even though at times, when I'm superstressed, the words don't come easily. When that happens, I call on just a few go-to prayers. Short ones. One word. Two. The longest is only six words. Sometimes I pray just one, over and over. Other times, I pray several, in order, more or less. See if any of these prayers for coping with stress help you:

- **A one-word prayer: *Breathe***—Sometimes when I'm stressed, I hold my breath. I don't even know I'm doing it. But when

I realize it, I remind myself and turn it into a prayer of sorts: *Breathe.* My wife's watch even reminds her to breathe! It's a helpful practice. Stop. Slow down. Breathe.

- **A two-word prayer: *Hide me*—**David sang, "Keep me as the apple of your eye; hide me in the shadow of your wings" (Psalm 17:8, NIV). Oh, I pray that often, and I frequently condense it and simplify it into just two words: "Hide me." While the storm rages. Until the storm passes. Until the stress evaporates like summer rain on a hot sidewalk.
- **A three-word prayer: *Peace, be still*—**When His closest friends were stressed and scared by a storm at sea, Jesus rebuked the storm, saying, "Peace, be still" (Mark 4:39, KJV). And the squall surrendered. It's a great prayer at any time, for any soul in stress: "Peace. Be still."
- **A four-word prayer: *I come to You*—**Jesus said, "Come to me, all of you who are weary and carry heavy burdens, and I will give you rest. Take my yoke upon you. Let me teach you, because I am humble and gentle at heart, and you will find rest for your souls. For My yoke is easy to bear, and the burden I give you is light" (Matthew 11:28–30, NLT). Remember these words in the midst of a stressful situation, and pray, *I come to You.* Let Him give rest to your soul.
- **A five-word prayer: *My help is in You*—**On one occasion, I was so stressed—panicked, even—that I spent a half hour on my face on the floor of my study, praying, *My help is in the name of the Lord, the Maker of heaven and earth* (see Psalm 124:8). Over and over. Until my heart and mind began to agree with my lips and my voice. And calm and hope returned to my soul.

- **A six-word prayer: *I have calmed and quieted myself*—**One of the shortest psalms in the Bible, Psalm 131, is a lullaby. I love it and pray it often when I'm stressed—especially the second verse: "But I have calmed and quieted myself, I am like a weaned child with its mother; like a weaned child I am content" (Psalm 131:2, NIV).

The picture is that of a child contentedly snuggling with his mother, not complaining or clamoring, but simply and completely content to be in his mother's arms. Those six words remind me that I am in the arms of a loving and protective God, a realization that relieves stress and revives my soul.

That's it. Altogether, just twenty-one words. But they do often soothe me and save me from stress. I hope they do the same for you.

Seven Prayers to Help Embrace Change

– BOB HOSTETLER –

Maybe you'll soon be getting married. Or starting a new job. Or launching a business. Or moving somewhere new or speaking publicly about something you're passionate about. Or in some other way, boldly going where you've never gone before.

At such times, prayer can be your terra firma, your force field, and your fuel. If you're about to take brave new steps of any kind, try adopting—or adapting—some of the following prayers:

1. Lord, as you were with Abram when you called him out of Ur, so be with me in this new venture. You are my shield, my very great reward, and I know that nothing is too hard for You. (Based on Genesis 15:1, 18:14.)
2. May the God before whom Abraham and Isaac walked, the God who has been my Shepherd all my life to this day, bless these steps I now take. (See Genesis 48:15–16.)

3. Lord, Your Word says that You direct the steps of the godly and delight in every detail of their lives. Let it be so with me as I take the next steps on this path. (Based on Psalm 37:23, NLT.)
4. "May the favor of the Lord our God rest on us; establish the work of our hands for us—yes, establish the work of our hands" (Psalm 90:17, NIV).
5. I trust in You, Lord, with all my heart. Help me not to lean on my own understanding but to acknowledge You in everything. Make my path straight. Help me not to be wise in my own eyes but to hear Your voice telling me, "This is the way; walk in it." (Based on Proverbs 3:5–7 and Isaiah 30:21.)
6. Lord Jesus, never let me forget that, whatever happens, You have promised to be with me always, all the way to the end of the age. (Based on Matthew 28:20.)
7. Father God, please grant that whatever I do, whether in word or deed, I may do it wholeheartedly, in the name of the Lord Jesus, giving thanks to You through Him. (Based on Colossians 3:23.)

10

The Power of Prayer

Prayer is not asking. Prayer is putting oneself in the hands of God, at His disposition, and listening to His voice in the depth of our hearts.

MOTHER TERESA

Four Key Elements of Prayer

"Mom, can I use the car tonight? Oh, and can you pay for my friends and me to go to the movies on Friday night—there's only three of us. And can you pay for a new shirt and a couple of leggings for my friend, Stella—her family is going through a hard time right now. And while I'm at it, can I pllleeaassse buy a new pair of Vans? Mine got scuffed, and I've had them over a year. Please, please, please? And do you mind giving my friend Gavin a ride to and from work tonight? His car is broken down, and he needs help. I'd do it, but I'm planning to be out already—you can use Dad's car . . ."

When you're a parent of a teen, the requests can make your head spin! And while we love helping our kids and taking care of them, and even helping their friends occasionally, it's easy to get tired of the endless requests and maybe even feel . . . taken advantage of? Sometimes, we wonder if our kids actually love us or just love the things we do for them and give them.

A relationship that's solely about one person asking and another person giving can be an unbalanced relationship.

Let's look at that in a spiritual sense.

Although God invites us to bring our requests to Him, when prayer becomes a continuous string of asking, asking, asking, it's not healthy or complete.

To keep your prayer life fresh, you might consider trying the ACTS method of praying.

Adoration

In the ACTS method of prayer, adoration is the first step. Before we do anything else, we express our love and reverence for God. Does that mean we sit around and cry, "Oh, I love you, I love you, I love you"?

For some people, yes. Some people are so in tune with God and so constantly aware of His presence and blessings that they can immediately move into a sense of pouring out a heart of praise and love to God.

For others, that awareness takes some concentrated focus and some practice and maybe even some education on why God is worthy of adoration.

To help better understand the fuller scope of who God is and why He deserves our adoration, let's look at His attributes.

God is faithful. Scripture tells us that even if we are faithless to Him, God remains faithful to us, for He cannot deny Himself. He cannot change this characteristic about Himself, so He will be with us no matter what. His love for us is everlasting. He loves us and He likes us . . . and He always will!

God is glorious. God is awe inspiring. He is stunning through and through. He is filled with splendor and striking beauty in all ways, and when we see glimpses of Him, we cannot help but be filled with overwhelming admiration.

God is good. Forget the image of the traffic cop God trying to catch you doing something bad! Instead, think of the kindest person you know—and realize that God is even kinder. He is infinitely, unchangeably kind and full of good will! According to A. W. Tozer, the goodness of God "disposes Him to be kind, cordial, benevolent, and full of good will toward men. He is tenderhearted and of quick sympathy, and His unfailing attitude toward all moral beings is open, frank, and friendly. By His nature He is inclined to bestow blessedness and He takes holy pleasure in the happiness of His people." We can trust a good God with the most intricate, intimate desires of our heart.

God is gracious. God desires that all would come to Him. When we confess our sins, He removes our sins and casts them into the depths of the sea. Holocaust survivor and author Corrie ten Boom said, "God takes our sins—the past, present, and future—and dumps them in the sea and puts up a sign that says No Fishing Allowed." God is all about grace, about giving us goodness that we don't deserve!

God is holy. He is perfect. God cannot sin because He is holy. He is unlike humans. He can do no wrong. He is above all His creations. He is the standard for everything.

God is immutable. He never changes. His character doesn't change. What we see is what we get! There's no shift, no adjustment. God is dependable, and we can count on everything about Him, including His love for us and that He hears our prayers.

God is infinite. He is self-existing and has no beginning or end. He is. He has no limits as humans do and no time frame—He created time!

God is just. Humans have prejudices that keep us from being perfectly fair at times. That is not a challenge with God. He knows all so He always is aware of exactly what is going on in any situation.

He is more than fair; He always does what is right and good toward all. He acts with compassion, but He acts with ultimate justice.

God is loving. Have you ever been loved? Unquestioningly loved no matter what you do? God's love for us is way more than we can even imagine. His love laces every interaction He has with us and surrounds every answer to prayer.

God is merciful. Hand in hand with God's justice is His mercy. Because He is all-knowing, faithful, good, and holds these other attributes, He is also compassionate toward His humans. He understands our failings, our humanity, our weaknesses.

God is omnipotent. He is all powerful. He speaks and things happen! God's power is unlimited. He is a good God with unlimited power, so He is able to care for His humans perfectly.

God is omniscient. He knows everything. He can be everywhere. He knows the solution for every problem.

God is self-sufficient. He has no needs. He needs nothing outside Himself to make Him who He is. He is enough. Because He has no needs, we can go to Him with our needs and find answers at any time. He never needs to rest or take a break from us.

God is wise. Wise is not just smart, even though, of course, He has the ultimate, perfect, all-knowing brain. Wisdom means also knowing what to do with that intelligence, knowing and understanding all the facts, and making the best decisions possible. It includes understanding people, their emotions and their perspectives, and using ultimate fairness.

As we look at God and spend a few moments reflecting on Him, we can't help but appreciate Him. This helps us come to Him with the proper respect. And it draws us into awe that this amazing One would want to have a relationship with us! As we come to Him reflecting on who He is, we realize that not only is He the Lord of the universe but He personally meets our needs.

And while it humbles us to think that this magnificent God would invite us to come to Him in prayer and enter a relationship with Him, thinking of His attributes and how they play out in His goodness and love for us gives us confidence to approach Him as the ultimate more-than-parent.

Confession

Another important element of prayer is confession—called contrition by some who use this model. When we come to God in prayer, it's important for us to confess to Him ways we have failed or have not done as well as we could or any sins we have committed.

Why is confession important? Scripture tells us of a time when the Israelites called out to God and got no response. The Israelites were told, "Listen! The LORD's arm is not too weak to save you, nor is his ear too deaf to hear you call. It's your sins that have cut you off from God" (Isaiah 59:1–2, NLT).

Our relationship with God is just that: a relationship. When something is wrong in that relationship, communication becomes hindered. A successful prayer life and good walk with the Lord means that we need to be in good relationship with Him. When we don't confess our sins, they become like bricks—they become piled on top of each other like a wall. And that wall blocks our view of God and keeps us from being able to see and hear Him clearly and from walking in fellowship with Him.

The act of confession doesn't have to be just a quick "Yep, I did it." Sometimes the steps of our ACTS model overlap a bit. For instance, in a time of confession we may want to talk to God about why we did what we did, about the situation that is plaguing us. And it may be a good time to ask God to help us overcome the temptation or other negative situation we face. This can be a relational conversation, not just reciting a list of bad things we've done and checking them off.

As we confess our sins, God has promised to forgive them. The bricks disappear, and we see God once again and can enjoy communion with Him.

That forgiveness we find through confession helps us realize how much our Father loves us. Our sins don't change His love for us . . . they may cause consequences, but they don't change His love.

As we see where we have fallen short of living for the Lord, we also begin to realize just how human and fallible we are. We realize how much we depend on Him. And that's good for our souls!

Thanksgiving

After we've noted the wonder of our fabulous God and made sure we're in right relationship with Him, it's not quite time to start making the requests yet.

In fact, the next step in the ACTS model, thanksgiving, is actually an outpouring from or natural response to the first two steps. As we see how marvelous God is, we become filled with gratitude that the Lord of the universe cares for us.

As we come to Him confessing our sins and we experience His forgiveness, our hearts rejoice with deep appreciation. Take a few moments to consider all the prayers He has answered for you. Consider the ways He's been good to you or shown His divine protection—like maybe that car with the distracted driver who almost hit you on the way to work! Thank Him for the gifts of friendship, of material possessions, of a good church home, and of a family. Thank Him for the promises in His Word.

Don't be surprised if, when you start thanking God for things in your life, you start to see more and more and more reasons to thank Him! How great is His love for us that He provides so many good things! It's not difficult to pray in faith when we realize how good God is to us!

Supplication

Now, according to the ACTS model of praying, after we have expressed adoration for God, have confessed our sins with a sincere heart, and have thanked Him for His goodness, it's time to bring our requests to Him.

What kind of requests do we bring? Jesus showed us several in the Lord's Prayer:

- We can ask for God's will to be done, for His help in living like Him and for Him on this earth.
- We can ask God to bring the provision we need for our ordinary, daily lives. God delights in providing for us. In fact, one of His names in the Bible is Jehovah Jireh, which means "the Lord will provide." Don't hesitate to ask God to take care of the needs in your home, for you, and for your family—He cares about what you eat, drink, and wear and how you pay your bills. God shines in the details of life! He also cares about your family's emotional and spiritual needs. Bring them all to Him.
- Relationship needs are also important. Not just forgiveness with God, but forgiveness with others. In our prayers, we can ask God to help us with these.
- We can talk to God about the temptations we face and ask Him to help us through them.

What else can we pray about? Anything at all that concerns us. Again, God is in the details of life. If something concerns us, our heavenly Father wants us to talk to Him about it. We can ask Him to provide help and meet the needs!

Remembering others is also a vital part of our prayer life. Who in your circle of family and friends needs prayer? When we pray for others, it's as if we're taking a journey with them. Our prayers may help them over rough spots or help them understand insights God is giving them. We may never fully understand how praying for others helps them, but we can be sure that it does because Scripture encourages us to do this.

Pray for corporations or organizations that are important to you—like leaders of schools or ministries or those who lead at the company where you work. Also pray for our national leaders. Ask that God's will be done in their individual lives and in our country. Pray for people in your community.

When you pray, feel free to have notes beside you to help you hit the highlights—and you may even want to write down some of the insights you have *while* you pray! If this model doesn't work for you, as you try it, you'll soon find an adaptation that does. Then you can enjoy a communion with God that goes beyond the "gimmes"!

The Power of Praying Together

Nothing tends more to cement the hearts of Christians than praying together. Never do they love one another so well as when they witness the outpouring of each other's hearts in prayer. —*Charles Grandison Finney*

"Please pray for me . . ."

We see it often on social media these days as people reach out amid the hurts, heartbreaks, and fears in their lives. When something goes wrong in someone's life or a hurt is encountered, others console with words of hope and healing and the simple but profound promise: "I'm praying for you."

We humans are constantly reaching out in our life journeys to find others and know we are not alone. That's pretty normal. "No man is an island, entire of itself, every man is a piece of the continent, a part of the main," said the seventeenth-century English poet John Donne.

And it's true, especially, in a spiritual sense. We were never created to make it alone through this life. God established His creation to live, for the most part, in families and communities, in the spiritual realm that broadens into the people of God fellowshipping, worshipping, and serving in communities. And that's what the church is all about—becoming a family, sharing the good times and the bad times together.

Praying together is one of the intricate parts of living as Christians in community. Think of it—even Christ, in His most challenging hour, brought along His friends and spiritual community to pray with Him. In fact, scriptures give us various examples of people praying together, in both the Old and New Testaments.

Matthew 18:19–20 asserts: "If two of you agree here on earth concerning anything you ask, my Father in heaven will do it for you. For where two or three gather together as my followers, I am there among them" (NLT).

Praying with others brings several benefits into our lives. For one, as we open our hearts and share our needs with others, they become more intricately involved in our lives. Ecclesiastes 4:9–10 says, "Two people are better off than one, for they can help each other succeed. If one person falls, the other can reach out and help. But someone who falls alone is in real trouble" (NLT).

When we open our hearts to others and ask them to pray and they do so, they share our burdens and obey the law of Christ.

When we pray with and for others, we walk a spiritual journey with them. We become a cloud of witnesses (see Hebrews 12:1)—encouraging, supporting, and helping them succeed.

And what better place in which to do this than the church body?

As we pray together and see prayers answered, we can remind each other when the going gets tough of how God has worked in the past—and assuredly will again in the future!

Praying together builds our faith together. And as our faith grows, we pray with more power, and the whole body becomes stronger.

Prayer also bonds us together in unity. When you're praying with a fellow Christian and seeing that person's heart, you're less likely to let petty things divide you. You will find that your love for the others you pray with builds and grows. And the whole body of Christ reaps the rewards.

Fresh Ways to Pray with Others

How do we pray together? Many churches traditionally hold weekly prayer services. Some gather around the altar or in a circle of chairs and discuss personal needs, needs of the church, and needs of the community.

Often, the traditional format of prayer has become more of a routine, perhaps too much of one. So let's look at some ways to punch up the power of praying together in your community, prayer group, friendship circle, or church. Remember, the more senses you involve in your prayer time together (sight, sound, smell, taste, touch) and the more the prayer activity gets people involved, the more real the need becomes, giving participants the impetus to keep praying for the need as time goes by.

Not all of these ideas will work for your situation, but try some of these suggestions or use them as a catapult to your own ideas to make your prayer times more memorable and perhaps even more effective.

Church Prayer Walk

Gather a small group to walk around the church. Stop at various locations and pray. For instance, stand outside the youth room and pray for the needs of the students and for their leaders. Do the same for the children's room, the gym, the baptismal, or any other areas you have in your church. Pray in the foyer for those who will walk in the door, and pray over the visitors' packets that God will use them to draw people to Him through the church.

This is a great thing for a prayer group to do each week before members of the congregation arrive for small groups and services.

Corporate Prayer Journal

Keep a spiral-bound book or binder specifically for your small group, Sunday school class, or church prayer requests. Enter and date the requests, leaving blank spaces. When a prayer is answered, write down the date and how the prayer was answered in the journal.

Periodically—especially if some members are facing a rough time—make it a practice to go through the prayer journal and see how God has answered requests. This reminds us that God is faithful—that He's taken care of us before and will take care of us with new prayer needs.

Figurative Praying

Give each person in the group a small container of commercial Play-Doh or a strip of modeling clay. (If you're doing this for a large group of people, you can find recipes to make modeling dough using flour, salt, cream of tartar, food coloring, and water.)

Ask each member to mold the dough or clay into a symbol that represents a prayer need. Then have each participant show his or her model to the group and explain his or her need. Participants can take the pieces home to sit on a desk or counter. Encourage them to pray about the need each time they see their model.

You can also use dough or clay to emphasize prayer from another angle. Have each person form it into a symbol that reminds him or her of a prayer God has answered.

Art of Prayer

For an activity similar to the previous idea, pass out finger paints, watercolors, chalk, markers, construction paper, colored pencils, or other art supplies. Let each person design something that will remind him or her to pray about the need (or to help the person visualize God answering the prayer). You can either let participants take home their work or use it to decorate a wall in the church for a month or so. Let your craftsy people create prayer banners.

It doesn't matter if the participants are good artists. The experience will help them connect more intimately with prayer. Let people who want to share talk about what their prayer art represents so others can pray too. You might even want to post the art in a special place to remind participants to not only pray about these needs, but also just to pray. You can follow up the experience with more art—let people create artwork that represents the answer to the prayer and affix it to the original prayer request art.

Prayer Sticky Notes

Each time you have a new prayer request, jot it on a sticky note with the date. Place the sticky note on the edge of your computer or another place that you see frequently. It serves as a reminder; every time you see the note, pray about what's on it. When the prayer is answered or you no longer need to remember to pray about this need, throw away the sticky note. You can put the names of several people you need to pray for on one note, if you want to keep the notes a little more low key.

Prayer Wall

You have heard of the Wailing Wall in Jerusalem where pilgrims stick their prayers to God in cracks in the wall. Create a prayer wall in your church—perhaps in a corner or room complete with an area for people to linger in front of the wall and pray about the needs they see.

You can let people who have prayer needs jot them down on sticky notes and stick them to the wall. Or you can spray-paint the wall with a chalkboard surface and let people write their needs in chalk or erasable marker. You might even purchase some invisible ink and let the person write down an unseen request.

Exercising Prayer

How about this for an idea? A Nazarene church in Indianapolis has set aside part of their grounds and created a walking trail. At different points of the trail, the walker is instructed to stop and pray about certain needs, including the needs of the people passing along the highway running by the church. You can also mix it up by having people walk in groups of two or three to pray together at each point.

Interactive Prayer Room

This could be a permanent or temporary setup. Create different stations or scenes in a prayer room. At each station, the person is instructed to pray about a certain item—either topically or specifically. And the person is also instructed to do something interactive. This can be as creative as you like.

For instance, in one spot, you might set up a garden display that includes different elements of creation (plants, a goldfish pond, and a small sandbox). The person may be instructed to thank God for His creation and to write in the sand the aspect of creation that he or she is most grateful for. Another station might focus on praising God through prayer, and the person may be instructed to listen to some praise music on a CD with earphones placed there. Another station may include creating something the person can take home to remind him or her of the need to pray.

Even when the person is having an individual prayer experience, he or she is still benefiting from praying in a group by being part of the shared prayer experience in the same location and the same event. Perhaps the final station can be praying with another person, such as a prayer host, and talking about the experience.

Adopt a Prayee

You may want to do this to foster intergenerational communication in your church. Let a certain set of people adopt individuals to pray for. For instance, you might encourage your teens to each choose a senior citizen. You can even have a stat sheet printed about each of the prayees (name, personal information, specific prayer requests), including the person's photo. Or let the adults adopt teens.

This is also great for involving seniors and older parents to pray with understanding for young parents! Who can't use the blessing of prayer?

Children's Prayer Service

Once a month or quarter, have a prayer service for your children or grandchildren. Their prayers can be surprisingly astute and on the mark!

Cross Service

Have someone in your church create a cross out of wood, papier-mâché, or brown construction paper and place it on a wall in your sanctuary or a classroom.

You can conduct your cross service in different ways. Some churches will play music and show a video about Jesus on His way to the cross. Others may do this at the end of a special service or communion. This experience is especially good during the last night of camp or a revival. At the end of the service, invite people to come to the cross and place their needs, burdens, praises, or intercession on the cross. As each person approaches the cross, he or she receives a piece of paper and pen to write a prayer. When finished, each person tacks (or tapes) his or her prayer to the cross. Congregants are invited to stay and pray at the foot of the cross as long as they would like, then to return to their seats or leave the room when finished. After the service, the prayers are destroyed, maintaining the participants' privacy.

Prayers to Heaven Campfire

This prayer activity is similar to the cross service. At the end of an outdoor service around a large campfire, invite congregants to write their prayers on papers and then put the papers in the campfire. It will be a stirring event with or without music!

Prayer Charades

This is a lighter approach to prayer—combining a game with prayer. Have a prayer need written on a slip of paper. Stick to general needs, like nursery workers, the youth group, construction projects, or aviation missionaries. Have members take turns pulling the needs one at a time out of a container and acting out the need. This might just work well with your congregation. The process of acting out the needs will keep these requests returning to members' minds for months!

Neighborhood Prayer Walks

You can do the prayer walk as formally or informally as you like. For an informal prayer walk, choose a neighborhood and walk around it, praying for the people in the neighborhood.

If you want to make this a church-wide event, have a map of the area around the church and divide the area into territories, which you will assign to teams. Two or three people should walk together, praying for the needs of those in the homes and businesses they pass. Some churches use neighborhood prayer walks to pass out flyers, inviting people of the neighborhood to tell them their prayer needs or even pray on the spot with neighbors they encounter. Always be sensitive to people who may not be believers.

You can also follow the example of some Christians in the Kansas City area. They gather in a bus and drive through the streets of their community, stopping at certain points to pray over schools, stores, and neighborhoods.

Pass It On

Use this prayer exercise with people seated in a group. Give each person a sheet of paper, and ask everyone to write down a prayer request. Have people pass written prayer requests to whoever is on their right. Give the people time to pray. Then have people pass the prayer requests they have in hand to the person on the other side (or in the row in front of them or the row behind, or two to the left, or diagonal). Keep the prayers passing around for a while. You can also let people split into groups of two or three and pray for the needs they are holding.

Map It Out

Get a map of the world and pray for missionaries in different places. You can do variations of this idea, such as putting a map on the floor and letting people stand on a nation to pray for it. You can have prayer sheets listing facts about the countries to aid the participants. You can also use maps and facts to pray for various states and state leaders.

Popcorn Prayers

Have the leader say a word, situation, or person's name. Then let others "pop" in with a one-sentence prayer relating to that topic.

Prayer Board

With their permission, choose certain members of the church on a weekly or monthly basis. Put their photos and a fact sheet about them on the prayer board. You might even place a prayer sheet about all chosen members in the church bulletin or newsletter. Then encourage the congregation to pray for these members.

Directory-Based Prayer

Pass out copies of the church directory, and have each person in the prayer meeting pray for a page of members. You can also pray over school directories, neighborhood directories, nursing home directories, or even local business directories.

As a twist on this activity, take the "Most Influential Americans" or "Most Famous People" lists often printed in magazines, and pray for the spiritual condition of these men and women of influence.

Scripture Prayers

Choose appropriate scriptures before the meeting. At the meeting pray for the members or needs using these scriptures. You can also pray this way using devotional quotes.

Prayer Calendar

Create prayer calendars to hand out each month. Each day should list a focus point for prayers. You can also create specific calendars for church members in general or for the youth group and other specific departments.

Prayer Chairs

Before a prayer meeting, write needs on pieces of paper or sticky notes. Attach them to the bottom of chairs. When the meeting begins, have participants pull the needs from underneath their chairs and pray over them.

Prayer Pals

There are different ways to pray together on a smaller scale. Pair up people in your church, and give them the assignment of praying together at least once a week for a month. Perhaps they can meet before or after a service at church to pray together. Maybe they will want to meet at a local restaurant and pray over a sandwich. Or maybe they will want to call each other on the phone or have a text prayer session.

The next month, you can form new pairs and do it all again. Encourage the people to pray for personal needs, church needs, and other needs. This helps your prayer team get to know each other individually.

Some Words of Caution

No discussion of corporate prayer would be complete without a couple of cautions. First consider the Golden Rule in discussing prayer needs: share others' needs only in ways you would want shared.

For instance, a few years ago, the missionary in one denomination was flown from another country back to his home in the United States with a severe health need. Without thinking, well-meaning people who knew of the problem started broadcasting his problems for all the world, literally, so people could pray for him.

Prayer is good, right? Well, yes, usually. However, the man was a popular speaker. What if people who heard about the man's health issues assumed he would no longer be able to speak? A general perception that he could no longer do presentations at churches could circulate, and churches could stop inviting him. That perception could lead to the person losing part of his source of income.

Be careful with whom and when you share a prayer request about someone else's personal life. Get permission if at all possible—especially on health issues—before you share private information. Yes, your group should be trustworthy, but it takes only one person being indiscreet to cause unforeseen—and sometimes litigious—problems. If in doubt, go for the old unspoken need or the unnamed vague need: "Please pray for my friend who is having challenges with her daughter" or "Please pray for my coworker who is starting chemo."

And never, ever put a prayer request in print or on the Internet—including social media or e-newsletters—without permission. Yes, you might put it only on your church bulletin, but that bulletin may end up photographed and shared in places you don't expect.

There's power in prayer, but especially corporate prayer. Find ways to explore the effectiveness of praying with others.

How to Pray When You Don't Know How

Ideas to Get You Started

We know we need to pray, but *how* do we do it? What do we do when we don't know how to pray or don't know *what* to pray?

Prayer is simply talking to God. We can do it any place, at any time, for any length of time, about anything. Whatever is on our hearts and minds is fine to converse with God about.

We don't have to act any specific way to communicate with God. We don't have to use "thee" and "thou" or try to be formal. Imagine you're sitting in a restaurant with a close friend, just chatting. That's a perfect example of how comfortable we can be talking to God.

While some people have no problem being prayer conversationalists and chatting away with the Almighty, some of us may need a jump start sometimes. Here are some ideas to help you when you don't know what or how to pray.

Pray the Bible

Google the prayers in the Bible. Then pray the ones that are appropriate to your situation or thoughts and use them as a springboard for your own prayers. For instance, if you are tormented by a sin you have committed, you might turn to Psalm 51:1: "Have mercy on me, O God, because of your unfailing love. Because of your great compassion, blot out the stains of my sins" (NLT).

You can also adjust the scriptures to become prayers. For instance, Proverbs 3:5–6 says, "Trust in the LORD with all your heart, and lean not on your own understanding; in all your ways acknowledge Him, and He shall direct your paths" (NKJV).

You can pray, "Lord, help me to trust You with all my heart and to not depend on my own understanding, to realize there are things I don't know. Father, I know You are the One who guides me, and I ask You to continue to do that. Thank You for showing me the direction You want me to follow."

You can even address specific needs in such a prayer.

Another way to pray the Bible is to place others' names within the scriptures. For instance, parents can benefit from praying for their children using Ephesians 4:32: "Be kind to one another, tenderhearted, forgiving one another, even as God in Christ forgave you" (NKJV).The prayer could read like this: "Lord, I pray that my children, Anthony and Liz, would be kind to each other. Help them be tenderhearted and quick to understand each other, and help them solve problems together. I pray You will help them forgive each other when there is hurt, just as You forgive them."

Don't just pray scriptures over family members; carry anyone to the Father in this way.

Think through People You Care About

When you feel compelled to pray and don't know where to start, looking at those around you is a good exercise. Here are some ideas of individuals to pray for:

- Your family, even extended family. You don't even have to be close to that cousin to pray for him!
- Your church family. Do you have a directory? That's a great way to pray—perhaps even cover a certain number of names daily!
- Coworkers. The people you work with have needs, and you might even talk with them about the challenges they face in their professional and personal lives. Are you remembering to pray for them?
- Children's teachers and other personnel in the schools, including cafeteria workers, bus drivers, and board members. They can all certainly use your prayers!
- Community leaders. You can probably find their names on community websites. Ask God to help them be wise rulers.
- First responders (police, firefighters, EMTs). Pray for their protection and blessing. You might even contact their departments and ask if you can at least have a list of their first names because you would like to pray for them specifically. Ask them about needs they might have beyond safety and wisdom.
- Politicians. Jokes aside, they all can certainly use prayer whether they realize it or not! Scripture tells us that the kings' hearts are in God's hands and that no one is in power except through God allowing it, so pray for God's will to be done in politics.
- Ministries. Start with your church and denomination. Then think about the ministries you respect and admire. Ask God to

fortify their energy and provide for their needs. Ask Him to help the leaders remain pure and hear the Lord's voice, for example.

- Don't pray only for the people at your own job; pray also for those at local businesses.

Make a List of Concerns

What things make your forehead wrinkle or give your heart a frown? Make a list of the concerns on your heart and mind. Don't keep nebulous or specific worries to yourself; take them to the Father and ask Him to provide solutions and give you peace.

You might even mark the date you pray about the concern—and leave a space to mark a response and date when God answers those prayers.

Write Down Your Prayers

Do you find it hard to focus when you're praying? If so, you might want to write down your prayers. Some people just communicate best through writing or typing. God can read as well as He can hear!

Use Art for Your Prayers

Perhaps your soul expresses itself best when you're creating something with your hands. Feel free to use your favorite art forms in your process of praying. Perhaps you can create a clay figure that will represent a prayer need. Maybe you can paint a picture that shows God answering your prayer. Maybe you would like something to place on your desk to help you remember to pray about a certain need—perhaps you would like to make a pen-and-ink drawing. Maybe you like to use calligraphy to write phrases of your prayers or scripture prayers. Maybe you can weave or quilt a special shawl to symbolically help your heart get ready to pray.

Pray through the News

Do you like to read the news each day? As you read the stories, stop and pray over the ones that you feel led to focus on. Pray for the young person who stabbed his friend, that he would find the Lord. Pray for the report about the new treatments for cystic fibrosis—ask the Lord to give the doctors wisdom. Pray for the family of the homicide victim. Ask for the Lord's will to be done on the new law being voted on.

If you watch a newscast on the internet or television, feel free to get vocal with it. Respond to the anchors' words with your prayers. Praying over the stories you just heard is a great way to make use of that pesky commercial time! If watching on the internet, feel free to pause the newscast to pray over the stories.

Pray through Social Media

As you go through your Facebook, Twitter, or Instagram feed, how about praying for those friends? Pray over the problems mentioned not only on your friends' pages but also in the chat rooms and groups.

Wait on the Lord

In our world of busyness and noise, sometimes we forget that silence can be golden. And we don't have to keep things moving. Especially in prayer. Sometimes when we don't know what to pray, it's best to simply enter our virtual prayer room with the Holy Spirit, let God know we're there, and wait for the Spirit to bring things to mind that we need to pray about.

Create a Prayer Calendar

Help yourself by having a plan. Organize what you want to pray about each day—perhaps family on Monday, coworkers on Tuesday, and so on, and write the topics in a weekly or monthly calendar.

These ideas are meant to get you started. Brainstorm for more ideas of how to make prayer most effective for you. Remember, the main thing about prayer is simply coming to God and taking the time to do it. There is no right or wrong way to sincerely come to the Father!

How to Wait in Faith for Answers

Sometimes when we turn our lives and our situations over to God through prayer, we don't receive answers immediately. Instead, God seems to say wait. To help us better understand a spiritual perspective on waiting in prayer, let's look at what Scripture tells us about waiting.

"Those who wait on the Lord shall renew their strength (Isaiah 40:31, NKJV). This is one of the "well-worn" verses of the Old Testament. It is a promise that is preceded by a condition: first wait, then God will act. The prophet Isaiah reminds us that God will act in such a way that we will mount up with wings as eagles, run and not be weary, and walk and not faint.

The promise attached to this invitation to wait was written to a nation in turmoil—a nation scattered, struggling, and vulnerable to chasing after idols of all kinds. Today a wide array of voices and choices are vying for the attention that is rightfully due to the God who has proven His faithfulness for generations. As it is for so many of us, the temptation for the people of Isaiah's time to do *something*—to act rather than be still—was great. However, acting for the sake of acting can often lead to foolish choices. Going when we are called to wait can have disastrous consequences. Just ask anyone who has received a false start disqualification in a footrace or a swim meet.

But God's version of waiting is not about twiddling our thumbs with nothing to do. With God, times of waiting are often times of preparation. Sometimes the preparation is obvious to us, but most of the time, we are unaware of the ways in which we are being prepared as we wait. When David was a shepherd fighting off wild dogs and bears with a sling and some stones, seemingly wasting away in a thankless job in the middle of nowhere, a time of preparation was taking place. Only later, when he faced Goliath, did he realize that his time with the sheep was not idle waiting but preparation.

As he faced the giant, David noted to King Saul in 1 Samuel 17:34–37, "Your servant has been keeping his father's sheep. When a lion or a bear came and carried off a sheep from the flock, I went after it, struck it and rescued the sheep from its mouth. When it turned on me, I seized it by its hair, struck it and killed it. Your servant has killed both the lion and the bear; this uncircumcised Philistine will be like one of them, because he has defied the armies of the living God. The LORD who rescued me from the paw of the lion and the paw of the bear will rescue me from the hand of this Philistine" (NIV).

At that moment, David recognized his time of waiting in obscurity as a time when God was preparing him for something great. Taking his preparation time seriously in the wilderness with sheep allowed David to be ready when it was time to apply that preparation in a life-or-death situation.

The old saying goes, "Don't pray for patience, because sure enough you will have to use it more than you ever imagined." Certainly, there are times when God develops our patience through times of delay.

However, the Bible reminds us that one "fruit of the Spirit"—the name given to those characteristics that develop as we draw closer and closer to Jesus—is patience. Another term for patience is *long-suffering*—the ability to endure suffering for a long period of time!

Living in our fallen world exposes us to all kinds of suffering. Jesus Himself promised His disciples that they would have trouble. But He quickly added that He has overcome the world. Once again, as Isaiah reminds us, we are able to rest and have peace during times of waiting because we are resting on the promises of God. The disciples could have peace and even hope in a world in which they would indeed suffer because of Jesus's promise. This overcoming would not always be immediately recognizable, but it would come because Jesus is trustworthy.

While we wait for the ultimate victory, we learn to watch for God's hand in the middle of whatever we are enduring, so that our waiting can be turned into something useful for God and beneficial for us.

The Gift of Waiting

When God says wait, scriptural stories and promises suggest we can engage in what could be called "useful waiting." That does not mean this waiting will always be filled with laughter or will be without struggle. However, God can turn even our sufferings while we wait for relief into something that brings glory and honor to His name and assists us in growing in His grace.

Educator and news anchor Charles Christian said that God tried to teach him this lesson in—of all places—the grocery store line! "I joke with friends and family that, regardless of the other spiritual gifts they may see in me, one gift I am quite sure I have is the gift of finding the longest line. Of course, I scan the lines for what appears to be the shortest. Sometimes I am fortunate enough to find a line that is extremely short—perhaps only three people. However, I end up still waiting to check out when the seventh, eighth, or tenth person in the other lines are checking out!

"This cycle has repeated itself so often that I no longer consider it a coincidence. It borders upon a spiritual gift . . . the gift of waiting. Ironically, my personality does not easily lend itself to waiting. The truth is, I hate waiting. Time and again, though, the lines just refuse to cooperate.

"After a while, these times of waiting went from times of frustration and aggravation to times of looking for opportunities. Once while standing in line, I thought of something my father was fond of saying to me. He told me, 'For us, the shortest distance between two points is a straight line. That is almost never true of God. God is always on time, but God is never in any hurry, and His way of getting us to our destination rarely has shortcuts.'

"So, I started exploring ways to make the most of my newly discovered spiritual gift of finding the longest line. Instead of wasting time and energy being frustrated and being short with those who were waiting with me or who were serving me in line, I chose to look around for opportunities to be more Christlike.

"Once I noticed a woman in line who used to be my mail carrier. She waved and recognized me as well. We struck up a conversation about why she was no longer the mail carrier in my neighborhood. She opened up to me about recent family problems, including the loss of her son to suicide. God used that moment to allow me to step out of line and ask if she would allow me to pray with her. We stepped to an empty cash register area, and I prayed for her, for her family, and for peace and provision. We both walked away (back into line) with the realization that God had visited us in—of all places—a grocery store line."

Waiting Is Not (Always) a No

When we are asked to wait by God or even by our circumstances, it helps to remember that this is not always the same thing as receiving a no.

In Exodus, God's people wandered in the desert for around forty years, living as nomads. However, they were continually reminded that they would someday reach a land that God had promised to them. Their delay did not mean that God was permanently denying their desire for a homeland. Similarly, when we tell our children to wait until *after* dinner for dessert, we are not denying them dessert. We are simply watching out for them and recognizing that, more often than not, timing is indeed everything!

In the Gospels, the temptations of Jesus came at what appeared to be the very worst time. Jesus had just been recognized publicly by a man who had recently gained a large following (John the Baptist). After Jesus's baptism, the voice of God Himself could be heard affirming the ministry of His "beloved Son," and commanding those around to "listen to Him!" (Matthew 17:5, NASB).

What better time to capitalize on all this free and obviously positive publicity? Why not begin right there to perform public miracles by the riverside? Why not begin the Sermon on the Mount right there, while startled and curious people are present? Why not strike while the iron is hot before the publicity and interest begin to cool?

That is not what happened, though. Matthew, Mark, and Luke explicitly record the temptation of Jesus in the wilderness. In all three, Jesus was *immediately* led into the wilderness by the Holy Spirit after this very public baptism. Surely, after forty days, some there were left wondering whatever happened to that young man that John the Baptist and God Himself seemed to make such a fuss about! God had different plans. Both during and after the forty days, God affirmed the messianic ministry of Jesus, of course. However, God's timing and means of promoting and blessing the ministry of Jesus had different methods. God chose not to use what we might call traditional means of marketing and timing in order to exalt the ministry of His beloved Son.

This was certainly not a no in regard to Jesus's ultimate ministry, life, death, and resurrection. Rather, it was a wait.

The waiting time in the wilderness, which we now commemorate during the season of Lent in the church calendar, sent a clear message that God's ways and God's timing are different from the measurements of the world. God has His own timetable. Furthermore, the *kind* of Messiah Jesus was to be would not be determined by worldly opinions or measurements. Instead, as Jesus put it, "the Son can do nothing by himself; he can do only what he sees his Father doing, because whatever the Father does the Son also does" (John 5:19, NIV). Likewise, we as God's children are often called to a different timetable, and we are almost always called to methods different from the world's.

When God Says Wait

We would like for things to work this way: waiting, the call of God, and then a new beginning. Actually, though, it often works like this (even in the Bible): the call of God, waiting, and then a new beginning!

This distinction is important because it strongly implies that when God calls, waiting is almost always part of the equation. God called His people in Exodus to a new land. They then waited in the wilderness for a while. Then they experienced a new beginning. God called and anointed David to be king of Israel. He waited until Saul completed his reign—sometimes while pursuing David in order to kill him. Then David and all Israel experienced the new beginning as David finally assumed the throne. Jesus was publicly acknowledged by the voice of God as the beloved Son of God after His baptism. He then waited in the wilderness (forty days and nights). Then His public ministry experienced its focused and powerful beginning.

The similarities here are obvious: waiting was involved. This pattern can be seen in many more biblical stories, from Joseph to Paul! God calls, there is a time of waiting, and then there is a new beginning. Knowing that this seems to be a consistent pattern with God, what can we do while we wait?

First, we can rest in God's promises. Psalm 46:10 reminds us to "be still, and know that I am God" (NIV). In our times of waiting, we can experience God's presence and comfort as we still ourselves and allow God to speak into our silence.

Second, we can look for the lesson. We can consider if there is something God is trying to prepare us for in this time of waiting. Are we allowing what we think is wasted time to cause us to miss important lessons about ourselves, our surroundings, and even our future?

What if we seek to make the most of the time of waiting? If we are outside our comfort zones during a time of waiting or transition, we can let God use this time to develop skills or even patience that we did not know we could develop.

Third, we can bear witness to and provide comfort to others who are waiting. While we wait, we can find others who are waiting for a new beginning and become a source of encouragement and comfort to them. They will likely be on different journeys in many ways. They may be waiting for decidedly different answers. However, we can find opportunities to connect with others during times of waiting because, as we noted, it seems that God consistently builds in times of waiting for all of us at some point in our lives. While we wait, not only can we be sharpening our own skills as David did in his shepherding days, but we can also become a source of comfort and encouragement for others while we and they wait.

Finally, we can recognize that apparent times of waiting can become new aspects of our calling in Christ. Sometimes the apparent detour becomes the permanent road! As we wait for the way we think God is going to lead us, we may find ourselves going in a completely different direction, and that may end up being the answer to our prayer.

When you face a time when it seems like God's answers to your prayers are not forthcoming, wait patiently on Him. When His answers and direction do come, they will be perfect.

When God Says No

There's a story of two young girls who were praying on the same day in the same small farm town. The first girl prayed for God to please keep it from raining the next day so that she and her friends could play outside all day. The second girl, the daughter of a farmer, prayed for God to send lots of rain so that her parents' crops wouldn't die and so that they could have plenty of food for the coming winter.

The next day, it rained all day long and well into the night. As would be expected, two different responses emerged. The second girl—the farmer's daughter—rejoiced and expressed thanksgiving for the abundant showers. The first girl, the one desiring a playdate, was disappointed and asked why God sometimes says no.

This is a very simplistic example. We all know that things like weather patterns are complicated, and that God is not simply a giant Santa Claus in the sky who functions according to our will and desires.

However, this example can shed some partial light on assessing why God sometimes says no to our prayers. God's way of interacting is far more complicated and takes into consideration far more than we can comprehend.

In fact, sometimes our prayers seem to result in no supernatural action from God. Rather, God seems to allow things to run their course and demonstrates His faithfulness in the middle of the difficulties. At other times, it seems that God does supernatural things—also known as miracles—that further His purposes in the world. Also, there are, of course, times when we sense God saying no to a particular request or to a particular choice we are inquiring about.

At these times of no, we have choices to make about how we will adjust. Sometimes, like spoiled children, we see no as automatically bad. We want what we want, and when we do not get it, regardless of the reason (or lack of reason), we rebel. Some even choose to abandon faith when God does not answer directly or at least does not answer the way we hope He would. We are like the small child who stomps away in a fit of rage when she is not allowed to eat cake for breakfast. Or we behave like the preteen who becomes enraged when he cannot stay home and play video games instead of going to church! This is a conditional approach to our love and faith in God, who loves us without condition.

There are Christians who believe that nothing happens without God's direct intervention. Historically, though, even more Christians believe that God gives room for things like freewill and for the natural course of things to take place. Hence, miracles are *super*natural events—events where God intervenes "above nature."

This means that not getting what we want may not exactly be a no from God. Of course, it surely is not a yes, either. In order words, sometimes nature takes its course, and God sees us through the changes and even the difficulties that a fallen world sends our way. It could be that, as is the case in most of the biblical miracles, God reserves true supernatural miracles for occasions where an attention-getting event that will further His kingdom in a relatively untouched place is needed. Either way, it seems that God's desire for us is to trust Him, regardless of whether we get our way in answer to our prayers.

In the case of the two young girls in the illustration, if indeed the rain was a direct yes to one girl and a direct no to the other, we would assume that if the first girl—the one who wanted no rain for a playdate—knew that her no was based upon a "life-and-death" need for rain by the second girl, she would hopefully be content or even happy with the outcome. When we receive a no, our priorities are tested, and we are forced to ask, Does this thing I am asking for really matter?

Sometimes no is a direct result of our simply not being ready. Consider the preteen who wanted to drive his dad's old pickup truck. Fortunately for him and for the other drivers on the road, he did not receive his dad's permission. The dad was not trying to deprive his son of the fun and usefulness of driving. Instead, the dad wanted his son to be more ready (in regard to the law and his own maturity) to fully experience the yes when it was time.

Our immaturity can cause us to ask for a myriad of things for which we are either not ready at the moment or for which we may never be ready. In other words, we sometimes ask for things that are not intended for us to have.

Country singer Garth Brooks had a smash hit in the 1990s with a song called "Unanswered Prayers." In it, the singer recalls meeting his old high school sweetheart at a hometown football game. His wife is with him, and the meeting of the old flame is awkward. It then hints to an earlier verse, where the narrator says that this girl "was the one that I'd wanted for all time, and each night I'd spend praying that God would make her mine."

Whether God directly said no or if it was just a matter of the girl's freewill combined with a lack of attraction, the singer uses the event to exalt the wisdom of God—even when God says no. He says, "I guess the Lord knows what He's doing after all."

Trusting God intimately to know and to do what is best for us out of His love for us is the ultimate posture for participating in and understanding prayer. Prayer begins with trust. We interact with God in prayer because we are willing to begin to trust Him or because we have developed an ongoing relationship of trust with God. We do more than simply trust God's promise to always be there and to hear us when we call. We also pray trusting that God is wise, powerful, and loving in ways that we are not.

God knows more, loves more, and can do more, and so we pray. This means there is always the possibility that God will say yes in a way that exalts His faithfulness and love. This also means that there is a distinct possibility that God may say no. In His love and wisdom, God may look at the situation, at our maturity, and the impact upon His purposes, and say no.

That no is not a rejection of us, however, even though it may seem that way. A no from God flows from the love of God. God loves us too much to allow either our flawed desires or simple bad timing to move us into a place where our answer provides long-term trouble. God has a big-picture vision, and while a short-term yes may win the battle, God cares whether we win the war.

So what do we do when we sense a no from God? First, we must remember that this is not an uncommon phenomenon. We are not alone, and God is not picking on us or singling us out to shame us. Just as our earthly parents say no often for our own health and good, so too our all-loving, all-knowing heavenly Father says no.

Secondly, we must remember that not getting our way is not always a direct no from God. Sometimes, the timing is just not right, circumstances are not right, or we are asking something too far outside the realm of possibility. An extreme example would be asking to fly off the roof of our house in defiance of gravity. Not granting this would not really qualify as a no from God, since God did not create us to fly without the aid of something like an airplane. In that case, we would be asking something outside the realm of the way God has structured the universe. And while few would be comfortable with saying that God *could not* cause someone to fly, most everyone would recognize that if such a request is denied, it is not necessarily a direct no. In fact, the request could be construed in many cases as *tempting God*—putting God to a foolish test—as when the devil tempted Jesus to leap from the pinnacle of the temple.

Another response to a no from God should be self-examination: What are my motives for asking? Looking again to the temptation account of Jesus in the Gospels, we see that a key reason for all three of Jesus's denials in answer to the attractive temptations presented to Him was precisely about motives. All three temptations were centered on a basic question: What kind of Messiah are you going to be?

We recall that these temptations come very early in the ministry of Jesus—immediately following His baptism. Of course, the temptations were not exactly prayers from the devil to Jesus. However, Jesus's reasons for not giving into the temptations teach us much about why no is sometimes part of the equation when we pray and how we can respond when we do not get what we ask for. We can take the no as an invitation to examine our reasons for requests of God. We can also take a deeper look at what a positive answer could have meant, not only to us but to those around us as well. At times, what benefits us individually in the short run does not lead to a positive outcome in the long run.

Furthermore, what benefits us individually may not be best for our family, our community, or the overarching purposes of God.

Finally, we can remind ourselves that negative responses from God are often surrounded by myriad positive ones. Scripture reminds us that all God's promises are for our good and can be trusted, because He is trustworthy. Conversely, we can also trust God's negative responses. When the yes and the no go hand in hand, we see something of the fullness of God's nature come into play. A key example of this idea is seen in God's earliest interactions with Adam and Eve in Genesis.

God's first command to Adam (and eventually Eve) forbade eating from the tree of knowledge of good and evil, a proscription that was surrounded by an extremely generous promise and provision—they could eat from any other tree in the garden.

Perhaps it would help us to process negative responses we receive in light of the many positive ones God gives us: the abundant yes in Christ that we receive in regard to all the promises that come to us through our relationship with God through Jesus Christ.

Avoiding Extremes

First and foremost, the Christian life is defined by God's grace that we receive through faith: "For it is by grace you have been saved, through faith—and this is not from yourselves, it is the gift of God—not by works, so that no one could boast" (Ephesians 2:8–9, NIV).

Our call as Christians is full faith and trust in the love and provision (grace) of God in all situations of life. In fact, this calling extends even after this life and for all of eternity. Because of the loving grace of God, we can rely upon God to say yes to us in our deepest times of need: when we need comfort, when we need peace, and when we need to rely upon His ways above all else.

We can also confidently approach Him with our prayer requests, unafraid to present Him with our deepest desires. As Hebrews 4:16 puts it, "Let us then approach God's throne of grace with confidence, so that we may receive mercy and find grace to help us in our time of need" (NIV). Fully trusting His grace, we can ask with abandon, not worried that He will shame us or belittle us for asking too much.

However, we can also have confidence in the fact that God is wise enough and loving enough to at times say no. He is our Protector as well as our Provider. We can trust His negative responses as well as His positive ones. Sometimes our loved ones and friends say no for selfish reasons. Sometimes they say no out of simple lack: they don't have the resources to grant us.

God is different. God does sometimes say no, but His negative response is not because He lacks anything. Psalm 50:10 remind us that God owns the "cattle on a thousand hills" (NIV). Nor is it because God is somehow envious of us or wishes to shame us. God is all-loving and is certainly not offended or threatened by our desires. Rather, when God says no, it is motivated by love, a desire to protect, and a heart filled with the best desires for our present and our future. In response, we are called to seek and to ask within the will of God.

Jesus says that if you ask according to His name, He will do it. That does not mean simply invoking His name in a prayer or adding "in Jesus's name" at the end of the prayer. It means seeking to align our lives in such a way that what we ask for is in keeping with God's purposes and character. When we seek to align our lives within this boundary, we receive fewer negative responses and our prayers produce more observable fruit.

Conversely, we must avoid the extreme of blaming God every time we feel that we have received a no. In other words, we cannot blame

God if we don't always get our way. Sometimes we simply will not get our way, either because of natural boundaries or because of our own immaturity. To say that every no is God's fault as if He is to blame for us not getting our way stretches the boundary of a healthy prayer life.

An eight-year-old boy was at a church picnic that all the kids were excited about because of the games that would accompany it. Unfortunately, the picnic was moved indoors due to an East Texas rainstorm. The church had limited space, so the church members spread out all over the building. The boy and several of his friends ended up eating in the empty baptistery.

The pastor, who was walking around checking on everyone, saw the kids looking bored as they ate. He asked them, "Is it God's fault that this rain ruined our outdoor picnic?"

The eight-year-old swallowed his bite of fried chicken, took a breath, and said, "Well, if God did ruin it, I won't dare say that it is His *fault*."

The pastor smiled and nodded. It may not have been the most eloquent theological statement, but perhaps he smiled and nodded because at the heart of it was a child who was just beginning to learn that God does not make mistakes. God didn't commit an error, even if God did send the rain. God's heart was in the right place, even if the children were not outside enjoying games and running around the church grounds.

As Charles Spurgeon said, "God is too good to be unkind and He is too wise to be mistaken. And when we cannot trace His hand, we must trust His heart."

When you go to God in prayer and He seems to say no, trust His heart and His love for you.

The Sweet Scent of Prayer

May my prayer be set before you like incense; may the lifting up of my hands be like the evening sacrifice. —*Psalm 141:2 (NIV)*

Scents are important. The *Journal of Marketing* reported in 2014 that people spent more money when they were in an environment with warm scents, such as vanilla or cinnamon. A 2017 study found that people stay up to 44 percent longer in businesses that smell good . . . and the more time they spent in a store, the more they would purchase.

When someone is putting a home on the market, the sellers are encouraged not only to make sure the house is cleaned through and through and the trash taken out, but also to make it smell good by simmering scents, lighting candles, using diffusers, or even making cookies.

Think of all of the merchandise out there with a primary purpose of adding nice smells to our environments: perfume, air freshener, candles, body oil, body cream, diffusers, aromatherapy, incense, essential oils, cologne, deodorant, and more. Candle sales in the United States alone add up to roughly $2.3 billion each year, not including accessories such as candleholders.

Scents are important in the Bible too.

In the Old Testament, the tabernacle represented God's dwelling place on earth. People worshipped God in the tabernacle and brought their sacrifices there. The tabernacle included an altar of incense. While other items in the tabernacle represented God's work to provide for His people, the altar of incense represented the offerings of the Israelites to the Lord through prayer.

Just as we appreciate our favorite scents, God relishes the "scent" of His children praying. He never grows tired of hearing us call His name. He never becomes disgusted with our requests—even when we ask the same thing over and over. He never holds our confessed and forgiven sins against us or scolds us for being spiritually frail.

Remember, when you pray, it's as if God takes a deep spiritual breath and smiles. You are His child, and He loves to hear your voice.

Call out to Him often, and enjoy the fellowship with the almighty Creator and Sustainer of the universe . . . and your personal Father. Enjoy communion through the sweet scent of prayer.

About the Author

James Stuart Bell is owner of Whitestone Communications and has compiled and edited over forty volumes of inspirational stories for various publishers, including Guideposts. He dedicates this book in memory of the life and ministry of Mark Littleton.

Acknowledgments

The editors of Guideposts wish to thank Jeanette Littleton for her contributions to this book.

A Note from the Editors

We hope you enjoyed *Divine Interventions,* published by Guideposts. For over 75 years, Guideposts, a nonprofit organization, has been driven by a vision of a world filled with hope. We aspire to be the voice of a trusted friend, a friend who makes you feel more hopeful and connected.

By making a purchase from Guideposts, you join our community in touching millions of lives, inspiring them to believe that all things are possible through faith, hope, and prayer. Your continued support allows us to provide uplifting resources to those in need. Whether through our communities, websites, apps, or publications, we inspire our audiences, bring them together, and comfort, uplift, entertain, and guide them. Visit us at guideposts.org to learn more.

We would love to hear from you. Write us at Guideposts, P.O. Box 5815, Harlan, Iowa 51593 or call us at (800) 932-2145. Did you love *Divine Interventions?* Leave a review for this product on guideposts.org/shop. Your feedback helps others in our community find relevant products.

Scriptural Reference Index

Topical Index

R

S

Printed in the United States
by Baker & Taylor Publisher Services